Praise
The Jesu

MU00776712

"All I can say is that Ronnie McBrayer 'gets it.' He's a superbly talented storyteller and writer who challenges us to live with courage in a world where society's rules don't always match what is taught in the Gospels. Refreshingly honest and poignant, Ronnie McBrayer's *The Jesus Tribe* will make you think and inspire you to reach higher in your spiritual journey."

—Faith Fuller
Director, *Briars in the Cotton Patch: The Story of Koinonia Farm* (PBS documentary)

"In *The Jesus Tribe*, Ronnie McBrayer picks up on a tribal theme that I discovered while researching my book *Jesus Died for This?* I keep finding pockets of Christians from a diverse range of backgrounds who have gathered together to explore what it means to follow the Living Christ in the twenty-first century. Throughout this book, Ronnie offers spiritual seekers suggestions for how to shift from worshiping a Constantinian Christianity and move towards following the living Christ"

—Becky Garrison
Author of *Jesus Died for This?* and *Red and Blue God: Black and Blue Church*

"This vividly written book on the Sermon on the Mount and the way of Jesus Christ deserves very wide attention. Fast-paced and readable, filled with memorable stories and illustrations, McBrayer makes the distinctive way of life of the 'Jesus Tribe' both clear and appealing. He also joins a chorus of voices these days contrasting that way of life with the way of the American Empire. I warmly endorse this challenging and important book."

—David P. Gushee
Professor of Christian Ethics and Director, Center for Theology and Public Life,
Mercer University

"Ronnie McBrayer's *The Jesus Tribe* speaks directly to the heart of so-called 'American Christianity.' McBrayer challenges the very notion of a Christianity aligned with the ways of empire. Instead, drawing from his Cherokee roots, he offers unique perspective on the American relationship between God and country and lifts up an alternative 'way'—the Jesus way. McBrayer's is a welcome voice added to a symphony of contemporaries whose interwoven themes call forth and chart the twenty-first-century 're-formation' of our evangelical faith."

—Lisa Sharon Harper
Author of *Evangelical Does Not Equal Republican . . . or Democrat*

"What a treasure! Ronnie McBrayer is never at a loss for a good story or illustration to reveal the authentic Good News of Jesus that has so often been taken captive by Empire. His book is grounded in solid scholarship, the witness of countless true disciples across the ages, and his own life experience, as he unfurls the Way of the Jesus Tribe. For those tired of a Jesus wrapped in the flag or imprisoned within dried up churches, this book is one big banquet of satisfying, holy food."

—**Wes Howard-Brook**
Professor, retreat leader, and author of *The Church before Christianity*

"In a lively and engaging style, Ronnie McBrayer cuts through theological jargon and unwraps the central teachings of Jesus and his upside down Kingdom. This is must reading for all those who seek to follow the way of Jesus."

—**Donald Kraybill**
Author of *The Upside Down Kingdom* and Senior Fellow, Young Center for
Anabaptist Studies, Elizabethtown College

"Ronnie McBrayer's *The Jesus Tribe* offers a gutsy, folksy embrace of the Way of Jesus as expressed in the Sermon on the Mount. Drawing from his own Cherokee heritage, McBrayer utilizes the idea of *tribe* as over against *empire* to call followers of Jesus to embrace an alternative lifestyle, one that goes against prevailing notions of national idolatry and that understands Jesus' followers as a tribal family living out the radical commitments of the gospel. At moments humorous and at other moments passionate, *The Jesus Tribe* is a page-turner that ordinary church members will understand and that, perhaps, will change their lives. Don't read it . . . unless you are ready to look honestly at what it means to really follow Jesus."

—**Rob Nash**
Global Missions Coordinator, The Cooperative Baptist Fellowship

THE
JESUS

FOLLOWING CHRIST IN THE LAND OF THE EMPIRE

TRIBE

RONNIE **McBRAYER**

Smyth & Helwys Publishing, Inc.
6316 Peake Road
Macon, Georgia 31210-3960
1-800-747-3016

The paper used in this publication meets the minimum requirements of
American National Standard for Information Sciences—
Permanence of Paper for Printed Library Materials.
ANSI Z39.48–1984. (alk. paper)

Library of Congress Cataloging-in-Publication Data

McBrayer, Ronnie.
The Jesus tribe : following Christ in the land of the empire / by Ronnie McBrayer.
p. cm.
Includes bibliographical references.
ISBN 978-1-57312-592-5 (alk. paper)
1. Christian life—United States.
2. Christianity and culture—United States.
I. Title.

BV4501.3 .M3239

248.0973—dc23

2011021073

Also by Ronnie McBrayer

But God Meant It for Good

Leaving Religion, Following Jesus

Keeping the Faith

For my sons Blayze, Bryce, and Braden;
and in memory of my Cherokee ancestors, known and unknown.

About this time there lived Jesus. . . . And the Tribe of the Christians, so called after him, has still to this day not disappeared.

—Josephus, Jewish historian, circa 90 CE

Acknowledgments

"No man is an island entire of itself," the great John Donne famously wrote, and neither is a book. I am indebted to the cloud of witnesses that surrounds me, as these are also their words and not mine alone. A few of those witnesses deserve special thanks.

Thank you to Chad K. and Robin K. (and your beautiful children) for your love, faith, and resilience; sleep well, sweet Robin.

To Chris P., Chris H., and Bobby R.: Thank you for reading and critiquing this manuscript in advance and along the way. Most of all, thank you for your friendship.

Oh my dear Bridget B. and Larry B.: your tireless editing, e-mailing, assisting, and urging keep me going (and on my toes). Keep flying and keep rocking. Muchas gracias.

My gratitude goes to Tricia N., whose early reading of the manuscript pointed me in the right direction. Thank you.

To *A Simple Faith*, my community of faith in Seagrove Beach, Florida, that has sustained my family and me through the years: you will always have my heart.

To Match Point, the Fuller Center, the staff of the New Echota Historical site, Koinonia Farms, Ann Denson Tucker and the Muscogee Nation of Northwest Florida, and the Lenca Indian Tribe of Central America: your contributions were priceless.

The leadership and editorial staff of Smyth & Helwys Publishing are gifts to me, especially Keith G., Leslie A., and Rachel G. Thanks always.

All the readers of my syndicated newspaper column, "Keeping the Faith," make me a better writer. Some of these readers have become marvelous friends. Thank you for letting me into your homes and hearts week after week.

My aunt Betty Bearden Garrett, my beloved grandmother Artie Whitfield Bearden, and my great-grandmother Elizabeth Odom Bearden (all now deceased) taught me my Cherokee heritage. I am thankful for that and so much more.

Of course I must thank my sons—Blayze, Bryce, and Braden—to whom this book is dedicated. Boys, you are my best teachers. May it always be so.

And finally, to my wife, Cindy Cooper McBrayer: you are God's greatest act of personal grace to me. You will always be my *anamchara*.

Contents

Introduction

There is an ancient story from the Cherokee tradition that was used to illustrate the folly of getting too close to something dangerous. I first heard it as a child, though variations of the tale are found in the histories of most early tribal societies.

A young boy who was soon to be initiated into manhood was making a journey through the forest. Walking along the path, he came across a rattlesnake. The rattlesnake was very old and seemed almost dead. Yet there was enough life left in the serpent to speak to the young Cherokee.

"Please," said the snake, "can you take me to the top of the mountain? I hope to see the sunset one last time before I die."

The Cherokee highly respected the rattlesnake, the *utsanăti* they called it, and great care was taken never to offend this chief of the snake tribe. So the young brave responded cautiously, "No, Mr. Rattlesnake, this I cannot do. If I pick you up, you will bite me, and it will be me who will die."

The rattlesnake began to compromise. "No, my son; hear my promise. I will not bite you. Just take me up to the top of the mountain, as I do not have the strength to travel there myself. I must see the sun set a final time."

The young man thought about it, and finally, he carefully picked up the old rattlesnake. After a while, he was able to hold the snake confidently to his chest as he carried it to the top of the mountain. There they sat and watched the sun set together. Afterward the rattlesnake turned to the young man and said, "Take me home now. I am very tired and very old."

The young Cherokee carefully picked up the rattlesnake once again and held it to his chest, tightly and safely. He came all the way down the mountain, now accepting the old *utsanăti* as his newfound friend. He even took it to his home to give it food and a place to sleep.

The next day the rattlesnake turned to the boy and said again, "Please, my son, will you take me back to my home now? I have enjoyed my time with you, but it is now time for me to leave this world." A third time, the boy did as he was invited. He carefully picked up the snake, held it close to his chest, and carried it back into the woods. But just before he laid the rat-tlesnake down, the snake turned and bit the boy in the chest. The boy cried out in shock and pain. Staggering backward, he threw the snake to the ground.

"Mr. Rattlesnake, what have you done? You promised not to harm me! Now I will surely die!" he cried.

As the life slowly began to slip from the deceived Cherokee's body, the rattlesnake could only offer a sly grin with this slithering answer: "You knew what I was when you first picked me up."

The lesson is obvious: some things are best resisted by leaving them alone, and the above story is usually employed in a chiding, moralizing way to warn about what the preachers of my childhood called the "sins of the flesh"—sex, alcohol, card-playing, dancing, and the like. That's how I always heard the story used. But for centuries, the Christian church has been cuddling with something that is far more dangerous than any of these moral potholes. That something is power. It is the Empire. And it is killing us.

Put This Book Down Now!

Regardless of their particular denominational flavor, the majority of this country's churches are fiercely joined to American goals, ambitions, ideals, and nationalism. On most any national holiday, particularly Independence Day, "God and Country" patriotic rallies take place inside churches of all theological brands. Stars and stripes are draped from the ceiling. A recording of Lee Greenwood's "God Bless the USA" booms across the room or is sung by the church's best soloist. A military color guard brings weapons of war before the altar of the Prince of Peace. Stories of American economic and armed supremacy mingle with the Sunday school stories of faith.

If all this seems "Yankee Doodle Dandyish" to you, put this book down now and walk away. Don't read another word unless you have a handful of beta-blockers to keep your elevated blood pressure from blowing your eye-balls out. But if you are like a growing number of Jesus followers in North America, you've had this splinter in your mind for a while now that tells you there is something suspicious about attaching a national flag—any national flag—to the cross. It doesn't feel right. In fact, it feels a bit slithery.

The first time I sensed something was wrong, I was participating in one of the most recognizable and highly anticipated events on the church calen-dar: Vacation Bible School. It is a familiar scene. Children gather on the front porch in tightly regimented lines. Divided by age and gender, and all wearing the standard-issue t-shirt uniform, they wave their flags and banners, giggle, smile, and proceed into the building. Leading these marching Christian soldiers are brave lieutenants drafted into hazardous service. For some of these leaders, this will be their first and last tour of duty; the demands of combat will prove too much. But for others—the battle-tested and grizzled veterans—you can bet they will be back next summer to lead a new class of young recruits.

By my thirteenth year, I suppose I had dutifully marched into a church sanctuary for Vacation Bible School at least a hundred times. I not only participated in the weeklong affair at my own church but also made the rounds each summer with friends and cousins to the VBS at their churches. Songs. Bible stories. Cookies. Crafts. Games. Sticky red fruit punch in Styrofoam cups. Dirty little hands running along the church hallway walls. More cookies. It is no wonder why children enjoy it so. Eventually I moved up to lieutenant, leading my own group of conscripts, and finally I made general, that is, the pastor who presided over the opening ceremonies each evening.

Every year—as a child, teacher, or pastor—some things changed about Vacation Bible School: the director, the curriculum, the crowd, the theme, the color of the punch. But some things did not change. As constant as that summer gathering of children on the church's front porch was the processional of flags and pledges. Once the little marchers were settled into their pews to begin the evening, every Vacation Bible School I ever attended or presided over began with a familiar phrase: "I pledge allegiance to the flag of the United States of America." I once considered this pledge an indispensable part of the VBS experience. Now I can't in good conscience ask children to offer enthusiastic allegiance to the present Empire while in a place of worship. It is a muddy conjoining of allegiances.

We operate under the notion that America actually belongs to us Christians and that we belong to it. We believe the church and the state can make beautiful music together if only they would cooperate. We believe the preaching of the Kingdom of God and the rallying around the red, white, and blue are always compatible. We believe the lie of the Serpent that we can hold to the sacrificial, life-giving, peace-pursuing, cheek-turning way of Christ *and* hold to the poisonous, domineering, power-hungry, least-of-these-abusing systems of the Empire. But this is impossible.

"Wait a minute!" your patriotic soul may object as you throw back that beta-blocker and the room begins to spin. "What is wrong with a little flag waving in the church sanctuary? What's the problem with a pledge or two to the nation of our birth during VBS? We can be American and Christian, you know!" Yes, I know this—as long as we remember that there is no such thing as an *American Christian*; but there are Christians who *happen to reside* in America.

Understand that I love America, but not at the expense of marginalizing the Lordship of Jesus. I will say the pledge, but I will not intentionally put up barriers between me and my brothers and sisters in Christ who do not share my nationality (yes, there are Christians in other countries, and being Christians, our connection with them is stronger than the bonds of nationalism). Yes, I will sing the National Anthem, but I will not ask Jesus to share his place of supremacy with the flag. In short, I am more committed to Christ than I am to country, and my home is in the Kingdom of God, not in the Empire of the present world.

For when the church gathers to worship, it is gathering as a distinct people who have one primary allegiance. It is a gathering of people held together not by the accidental place or country of our birth, the War on Terror, or Jeffersonian documents stored in the basement of the Smithsonian. The bond that unites all believers is the person of Jesus Christ. Our allegiance is to him. He is our King. He is our Lord. It is his kingdom we serve. All other kingdoms and empires—including the United States— are in competition with the Kingdom of God, and these cannot demand our principal loyalty.

A great many Christians have never seriously considered the obvious truth, distracted as we are by trying to reclaim a Christian nation that never existed. That truth is this: *As an empire (simply a diverse group of people under a single sovereign authority), the United States does not value the way of Jesus, no matter what is printed on its coins or what hangs or does not hang on local courthouse walls. The Empire only values power: the possession of and control over others.* The church does not fit into this power game and should never seek to do so, for whenever the church receives the approval of the Empire at large, this is a sure sign that something is dreadfully wrong. It is a sign that we are holding the snake terribly close to our hearts.

Of course this relationship with power is nothing new. For all of us living in North America, the connection between the church and power is basically all we have ever known. When Spanish explorers landed in the New World, they made it a habit to read "The Requirement" to the native tribes they encountered, a note of welcome from the king and the pope. In part, it read, "I implore you to recognize the Church as a lady and in the name of the Pope take the King as lord of this land and obey his mandates. If you do not do it, I tell you that with the help of God I will enter powerfully against you all. I will make war everywhere and every way that I can. I will subject you to the yoke and obedience of the Church and to his majesty."[1] Church and power have been fused together since the first Euro-American Empire began, but even that is not the beginning.

Not many decades after the resurrected Jesus ascended to heaven and the first Apostles died, somebody—several people actually—decided it would be a good idea to join forces with the powers that be. After all, imagine how many people could be converted, helped, enrolled, and evangelized if the church were more powerful, more organized, and more efficient (it's amazing how often such thoughts arise). The church went for power and won it in spades. The coffers ran over with gold; people of influence, including the emperor, began to seek the ministers' approval on public policy; the pews were full every Sunday; there were no more martyrdoms (unless you were someone who opposed this new arrangement); and the "church's computers jammed trying to move all the names from the 'Pagan' column to the 'Christian' column until somebody realized it was just easier to switch the headings."[2]

Ever since, and this was more than fifteen centuries ago, Christians have more or less followed whomever was in charge, believing that such a union would enhance the work and mission of the church. What actually happened was the Empire gained everything by becoming "Christian" (but didn't really have to change anything), and the church lost everything by picking up the poisoned means and ways of the world.[3]

Just Imagine

This may be unsettling to some, but the earliest followers of Jesus did not refer to themselves as Christians. I am rather glad about this because the word "Christian" has too much baggage attached to it. It has come to mean a type of religion, or it is used as an adjective to describe music, politics, or schmaltzy merchandise. In the first century, those *outside* the community of Jesus coined the word "Christian" to describe people who had adopted the words and way of Jesus as their own. The first believers in Jesus referred to their pursuit as "The Way," a much better description.

Being a "Christian"—a word used only three times in the New Testament—is not Jesus' goal for his people. But making a community of revolutionary followers or "disciples"—a word used nearly three hundred times in the New Testament—seems to be exactly the goal. The church must return to these roots. The church must become a way of life, an alternative lifestyle, a counter-community of Christ followers. Church must once again become a people who are on "The Way" formed by the words and way of Jesus.

Most of the time we call this community of people the "church." But that is another word that doesn't seem to work anymore, at least not for me. Oh, I still believe in that living thing known as the Body of Christ. I still believe in the *ecclesia*, those whom Jesus has "called out" from the world. I still believe in the local congregation and its Spirit-infused witness that can transform individuals and communities, but I have lost faith in the English word "church." In the imagination, the word too often conjures up pictures of somber robe-clad clergy, of closed and suffocating systems of legalism, of places where the doctrines and the pews are screwed to the floor, of angry picketing Christians, of multi-million-dollar mega-façades or cold, damp, deteriorating cathedrals.

Going further, many people think of church as nothing more than a place—a building, something constructed with brick and mortar, stained glass, tiled floors, pointy steeples, and heavy wooden furniture. This does not take into account our two-millennia history littered with moral failures, doctrinal squabbles, dissention and separation, crusades and inquisitions, bloodshed and war in the name of the "holy." But if you really want to know what pops into people's heads when they think "church," conduct an interview on any street corner (make sure that blood pressure medicine is still in your hip pocket). Likely, it will not be a pleasant experience.

Most of us can accept the failures of the church, as it is filled with flawed, imperfect people and it will never be a utopia. That is fine, as the church does not exist for that purpose. It does, however, exist to bear witness to the words and way of Christ, and we cannot accept less than that. When bestselling author Anne Rice made a public departure from Christianity, her words—"Today I quit being a Christian . . . . I remain committed to Christ as always but not to being Christian"—rattled around the Internet like marbles in a tin can. Some defended her. Some attacked her. Some were confused by her. Some took the opportunity to preach her a sermon. But one thing was clear through all these conversations: the disconnection between Jesus' way and the church that bears his name produces a dissonance that some people simply cannot hold in their minds, including me.

For this reason, and because of all the baggage cataloged above, I am introducing here a less common metaphor to describe the church. That word and metaphor is "tribe," specifically the "Jesus Tribe." Seth Godin defines a tribe as a group of people connected to one another, connected to an idea, and connected to a leader.[4] Jesus is our leader, the Kingdom of God is the idea, and those of us who have heard and heeded the words "Follow me" form the people connected one to another. This is the Jesus Tribe.

This metaphor is not my invention. It is actually found in the Scriptures. Our ancient tribal roots run all the way back to Father Abraham. The Jesus Tribe has been forged in the fires of slavery, struggle, and adversity. Our forbearers were a people who played hide-and-seek under the canopy of the Old Testament prophets, whose voices echo through the history and songbooks of old, and whose identity rings out in the Apostles' preaching. Simon Peter articulated our heritage, character, and coming challenges when he said,

> You are a chosen people. You are royal priests, a holy nation, God's very own possession.... Once you had no identity as a people; now you are God's people. Dear friends, I warn you as "temporary residents and for-eigners" to keep away from worldly desires that wage war against your very souls. Be careful to live properly among your unbelieving neighbors. (1 Pet 2:9-12)

Promised to our forefathers, anticipated in the Christ, and fulfilled in Jesus of Nazareth, this Tribe has a lineage that endures to this day. While we must live in this world, we do not belong to it, for our citizenship lies within the Kingdom of God as we join him in his creative work of redemption. But until that Kingdom completely comes, we are compelled to live as aliens and strangers in a world we can no longer call home—even a world called America.

If you read on, you will find this book to be about

- waking up to the opportunity now before the church, the opportunity to reclaim our unique tribal identity as followers of Jesus in the shadow of the Empire;
- forsaking our addiction to, dependence on, and dangerous handling of the seductive powers of the world;

- the "category-smashing, life-threatening, anti-institutional gospel that spread through the first century like wildfire but was considered by those in power to be dangerous";[5]
- and committing to a life of radical discipleship that graciously resists and defies "how things really work" in the world.

Imagine what could happen if any of this takes root in our hearts! If we finally decide that the Dow Jones Index is not god; that the winner of elections, now or whenever, is not Lord; that the rules and stories that control our society are wrong; that the way into the future is not paved with more and more possessions, with higher and higher standards of living, or with the blood and corpses of our enemies. Imagine if we could be free from the materialistic, pleasure-driven, individualized, greedy rules of the world. Imagine what would happen if we held intensely to our identity-shaping, life-giving commitment to Christ, rather than being anesthetized by the sedative of the religious status quo. Imagine a place where we offer others a powerful, life-changing, life-forming story of what it means to be the people of God on mission in the world.

Imagine a day when followers of Jesus do not choose the path that leads to the highest corporate salaries, the greatest personal success, or the most profitable bottom line. Rather, they learn to become men and women of "The Way" who will care for the poor, work to heal and help others in Jesus' name, and refuse to participate in systems of abusive power. Imagine a people who understand that the most radical and world-changing thing they can do is "stop believing in the dominant systems and rules of this world," for these are all passing away. Imagine a church that exists not to sustain the world around us but to live as "a contradiction full of hope and promise."[6] If we can begin to imagine some of this, we can imagine life in the Jesus Tribe.

Come to Qualla

To develop this tribal metaphor further, I need to look no further than my own genealogical record. In the middle of the nineteenth century, when the Cherokee Nation was being uprooted and expelled from their primeval home by gold-crazed Georgians, one of my Scotch-Irish ancestors took a bride who was a proud daughter of the Cherokee Nation. I still remember how my great-grandmother's skin was as burgundy as red wine, and how she would say a brief Cherokee blessing over Sunday dinner from time to time.

And though it has now been bred down to less than fractional amounts, that tribal blood still runs in my family's veins.[7]

This heritage was reinforced by the fact that I grew up a five-minute drive from the last eastern capital of the Cherokee Nation before the Trail of Tears. That capital is called New Echota or "New Town." This was a thriving community once, before the Empire arrived. But today, while part of the site is preserved by the State of Georgia, most of the former glory of what was New Echota lies beneath a community golf course and a state highway, a casualty to the powers that prevailed.

As the sprawling Empire of the United States populace came crashing and intruding upon the Cherokee shores, those ancient people found themselves trying to answer a twofold question: (1) How do we sustain our unique way of life against the onslaught of a greater, prevailing culture, and (2) when and to what extent do we adapt to engage this new civilization around us? The Cherokee dealt with their situation with varying degrees of success. But typically, they opted for one of three alternatives. These alternatives are now put squarely before the church.

First, *conform*. Become like those who have now entered the land. United States Secretary of War John C. Calhoun (whom, ironically, my hometown is named after) saw this option playing out clearly in the future. He stated to the Cherokee chiefs, "Your great object ought to become as your neighbors; and to live and bring up your children in the same way they do, and gradually adopt their laws and manners."[8] His answer to the Cherokee question was simple: "You will be assimilated." Similarly, conformity could spell the death of the church's witness in North America, a slow suffocation of sorts as the unique identity of the Jesus Tribe is absorbed by the broader culture.

Second, *combat*. Many Cherokee did just that. Native blood soaked the red clay of the Appalachians as the people fought against the white-skinned invaders who had come to take their land. Likewise, Christians have often opted for this path. Yes, with the sword, but in our more "civilized" nation our brutality is committed with words, court battles, and angry letters to the editor. As our land is "stolen," many believers wage the violence of holy cultural crusade in an attempt to stave off the invaders who have come to destroy our way of life. Hate and blood scorch the ground beneath our feet once again.

Third, *concede*. Most of the Cherokee, unwilling to comply or raise their weapons in aggression, finally went quietly into the night. They packed what goods they could carry, and, fighting starvation, dehydration, and disease, were forcibly marched to the margins of the American continent where their strange ways and customs could not impede the progress of the Manifest Destiny. Again, this is an option for the church. We can just give up and wait for the inevitable. Our houses of worship will become reservations—museums that memorialize a day long gone.

Conformity.
Combat.
Concession.

These seem to be the only options when handling the snake that is the Empire. Surely we can maintain our unique character as those "called out" while graciously interacting with the dominating powers around us? Surely there is a more authentic and redemptive way forward than these options that are nothing more than dead ends. Surely that portion of the Jesus Tribe found living in the shadow of the American Empire's power can live differently than this. I think there is a better option. It is something the Eastern Cherokee called *Qualla.*

The Eastern Band of the Cherokee, my distant ancestors, traces its descendants back to a small group of tribespeople who did not wage war against the Americans and who managed to elude the forced removal. Chief Yonaguska, also known as Drowning Bear, and his adopted Caucasian son William Thomas, carved out 640 acres in the North Carolina hills, a meager homeland in light of what the Cherokee Nation once held. This land, now more than 57,000 acres, is commonly referred to as the *Cherokee Indian Reservation*, but that is not completely accurate, for it is not a reservation. Officially this ground is called the *Qualla Boundary.* This is sacred space that has never left Cherokee possession. It is holy ground held in common and in trust, where the Cherokee perpetuate their way of life. It is within the boundary of the Empire—there's no doubt about that—but it does not belong to the Empire. To use biblical language, it is "in the world, but it is not of the world" (see John 17:15-18).

Today, when you visit the Qualla Boundary, you will find a thriving hub of tourist activity. All the customary attractions are there: native arts and dance, more than one staged photo opportunity, a wonderful museum, archaeological sites, and, yes, the obligatory casino. But if you look closer you will discover much more. You will find some of the oldest craft-making traditions in North America. You will hear the Cherokee language, almost extinct a generation ago, being spoken and taught. And you will visit the mother villages of the Cherokee Nation, a constant reminder of where these people came from, where they are going, and who they are.

At Qualla you can enter into a culture and a people who study, work, play, worship, remember, plan, believe, and behave differently than "the rest of the world." That is uniqueness. That is a way of life. That is an alternative existence in the shadow of power. That is counter-community, and we must become that kind of people again, a people who persist in sustaining the Jesus way of life, a people who live out a distinctive, radical discipleship in the world.

Of course, the Jesus Tribe's Qualla is no pine-laden forest in the hills. It's not a church building, a mountain retreat center, a bunker in the Montana wilderness, or a hoped-for skyhook rescue whereby we escape while everyone else is "left behind." Our holy ground is Jesus himself—his words, his way, and his power that comes from a cross and a resurrection, not an Empire of the world.

As we explore these words and way of Jesus, my constant reference point will be the greatest sermon he or anyone else has ever preached: the Sermon on the Mount. Matthew, it seems, collected these words of Jesus as the bedrock of our Lord's instruction. In fact, these may be the words Matthew has in mind when at the conclusion of his Gospel he quotes Jesus saying, "Go and make disciples of all the nations, baptizing them in the name of the Father and the Son and the Holy Spirit. *Teach these new disciples to obey all the commands I have given you*" (Matt 28:19-20). We might think of these chapters as "Jesus' Greatest Hits,"[9] a summary of what it means to be his disciple, a member of his tribe. These words serve as a means—maybe the most practical means—of actually following Jesus.

This does not mean that Jesus' words from the Sermon on the Mount will answer all our questions about what it means to follow him. These words will not defuse the tension or untangle the knot of clinging to the radical and revolutionary Christ while living in a violent, hateful, power-hungry world. These words may in fact produce even more angst for us than if we had just left them alone. But for those of us who have grappled with what it means to pursue Jesus in these uncertain chaotic times, I hope this book will begin to flesh out the implications, possibilities, contradictions, and complexities of what it means to live within the Jesus Tribe in the shadow of the American Empire, and to keep us from picking up the rattlesnake.

One last beginning note: When Chief Drowning Bear came to the end of his life, the future of his people at Qualla was uncertain. He called the tribal elders together for one final word. Wrapped in a blanket, holding back the chill of death, he charged his people to live peaceably alongside those who had come to share their ancient hills. But the Cherokee Nation could never—under any circumstance and no matter how tempting—trade in their unique way of life. To do so, he warned, would be to give away their identity and their very existence. The challenge before the Jesus Tribe is no less different and no less critical.

Chapter 1

A Three-legged Stool

Then Jesus was led by the Spirit into the wilderness to be tempted there by the devil. For forty days and forty nights he fasted and became very hungry. During that time the devil came and said to him, "If you are the Son of God, tell these stones to become loaves of bread." But Jesus told him, "No! The Scriptures say, 'People do not live by bread alone, but by every word that comes from the mouth of God.'"

Then the devil took him to the holy city, Jerusalem, to the highest point of the Temple, and said, "If you are the Son of God, jump off! For the Scriptures say, 'He will order his angels to protect you. And they will hold you up with their hands so you won't even hurt your foot on a stone.'" Jesus responded, "The Scriptures also say, 'You must not test the Lord your God.'"

Next the devil took him to the peak of a very high mountain and showed him all the kingdoms of the world and their glory. "I will give it all to you," he said, "if you will kneel down and worship me." "Get out of here, Satan," Jesus told him. "For the Scriptures say, 'You must worship the Lord your God and serve only him.'" Then the devil went away. (Matt 4:1-11)[1]

The book of Genesis opens with the familiar phrase, "In the beginning," and one does not have to look much further than that to find the roots of the first empire. The voracious thirst for power has been present since the beginning of recorded history. God created humanity to live in trustful dependence on him, but our ancestors reached for the forbidden fruit of self-rule. They aimed to replace the Creator with themselves (see Gen 3:4). They succeeded, of course, and reaped the whirlwind.

A few pages later, we move from the lush, green garden of Eden to a wide, open desert—an alluvial plain now pounded by the boots of American soldiers, the plain of Shinar in the Tigris-Euphrates River valley of modern-day Iraq. There the civilization of the Middle East gathered to build a tower to heaven, the first human attempt at wholesale consolidated power. Genesis 11:4 captures their motivation: "Come, let's build a great city for ourselves with a tower that reaches into the sky."

This early effort at empire building was named "Babel," which means "gateway to the gods." This was more than a tower to the heavens. It was the corporate abandonment of divine dependence for human supremacy. It was the same sin as the sin in Eden, a declaration of extreme independence and an attempt to storm the gates of heaven and wrestle control of human destiny from the hand of God. God saw those bricks rising to heaven and came down to visit as the most exacting of building inspectors. Calling a heavenly council to deliberate (Gen 11:5-7), God elected to confound human language, creating a myriad of tribal cultures, and scattered humanity across the face of the earth.

Every empire, from Babel to the current nation-state, operates under the same unifying principle: to commandeer heaven; to depose the Creator and play the role of God in the world. After thousands of years, and countless monuments to our hubris dotting the planet, the spiritual pathology of Babel has yet to be removed from the human heart.[2] But into this soul sickness and commotion God clearly speaks. Turning from the confusion of Genesis 11, we flip the Bible's page to read, "The LORD *had said* to Abram, 'Leave your native country, your relatives, and your father's family, and go to the land that I will show you'" (Gen 12:1, italics added).

Note that God *had already spoken* to Abram (who would become Abraham), and had called him away from the building of empires. With the tower of Babel eroding away in the Iraqi desert, and maybe Abram as one of its former, now disappointed brick masons, God speaks to him again and calls out a tribe—aliens and strangers in a strange land. God seeks to create a people who will follow him, submit to him, and trust him. The result of this will be a unique people whom God will use to bless and grace the entire world.

It is in this context of Babel and human empires that "tribe," and more specifically the "Jesus Tribe," can be accurately defined. By using words like "apart," "separation," and "tribe" to describe the church, I am not advocating sectarianism, rebellion, seclusion, or isolation. Instead, we must become a community of faith that so heeds the voice of Christ, that is so shaped and formed by the words and way of Jesus, that we become a genuine, alternative society that lives in hopeful, peaceful defiance, subverting and resisting with grace the world of empire. As followers of Jesus, we are not Babel builders. We are not power seekers. While once we may have plied away within the systems of the world, we do so no longer. It is now our vocation to "hold the Powers, their seduction, and their enslavement, at a distance," allowing our very existence to be our greatest witness.[3] In the desert, Jesus shows us how to do this.

Feeding the Belly of the Beast

Jesus' baptism signaled the beginning of his public ministry and served as a prelude to the Sermon on the Mount. At such a beginning, the looming questions hanging over Jesus' ministry would have been, "What kind of power will this Jesus use to accomplish his purposes? What method will this man employ to bring his ambitions to bear on the world around him? What path will he take to the throne of the nation?" The answers to these questions begin to take shape as, still dripping wet from his baptism, Jesus is driven into the desert. After spending forty days and nights fasting, like a landlord showing up at the most inopportune time to badger a tenant for rent, the devil comes a calling with temptations of bread, skydives, and mountain climbing.

Though I grew up in the church and heard this text preached many times, I never understood the desert temptations of Jesus. Preachers and evangelists often spoke of the heavyweight boxing match between Jesus and the Tempter, but I didn't get the point. How could the invitation to bake a little wilderness bread be classified as a sin? And what was the whole "cast yourself down" at the temple about? The only temptation that made any sense to me was the last one, when the devil invited Jesus to fall down in submission. Such an act was so obviously wrong, the act of worshiping the devil, that it hardly seemed like a temptation at all. My childhood preachers always resolved my questions with a Puritanized discussion about the "lust of the flesh" and told me to stay away from liquor, naked-picture magazines, the opposite sex, and HBO. That was their solution for most temptations.

However, these temptations were real options presented by the devil that went far beyond appeals to Jesus' hunger, lust, or pride and represented far more than baking bread, taking bungee jumps off the church steeple, and drawing pentagrams on the ground. These temptations were attempts to provide Jesus with an easier means for achieving his mission, to build an empire through systematic force and domination rather than establishing the Kingdom of God through love, justice, and suffering sacrifice. The devil invited Jesus to reach a sanctified finish by following an unsanctioned path. This path was paved with the bricks of the tower of Babel: bread, temples, and mountains—or, put another way, economics, religion, and political/military power, the major structures upon which all empires are built. This is what Donald Kraybill calls the three-legged stool of human power.[4]

Jesus answers these temptations and the questions surrounding the onset of his ministry loudly and clearly. He will not employ the established human systems of power offered by the empire for his own purposes. The entire episode in the wilderness and the intent of the Sermon on the Mount are about Jesus' refusal to slap mortar in between Babel's bricks and joints; he knew that no human power can serve God's ultimate will. And his followers (if we take his example and words as our own) can learn to do the same: refuse to collaborate with the fallen, abusive systems of the world.

But first temptations first: Why did Jesus refuse to turn stones into bread in the wilderness? God knows the people to whom Jesus preached could have benefited from a good meal. In his day, eight out of ten people were in the peasant class or lower—the unclean and "expendable." Most lived in extreme poverty, often not knowing from where their next meal would come. Meanwhile, the aristocracy of the upper class grew more and more wealthy. The Jewish society of the first century was rotting from within as the gap between the "haves" and the "have-nots" grew wider almost daily.[5] The American Empire that now surrounds us isn't much different.

The United States Department of Agriculture (USDA) issues a hunger report every year. It is a barometer of sorts that gauges Americans' access to food. One of the latest reports has determined that no one in America is going hungry. Sound like good news? Think again. Authors of the report have determined that hunger is "not a scientifically accurate term for the specific phenomenon being measured in the survey." The geniuses at the USDA have concluded that hunger is incalculable and thus the term should be dropped. In other words, there are no hungry Americans. But 35 million Americans cannot put food on their tables at least part of the year. Of these, 11 million consistently do not get enough to eat. But they are not hungry, mind you. No, these 11 million Americans are experiencing, and I quote, "very low food security." But they are not "hungry." That term no longer applies.[6]

When there are so many people hungry, or "experiencing low food security," in this country and another 800 million plus in the world community, couldn't we stand a little boulders-into-bread action? Why not get that divine Easy-Bake oven working in a hurry? Because turning stones into bread was not an invitation to feed the hungry. It was incitement for a pitchfork-waving, torch-burning, castle-storming peasant rebellion. Jesus, starved himself after forty days without food, personally felt the hunger of Palestine's disadvantaged masses. He identified easily with their desperation and would have known the truth of the old adage that the quickest way to a man's heart was though his stomach.

With his supernatural breadline working around the clock, Jesus could soon have an army of devoted revolutionists at his disposal. But Jesus refused the temptation to become a welfare king who would satisfy the needs of the people by means of economic domination and dependency. He knew that baskets full of bread were only a quick fix, and the crowds would follow him only because their stomachs and savings accounts were full. Miraculous feedings, a "chicken in every pot," did not produce serious discipleship; nor will it ever.

Later in his ministry, at the feeding of the five thousand (see John 6), this reality was graphically illustrated. With stomachs full of sardines and crescent rolls, the crowd pressed Jesus so hard to become their king that he literally had to hide in the hills. Jesus would later explain to the masses, "You want to be with me because I fed you, not because you understood" (John 6:26). But this is something powerbrokers understand well: "It's the economy, stupid." Bread for Jewish peasants, circuses for the Romans, and a double-digit return for the American investor: deliver these goods and all will go well for the elected officials, regardless of the particular empire. The economic systems of the world are based largely on the belief that economic prosperity (bread) is the surest means of happiness and security. Thus, those who steer these economic systems are powerful people indeed.

Yet empires cannot succeed among a people who refuse to be economically dependent (a topic that unfolds later in the Sermon on the Mount). This was the wonderful rebuke lived out by the early church. They took care of one another, shared everything in common, and built a community of partnership. They chose to rely on God and one another rather than on the empire. Out of this dependence on a greater Power than the empire in which they lived, they were able to meet the growing material needs of their Tribe. And when they could not meet these needs, they were willing to do without and to sacrifice rather than capitulate to the empire. This willingness to sacrifice gives the church a unique and powerful witness when it is God who provides for our needs, and not our preciously guarded 501c3 empire-approving, tax-exempt status without which we feel we would not be able to function, as "charitable giving" would collapse almost overnight.

Wake Up!

From 1981 to 1990, hundreds of mysterious deaths were reported to the Centers for Disease Control in Atlanta, Georgia. Healthy adult men, most of them members of the immigrant Hmong community from the Laotian Highlands, were dying in their sleep. After some research, the death-sleep was also found to affect males in Singapore, the Philippines, and other parts of Asia. At the time, no medical cause of death could be determined. The only evidence doctors had was the victims' apparent struggle in violent nightmares just before death. With little else to go on, the deaths were simply labeled "Sudden Unexplained Nocturnal Death Syndrome."[7]

The Hmong people, however, had their own explanation. They claimed that these young men were the victims of a nocturnal visitor they called the Dab Tsog. Dab Tsog, the Hmong said, was a nightmare in the old meaning of the word: an evil spirit that visited the victim while he slept and took his life. Dab Tsog would enter the bedroom, so the Hmong said, and climb on the victim's chest. With crushing weight, he would sit there suffocating and slowly squeezing the sleeper's life away. The only way to escape the Dab Tsog was to wake up before it was too late.[8]

The second temptation of Jesus is about waking up and shaking off the Empire's most effective tranquilizer: religion. While throwing around God's name and giving Jesus the occasional pat on the head, Christians in this country are sung to sleep by "God Bless America" speeches and National Prayer Breakfasts. Christian groups of all stripes (right/left/liberal/conservative/other) seek to enforce religious power over the American state as they view the mission of the church as synonymous with North American Judeo-Christian culture. We have created a Jesus in our nation's image, wrapped in the flag and leading us into war, allowing us to fuse religion with empire. Many a believer in America has bought into the devilish lie that this country is uniquely superior to all other nations or people groups, and that she has a unique mission and blessing from God to redeem the world. We remain so sedated and still that we do not open a discerning eye to take a closer look.

This is the opposite reaction from the Jesus Tribe that first emerged in the world. Those early Christians referred to empire and power systems with a single word: "Babylon." Babylon was the heathen nation that crushed the Israelites and carried them into exile some five hundred years before Christ. It was a cataclysmic event, an ancient Holocaust, that stuck in the Jewish and early Christian memory. In Babylon, the Jewish nation was forced to live as aliens and strangers, maintaining their unique culture in the face of domination and assimilation. The exiles understood that they did not belong in Babylon, and they lived unique lives not for uniqueness sake but to survive as a people.

This Babylonian experience shaped how the first generations of Christians, particularly the writer of Revelation, related to the empire around them. They too did not belong in Babylon and imagined its economic, religious, and political domination as a drunken whore riding a terrible, destructive beast that trampled the world beneath its feet (see Rev 17). First-century Christians saw their faith communities as incompatible with the Roman Empire of Caesar—they would have been horrified to be joined to that ugly beast. And while the names of empires change, their means and methods do not. We still live in Babylon, and it is still incompatible with the way of Jesus.

Tony Campolo says it clearer than most: "America may be the best Babylon out there, but it is still Babylon."[9] The shock and awe most of us feel at reading Campolo's words reveals just how drunk and seduced we are by the whore on the beast. It shows us how dead asleep we are. But Jesus was a man very much awake, and he wants us to be the same.

The religious climate of Jesus' day was a seething cauldron of tension and conflict, as much as or more so than our own. Pharisees, Sadducees, Essenes, and bands of violent Zealots all stirred the religious soup pot, each group looking for a specific type of Messiah. A miraculous appearance by the Messiah as he floated down to the temple court unharmed by a divine bungee jump would unite the differing religious groups of the day and forge a new nationalism that not even Rome could squelch. This was the sleeping pill the Tempter offered, but again Jesus would not take up religious muscle to accomplish his mission, understanding the eventual nightmare if he did.

Not far from my home is a Baptist church. I suppose it's like most Baptist churches that dot the highways of the south. They have a modest sanctuary. The former worship space has been converted into the "fellowship hall." I'm sure the hallways of the buildings have crayon and worn marks from little hands and the foot traffic of many a covered dish gathering. Perhaps the men's group meets monthly to eat, burp, and talk about who is going to cut the grass. And if it is like most Baptist churches, the Women's Missionary Union (WMU) is actually in charge, though no one would admit it. Historically the WMU has gotten more done than any other group in the Baptist church and probably deserves to be in charge.

In front of the church is a huge sign stating the times of worship, Sunday school, and the midweek prayer service. There is also space for a pithy message for the public to read. Typically it says something like "The family that prays together stays together," or it holds some other harmless, well-worn cliché. I'm sure the poor pastor is usually the one who has to change those signs in addition to preaching, presiding at committees, visiting the sick, and minding the old ladies' Sunday school class, so I cut him some slack on the creativity test. But in the days leading up to a national election, the sign read, "Vote for Jesus!!!"

Jesus' name will never appear on a Tuesday ballot, but many Christians of variegated political leanings pull the lever each November, thinking they are in fact voting for Jesus because of their particular stand on issues or party affiliation. Religion is used as a tool to garner votes, sanction candidates, and justify all manner of policy decisions. In the end, everyone is saluting the flag and their particular version of the Christian faith, but I don't think Jesus is much involved. Christians of all stripes and shades have put far too much confidence in human government as the means to transform the world. Many of us vote under the assumption that if only the right man/woman/party/ideology could get seated in the White House, the court house, or the school house, then the Kingdom of God would come. That is an illusion. As members of the Jesus Tribe, we do not look for the church to assist in or endorse the building of a made-in-America utopia that is only a Babylon with red, white, and blue curtains. We look for a city whose builder and maker is God. To him, and only him, we must pledge our primary allegiance.

A word of warning: this kind of thinking is exactly what got the first Christians in heaps of trouble. They would not bring their faith under the Roman pantheon or collaborate with state power. Our Christian ancestors found themselves on the business end of the "Patriot Act" of their day not because they believed in the afterlife, because they believed Jesus died for their sins, or even because they claimed Christ rose from the dead. They were thrown to the gladiators and lions, crucified, exiled, marginalized, and otherwise persecuted "for following a way that ran counter to the prevailing direction" of the empire.[10]

We must understand that Jesus offers a profoundly different way to live in the world today—not just a comfortable afterlife in the by and by. This contradictory way that resists the powers of the world has real social consequences. This does not mean Christians should not speak to or act within the systems of the world. It means we speak and act as Christians within those systems, refusing to accept the world's definition and rules of power.

And it means we should not be surprised if and when these systems do not tolerate our voice and presence. We won't belong. We will be branded as unpatriotic. We will be odd and eccentric. We might be persecuted. I am not intentionally seeking this kind of reaction, but when forced to choose—and we must all choose—we must call Christ the Lord.

Death in All Directions

The Palestine of Jesus' day could be any number of Middle Eastern nations of our own time. Political unrest, rebellion, civil uprisings, guerilla fighters, sectarian violence, bleeding patriots, acts of terrorism, decades of oppression, wars and struggle for independence: Palestine had these in spades. Read a modern newspaper or online news feed from Afghanistan, Beirut, the West Bank, or Pakistan and you will have a close appreciation for the situation in the Holy Land in the first century. It was a quagmire.

With the third wilderness temptation, the Tempter leads Jesus to a high mountain and then draws his attention to an area where Jesus' superhuman powers could do some real good—the kingdoms of the world. The traditional site of the Mount of Temptation is a steep incline about 1,200 feet high. This height is deceptive as the Mount of Temptation is west of Jericho in the valley along the Dead Sea. This location, the Dead Sea being the lowest place on earth, makes the mountain appear much taller. From this vantage point, Jesus could see death in every direction. The nations, as always, were a mess of violence, bloodshed, and injustice.

This final temptation of the three was overtly political and militaristic. The possibility of Jesus becoming what his nation wanted most, a political or military leader, was real. Someone with the right charisma, revolutionary strength, and idealism could unite the people of God and reestablish Israel's glory. This had been attempted with varying degrees of success in Israel's past, most strikingly during the Maccabean Wars only a century and a half before Jesus. The Tempter laid this option on the table for Jesus to take up as his own: "Re-institutionalize the nation and from there, rule and bring peace to the world. Jesus, you could straighten this out." Again, Christ refused, offering his strongest word of rebuke to the devil yet.

There are a few significant things about this third leg of the stool of power. First, Jesus did not disagree with or correct Satan when Satan offered him unrestricted politico-military dominance. Apparently, it was the Tempter's to give. The New Testament paints a fairly clear picture of Satan's role in the present world as the god of this age (see John 12:31; 14:30;

16:11; 2 Cor 4:4). I neither infer that a red-clothed, pitchfork-carrying cartoon character is the dominating force of planet earth nor necessarily mean the devil/Satan/Tempter is an easily defined and categorized literal being. Rather, I see Satan as described with Ephesians 6 language: the name attached to the real systems of domination and manipulation that enslave God's good earth. This lust-hungry power is, without a doubt, accurately defined as satanic, with the full force of the word.

Second, and this should give we who are Christians great pause, it requires a bowing down to the Tempter to get this kind of power. Do we really want to participate in or partner with a system that is inherently evil? Let me hurry to say that individuals serving in governments and empires are not necessarily evil, though some may be. My point is that the system itself is polluted, and trusting in these political power systems is an act of idolatry where we can be led to trust them to deliver safety and well-being instead of trusting God though Jesus. There is something dangerously dark in wielding political and military power within the empire because it requires compromise in following Jesus.

Third, the only way one can gain "the kingdoms of the world and their glory is to follow the Tempter's way of violence, a way that promises, but cannot deliver peace (this is a subject to which I will return in the coming pages). To hold political power in the land of the empire is to hold military power and use it in defending and expanding national borders against internal and external enemies. If one is going to rule an empire or even maintain the security of a nation, one must be willing to wage war. War, in this context, is a requirement of nations, particularly a nation like America whose borders and interests stretch over so much land and sea. That is simply what nations must do, and anyone who thinks differently is not being practical.

In December 2009, President Barack Obama delivered a historical speech at his acceptance of the Nobel Peace Prize ceremony in Oslo. For a speech about peace, his words acknowledged this absolute necessity to wage war in defense of empire. With words that could have been spoken from any United States President, he said,

> As a head of state sworn to protect and defend my nation . . . I face the world as it is, and cannot stand idle in the face of threats to the American people . . . . A nonviolent movement could not have halted Hitler's armies. Negotiations cannot convince al-Qaida's leaders to lay down their arms. To say that force is sometimes necessary is not a call to cynicism—it is a recog-

nition of history, the imperfections of man and the limits of reason. So yes, the instruments of war do have a role to play in preserving the peace.[11]

Speaking as one responsible for the Empire, Barack Obama said words that were exactly on target. America will fight against her enemies with bombs, soldiers, and priceless, sacrificial blood to protect the American way of life and preserve the nation. But I do not believe the church should employ or sanction these methods. Violence might be necessary in the world of the Empire, but if Jesus teaches us anything, he teaches us that what the world presumes as necessary may not be necessary at all in his view and in his way.

If what I have written thus far is true (and many will furiously deny as much), the obvious questions are, "Can Christians participate in the economic, religious, and politico-military systems of the Empire? Can't we Christians be in positions of power and use those position to do some good? Can't we take over and do what is right and just and pleasing to God? What is wrong with using the helpful tools at our disposal?"

Yes, participate as a Christian in society. Nothing about being a committed member of the Jesus Tribe should prevent us from working, and working hard, toward grace, goodness, and justice in the world. Just realize that anyone who reaches for power while remaining absolutely within the way of Jesus will not likely reach far. Something will have to give because, again, the way of Jesus and the way of the Empire are not compatible. The existing systems we often seek to improve, guide, endorse, seize, or reform belong to the Empire. As such, these systems are poisoned, and like a river flowing into the sea, if the river is polluted so will be the result. Yes, human society needs social structures and ways to meet the needs of others, but the Jesus Tribe is a society informed and shaped by a different kind of power. It is a society constructed on the inverted power of sacrifice, servanthood, grace, and willingness to suffer. It is a society built on a cross.

If we act differently, thinking we can pick up any empire's tools of power to accomplish justifiable ends, we are abandoning our identity for the Tempter's snare and doing nothing less than betraying the way of Jesus. We are risking the death of our unique culture and community, for when the church would rather be part of an economic, religious, or politico-military powerhouse than a collection of Jesus-like suffering servants, we have left the Tribe for brick building in the Babylonian desert. Yes, the Empire will bring power, influence, security, and safety. Following Jesus may not bring any of these things. But a church "addicted to security and safety is not the church of Jesus Christ at all. It is something else."[12]

Chapter 2

Abandon Ship

Jesus began to preach, "Repent of your sins and turn to God, for the Kingdom of Heaven is near." One day as Jesus was walking along the shore of the Sea of Galilee, he saw two brothers—Simon, also called Peter, and Andrew—throwing a net into the water, for they fished for a living. Jesus called out to them, "Come, follow me, and I will show you how to fish for people!"

And they left their nets at once and followed him. A little farther up the shore he saw two other brothers, James and John, sitting in a boat with their father, Zebedee, repairing their nets. And he called them to come, too. They immediately followed him, leaving the boat and their father behind. (Matt 4:17-22)

A century ago the mighty, unsinkable *Titanic* left the docks of Southampton, England, bound for New York City with more than 2,000 people on board. We know the disastrous history all too well. Just four days into her maiden voyage, steaming at full speed across the north Atlantic Ocean, she hit an iceberg, the steel plates of her hull buckled, and in a matter of three hours she had sunk to the bottom of the sea. Historians, authors, enterprising movie makers, and deep-water explorers have all made a hefty living off explaining and retelling the causes of this tragedy.

It has been determined that the crew was arrogant and overconfident in their abilities and in the ship's construction. The radio operators failed to deliver warning messages to the bridge about sea conditions. The captain waited too late to send out a call for help. Ships in the area that could have responded failed to do so. Further, the *Titanic* carried only half of the necessary number of lifeboats, and in the event of a disaster, a disaster no one could ever imagine, there simply was not enough room for everyone to escape. Yet that's not the truly outrageous role played by these infamous lifeboats.

When the command to abandon ship was finally ordered, unlike what we see in director James Cameron's cinematic telling of the story (1997), the *Titanic* was sitting calmly and evenly in the water. Her design was such that even while taking in water, she would list very little to one side or the other.

The *Titanic* simply began squatting in the water, and for the longest time she showed no outward signs of being in imminent danger. The electrical generators for the ship sat high and dry, so the lights were on, the ventilation systems were running, and all the cutting-edge luxuries of the day were unhampered. It was such a contradiction that as the crew repeatedly begged people to get into the lifeboats, the passengers on board refused to believe anything was wrong.

After all, this was the most technologically advanced sailing vessel in the world. It had been built by the best engineers, financed by J. P. Morgan, commissioned by the most experienced ship builders in Great Britain, and on board were some of the richest, most prominent people in the northern hemisphere. Abandon ship? Why leave the safety and comfort of the finest ship in the sea to enter a leaky, wooden dingy put afloat on freezing water in the north Atlantic? It didn't make sense. Surely this was some kind of pitiful joke. So when the moorings of the first half-dozen lifeboats were cut—lifeboats that could have held hundreds—the boats were set free from the *Titanic* with only a dozen or so survivors in each of them. Only later did the majority of the passengers realize the danger.

I use this story as an example of how the warning about the dangers of the Empire can sometimes fall on the ears of Christian listeners. "What can be the danger of the state and the church cooperating together? There's nothing wrong with the church flexing its muscles and showing we belong on the stage of power. Christianity has never been stronger or more influential! All this talk about keeping our distance is overblown; there's really nothing to worry about."

Many Christians keep plowing ahead, convinced that sailing aboard the Empire's vessel is the best idea out there. Safe, dry, and warm in their staterooms, they are oblivious to the fact that the Empire is fatally wounded. She is "passing away." She is sinking—all empires will sink—and the solution is not to bail water out of the belly of the beast. The solution is to abandon ship. For when Jesus invites us to follow him, that is exactly what we must do; we must leave the Empire's illusion of safety and launch out with Christ into the Kingdom of God. It might be cold, wet, and dangerous, but it will also keep us alive.

The *Mauerspechte*

If you conducted a survey of those leaving American churches on Sunday morning by asking, "What is the gospel that Jesus preached when he first called his disciples?" the answer would likely be consistent. It would go something like this: "Jesus died on a cross for my sins, and if I invite him into my heart I will get to go to heaven when I die." There would be some variation in the answer, but not much. This is the gospel typically preached, believed, and taken to the world by many a believer. Unfortunately, it is a confession of faith that is grossly disconnected from the world in which we live, it focuses almost entirely on the next life, and it is little more than an evasion technique to escape the devil's flames with which we have all been threatened. Worse, it is not at all what Jesus preached when he first appeared along the Sea of Galilee.

The gospel that Jesus preached was the good news that the Kingdom of God was near. It had actually arrived. This Kingdom wasn't a disembodied place whereby one got a guaranteed seat on the bus that would drive its passengers to heaven upon death. Rather, Jesus' message was that the rule of God had been brought to bear in the present world. "God has moved into the neighborhood," to use Eugene Peterson's vivid phrase.[1] The objective, according to Jesus, was not to get people inside of heaven but to get heaven inside of people. This is the gospel.

Does this mean there is no meaning in "asking Jesus into your heart"? Is there no meaning in individual salvation? I'm not saying that at all. But an understanding of the gospel that concerns itself only with getting my own soul into heaven—damn this world, it's all going to burn anyway—falls miserably short of the revolutionary message of Jesus. Jesus did not come to live in your heart like an imaginary friend. He came to bring you into the Kingdom that you might be a part of God's communal ministry of justice, grace, and mercy. He came not to give you a ticket to the afterlife per se but to revolutionize the life you live today. Any gospel that separates today from eternity is not the gospel, and those who follow a Christ who concerns himself only with the hereafter are not following Christ, for the Kingdom of God that Jesus announced, preached, and implemented is here today— right now.

As members of the Jesus Tribe, we should know more about this Kingdom of God than we do, for it was the subject most often found on Jesus' lips. With a little search, you will discover that Jesus spoke of God's Kingdom more than a hundred times. Matthew speaks of it the most, using the phrase "Kingdom of God" and its synonym "Kingdom of Heaven" on almost every page. Nearly sixty times Matthew puts it to use, and while he never defines it, it is clearly more than a mystical state, an intangible emotion, or a longing to avoid the netherworld. It is the reign and rule of God brought to earth in and through the person of Jesus. Wherever men and women submit their hearts, intentions, ideals, and relationships to the lordship of Jesus, there the Kingdom of God flourishes. So is this Kingdom of God only for today, in the here and now? Did the gospel Jesus preached have no future implications beyond resisting the current world's empires? Is the "pie already baked" rather than waiting for us in the sky?[2] The answer to these questions is not "either/or." The answer is "both/and."

When Jesus walked onto Palestine's stage, it was like the sun rising on the eastern horizon: "The people who sat in darkness have seen a great light. And for those who lived in the land where death casts its shadow, a light has shined" (Matt 4:16). A new day had dawned, but a day is more than the moment of sunrise. The sunrise begins the day but does not complete it. The timing of the Kingdom of God is not unlike this. God's reign has begun, but it is not yet complete. It is both a future consummation of all things, and it is a present, ongoing reality lived out by those within the Jesus Tribe. So while we do not have the timing for the completion of the Kingdom of God (something with which many Christians in America are consumed), we do have today, and today we can live out this dawning kingdom, not just wait for the sun to set.

Here is an example of what this might look like: On the afternoon of August 12, 1961, leaders of the German Democratic Republic, better known as Communist Eastern Germany, signed an order to close the border between East and West Berlin and erect a massive Wall dividing the city. Roads that ran into West Berlin were destroyed. Barbed-wire entanglements and land mines were set up. Apartment windows that overlooked the forbidden side of the city were barred. Concrete and steel were piled into place for the twenty-seven miles of city border, and guards were stationed along the Wall with orders to shoot anyone attempting to escape to West Berlin. But this Wall, like all things evil, did not last.

On November 9, 1989, following weeks of unrest, the East German government announced that its citizens would be allowed to visit West Germany and West Berlin. The border guards, unable to control the huge crowds who were eager to exercise this new freedom, abandoned their posts. Ecstatic East Berliners cascaded over, around, and through the iconic Wall that had separated families, friends, and a country for a generation. They were met on the other side by their brothers and sisters, who received them with open arms. In the weeks that followed that revolutionary November night, people from all over the world came to Berlin with picks, shovels, and sledgehammers to knock down a piece of the Wall. Some came for souvenirs. Some came to participate in a historical moment. Some came simply to get in on the action. All came to do their part in tearing down one of the ugliest symbols of restriction, oppression, and injustice ever created.

I remember watching these impromptu demolition teams at work on the cable news networks. I was a college student, just like the young men and women marching joyfully through Checkpoint Charlie, singing songs of freedom, and taking their swings at concrete and steel. It was years later that I learned the nickname given to these unnamed, unknown people who tore down the Berlin Wall piece by piece and blow by hammer blow. They were called the "*Mauerspechte.*" They were the "woodpeckers on the wall."

More often than not, it is those who have no names, unrecognized faces, or a small place in the world that actually knock the walls down. Bit by bit, year by year, with blood and tears, suffering mistreatment and injustice, they stay at it. They believe in the things that last longer than tyranny, unfairness, domination, greed, violence, and power as brokered by the forces of this world. With their work gloves on and their hammers in hand, they believe in and work toward peace, hope, justice, and nonviolence.

They believe every valley shall be filled, every hill and mountain shall be leveled, the rough places will be made smooth, the crooked places will be made straight, and the glory of the Lord shall be revealed. In short, they believe in the Kingdom of God and the eternal truth that Christ will conquer all, in the human heart, in the streets of Berlin, and eventually everywhere, when this world becomes "the Kingdom of our Lord and of his Christ, and he will reign forever and ever" (Rev 11:15). God knows the world could stand a few people joining this redemptive work today, a few woodpeckers on the wall who will persistently and defiantly chip away at what stands in the way of peace, justice, love, and mercy in service to the Kingdom of God.

Teach a Man to Fish

The first people to get in on Jesus' Kingdom were two sets of brothers with names Christianity knows well: Peter and Andrew, James and John. These men have become heroes of the faith over the millennia, but they certainly did not begin that way. They were just simple men doing what fishermen did: casting their lines, rowing their boats, selling their catch, and repairing their nets. They were up to their sunburned elbows in fish guts and scales, and if they were anything like the fishermen in the fishing town in which I live, they were up to their eyeballs in debt just trying to make ends meet.

Always scraping by and eager to get into a scrape with those who crossed their paths, with nicknames like "Rocky" (Peter) and the "Sons of Thunder" (James and John), these were not the level-headed wise men one would choose to perpetuate a movement, especially a movement as significant as the one Jesus was heralding. Nor were they religious professionals, rabbis in training, or seminary students. They were not gifted in public speaking or astute at dealing with people. They were fishermen. Still, these unlikely men were the men Jesus wanted, the ones he chose to serve on the inaugural tribal council that would carry out his intentions in the world.

For better or worse, in many ways, these men were just like us. They lived in a world of military domination, political posturing, grinding poverty, religious confusion, and economic uncertainty. Like us, they hoped and prayed someone could and would sort it all out and offer a better way to live in the future. If Jesus entered the world of the twenty-first century, he could just as easily walk onto a construction site or into a manufacturing plant and offer the same radical challenge as he did to these fishermen: "Follow me and I will show you how to really live in the world. Follow me and I will show you how to gain the Kingdom of God. Follow me and I will show you how to fish for people." At all times and in all places, to those who will enter the Jesus Tribe, this invitation is always the same: "Follow me."

This following of Jesus is not figurative or hypothetical. It is quite literal. It is the life of Jesus imitation, relying upon his words, way, and power. Those who follow Jesus along this path, like those first disciples on the seashore, are not called to be stoic students in a classroom (a strong contradiction of how most of Christianity operates, with its endless classes, conferences, seminars, and symposiums). Instead, these followers are to be more like apprentices or trainees learning a trade, gaining practical, hands-on skills and knowledge from Jesus so they will think, act, and be like Jesus. This life of Jesus imitation will pit us against the cultural, national, and religious mainstream in fundamental ways, but being pitted against the mainstream means we actually have something worth saying and a life worth living. This requires leaving behind the comfortable, safe, and familiar, but Jesus will not abandon us. He will show us the way.

A few years ago my wife and I finally faced a day that had been looming on the horizon for years. Some days we prayed it would hurry to us, but most of the time we dreaded it like the plague: our baby boy began school, and Braden McBrayer, all of his five years and forty pounds, slipped away from the surly bonds of home and his mother's apron strings and headed to kindergarten. This wasn't our first rodeo. Braden was the third backpack-bursting, lunchbox-bearing, pencil-packing McBrayer boy to climb onto the big yellow school bus. (Barring an Immaculate Conception of some sort, he will be the last to begin this journey, but I digress.)

When I began school so many years ago, I wept and cried every morning for a month. I clung to my mother's legs like a drowning man and had to be pried off of her to be put on the school bus each day. Most of my fears about school were unfounded. There was really nothing to be scared of except my school bus driver, Mr. Otto Walraven. He instilled fear into the bravest soul as he shook a switch the size of a tree limb at us in that large rearview bus mirror. More than once I saw him remove strapping high school students from the bus and throttle them along the side of the road. Old Otto would be in the penitentiary these days, God rest his soul (but again, I digress).

Braden, however, leapt aboard the bus with not even a hint of anxiety. As I walked away from the bus stop on Braden's first morning of school, I thought about how different our two school starts had been. Braden and I are a lot alike. Anyone who has ever seen us standing together could never deny that. But the biggest difference between father and son, besides my apparent cowardice, is that Braden has two big brothers. When I climbed onto that bus headed for school all those decades ago, I was the first in my family to do so. Sure, I had a twin sister with me that day, but she was as afraid as I was. This was a first for both of us. Braden, however, had been trying to get on the bus for more than three years. Why? Because he wanted to follow his brothers to school. With those brothers to show him the way, he had no fear, only anticipation. His first day of school was not a shove into the unknown alone. He had someone to go with him, someone who would lead him, and someone to follow.

As a Christian, I am glad Jesus is my Savior. Of course, by using the word "Savior," I mean a lot of different things. He saves me from sin and from myself. He saves me from fear and death. He saves me from all condemnation. I am grateful for all this. I am thankful that the Christian faith plants a hope in my heart that something marvelous exists beyond this present world. I believe the afterlife, as much as I do not know about it, is a life with the risen Christ. In short, I believe in a final resurrection. For this I am glad. But Jesus is also my guide for living today, in the here and now. To follow Jesus is not just to walk over the horizon of death into the sweet by and by, holding his hand singing a line of "Kum Ba Yah." To follow Jesus is to imitate him, to be like him, to chase after him and go where he goes, to take his ways and words to heart, and to live by them.

The way of Christ is the way of loving our enemies. He teaches us to do well to those who don't deserve it. He challenges us to give away our fortunes and the things we hold dear. He says, "Turn the other cheek." He calls us to take the path toward sacrifice and crucifixion that we too might arise from the dead. To follow Jesus, if I can be so simplistic, is not unlike a kid brother following in the steps of one who has gone before him. So every day when I rise, I do so not thinking about some future "graduation" date from this world. I get up, get dressed, grab my backpack and lunchbox, and follow Jesus into the school of life. He knows which seats on the bus I should stay away from. He points toward and warns me of compromising situations to avoid. He shows me with whom I should share my milk money and how to handle the bullies on the playground because he is an old hand at things and knows the ropes. He teaches me how to live, how to love, how to trust, and even how to die.

This takes more than a little fear out of living, for we never have to face the world without an example to follow. We don't cling to our perceived place of safety. Instead, we jump into each day doing what Jesus did, living the life he will show us.

A Demonstration Plot for the Kingdom of God

One of the tragedies of current Christianity in America is that we have so few compelling illustrations of this life that Jesus lived and the type of radical community he came to create. Leading pastors and preachers are little more than family-friendly celebrities or game-show hosts with all the razzle-dazzle and mass-media presence that accompanies the position. Congregations have become huge corporate machines chasing after the highest percentage of the local market share, and most of Christian writing, art, and music is so pathetically self-centered that you can't find the Suffering Servant Jesus in it with a red-letter Bible and a bloodhound. Christianity is awash with gimmicky, sappy pep rallies for Jesus, but it is not very interested in serious discipleship. In the words of Clarence Jordan, some Christians will "worship the hind legs off Jesus, but they won't obey him."[3]

Quoting Clarence Jordan is more than appropriate when speaking of the radical way of life disciples are called to live when following Jesus in the land of the Empire. Clarence Jordan spent his life pursuing Christ with a passion rarely rivaled, though he has been largely ignored by mainstream Christianity. His life is a modern illustration of serious discipleship, and if we Protestants canonized any of our peers, Jordan would be in that number.

With a bachelor's degree in Agricultural Science, Clarence Jordan attended and graduated from the Southern Baptist Theological Seminary, earning his PhD in Greek when he was only twenty-six years old. While at seminary, he met Florence, the woman who would become his wife. He said to her, "If you want to be the wife of a pastor of the First Baptist Church, you don't want to marry me. I'm going back to Georgia and farm and do something for the poor." Florence married him anyway, and in 1942 Clarence and Florence Jordan bought 440 acres outside of Americus, Georgia, and established Koinonia Farms.

Koinonia is the Greek word for community. And the Jordans set out to create just that: a farming community where men and women, blacks and whites, rich and poor would live together under the parenthood of God, employing love over violence and relying on one another in a self-sustaining, Empire-defying way. It was Jordan's dream that Koinonia be what he called a "demonstration plot for the Kingdom of God," a place where following Jesus worked itself out in practical, life-giving ways. Clarence understood that this would be a high ideal, and those taking Jesus serious enough to live such radical lives would be few. But a few people, Clarence thought, would be enough to witness to the world. A small number of committed disciples of Jesus were like dynamite in a coil or gasoline compressed by a piston, Jordan said. These were small, constrictive spaces, but in these tight spots, explosive, transformative power could be ignited. Koinonia became a place like that. It was never very large—no more than a couple dozen people and sometimes down to only the Jordans—but it was explosive in its influence and power. And sometimes it was explosive in the community.

In the 1950s, Clarence and members of Koinonia attended church on Sundays at the Rehoboth Baptist Church in Americus. One Sunday, a dark-skinned student from India went to church with Clarence. The student's presence caused such a stir that members of the church told Clarence it would be in his best interest and theirs not to come back—ever. He and all the members of Koinonia Farms were expelled from the church because they shared living space, worship space, meals, and life with those who were not Caucasian. Listen to Clarence's own words when the Koinonia tribe attempted to visit another church in the community with a young African-American man in their company:

So us-all went to that million-dollar church. When we sat down the folks in front of us moved away. The folks back of us moved away. There we were, a little island in the sanctuary. Shortly, the chairman of the hospitality committee came steaming up the aisle, face flushed. Pointing to the Negro fellow he said, "He can't stay here." So the fellow came around and stood right in front of the young black man, named McGee, and said, "Come on, nigger, you gotta get out of here. You are disturbing divine worship!"

Now, I didn't know where the divine worship was, but I did know who was disturbing it. The chairman got so infuriated, he lunged over the bench and grabbed McGee and started dragging [him toward the door]. When they got us outside, the deacons formed a big line and stood between us and the door to the sanctuary. The pastor was standing there with them. I turned to him and said, "You know, there's something wrong about tonight . . . for a man to be dragged out of the house of God [because of] the color of the skin with which the Almighty endowed him."

The pastor said, "Yes, I agree, but this is the policy of our church."

In the years that followed, the local community began a boycott of Koinonia's farming products. Jordan's fruit and produce stands were fire-bombed. For nearly a year, machine gun fire was sprayed nightly into Koinonia from the highway. Their fields were salted. Their pecan trees were cut down. Their tractors and farming equipment were sabotaged. The Ku Klux Klan regularly threatened Clarence's life and family. A grand jury began investigating Clarence and Koinonia under the accusation that they were Communists. Jordan responded to this accusation with a wink and his patented sense of humor, saying, "Sharing my goods with those I live with doesn't make me a Communist any more than me being with you makes me a jackass."

He always had clever slogans like that, including the phrase that saved Koinonia Farms. When it became clear that the farm would be unable to sustain itself selling its goods locally, Clarence began a mail-order pecan business that still thrives today. His marketing slogan was, "Help us ship the nuts out of Georgia!" And they did by the bushel loads, financially saving the farm. (Serious discipleship does not necessitate we lose our sense of humor. Rather, the opposite is true; those who follow Jesus truly have the "joy, joy, joy, joy down in their hearts.")[4]

An undeniable member of the Jesus Tribe, Clarence Jordan left a manifold legacy, but little is more powerful than something he called "Partners." In July 1968 a man named Millard Fuller moved to Koinonia Farms with his wife Linda and their family. Millard had been a multi-millionaire, but in struggling to follow the words of Jesus, he had given away his entire fortune. He and Clarence birthed the idea that poor people, God's people, could be provided simple, decent, affordable housing if the church would live out the Kingdom of God that Jesus preached. Millard and Clarence began building simple, decent houses with willing volunteers, and then the homes were sold to families who would pay back only the cost of building the house—no interest. As the house payments were made, those payments went into a Fund for Humanity that precipitated the building of even more houses.

The first such partnership homes were built in the early 1970s at Koinonia, and in 1976, Millard and Linda Fuller took the idea nationally. They started a small Americus-based organization named Habitat for Humanity and later established the Fuller Center for Housing, two organizations that have now built hundreds of thousands of homes, sheltering more than a million people. Clarence did not live to see even the first Partnership house completed at Koinonia Farms. In October 1969, Clarence died of a heart attack on his beloved farm. The greater community still reviled him to such a degree that the coroner and county medical examiner refused to come to Koinonia to pronounce him dead. The county instructed Millard Fuller that the best he could hope for would be to rent an ambulance and bring the body to town.

Millard thought about it and concluded that Clarence wouldn't want that kind of money spent for him in death. Instead, Millard buckled Clarence into one of the farms' station wagons and drove him to town, smiling all the way. Clarence Jordan was buried in an unmarked grave at Koinonia Farms, his coffin a large shipping crate. Though he is dead, Clarence Jordan lives still in the echoes of the Kingdom of God and in the Christ who says, "Follow me."

Chapter 3

The Blessed Community

One day as he saw the crowds gathering, Jesus went up on the mountain-side and sat down. His disciples gathered around him, and he began to teach them.

"God blesses those who are poor and realize their need for him, for the kingdom of heaven is theirs.

"God blesses those who mourn, for they will be comforted.

"God blesses those who are humble, for they will inherit the whole earth.

"God blesses those who hunger and thirst for justice, for they will be satisfied.

"God blesses those who are merciful, for they will be shown mercy.

"God blesses those whose hearts are pure, for they will see God.

"God blesses those who work for peace, for they will be called the children of God.

"God blesses those who are persecuted for doing right, for the kingdom of heaven is theirs.

"God blesses you when people mock you and persecute you and lie about you and say all sorts of evil things against you because you are my followers. Be happy about it! Be very glad! For a great reward awaits you in heaven. And remember, the ancient prophets were persecuted in the same way." (Matt 5:1-12)

Not far from where I live is a place called "Scenic Highway 30-A." It is a beautiful nineteen-mile stretch of beachside road along the Gulf of Mexico. There you will find vacation rentals, pricey real estate, some great seafood, and the jewels of Florida's Emerald Coast, something called the "planned community." These communities carry inviting names like WaterColor, WaterSound, Alys Beach, Rosemary Beach, and Seaside—where Jim Carey was filmed in the movie *The Truman Show*.[1] These are beautiful places filled with architectural masterpieces and natural wonder. Tourists visiting this part of our world walk the streets of these communities and see all the indications of deep connection: the designers of these neighborhoods have placed all the homes within easy walking distance of each other; small stores are run by local merchants; bicycles and golf carts dot the streets; families are laughing and playing together. It looks so perfect. But just like *The Truman Show*, it is largely a charade. It is a manufactured façade.

The majority of the people who populate those homes are, for the most part, vacationers. They are here for a few days and then are thrown back into the fray of living their lives. And for those who own the homes, it's hardly ever their primary residence. It is a second or third home, a millionaire's retreat from the world, not a place to engage or connect with others. I've often thought that the healthier communities along that stretch of road are those in the shadow of these artificial platforms; those old collections of cottages and fishing lodges where the architectural lines are not near as sharp, the paint on the walls has long faded, and the streets are filled with sand and oyster shells rather than cobblestones. These alternative neighborhoods are not artistic or aesthetically beautiful, but they are real, filled with real people who are interested in living life rather than perpetuating a façade.

Again, we look to the Cherokee nation for a similar comparison. Though the name "Cherokee" is an almost universally accepted name for this people group, this is a name attached to the tribe, again by outsiders. The earliest Cherokee didn't call themselves Cherokee at all. They called themselves *aniyunwiya*, meaning "we are the Real People." Or, literally translated, it can mean "we are the people of life." The early Cherokee understood that the way of life they shared together gave them their existence. Jesus understood this as well, and he didn't seem to be interested in façades either. We understand this from the beginning of his greatest sermon.

As the Sermon on the Mount, to which we now turn our attention, begins, Jesus goes up on a mountainside to instruct his newly called disciples. They gather tightly around him and the crowds hang on the edge, listening and wondering about this new rabbi who is already making such a splash in the local villages. Jesus begins his sermon with nothing less than an invitation to become a community of "real people," to become the "people of life."

In the tradition in which I was raised, an invitation was extended not before the sermon, but after it. And when I say "extended," I mean that one, an offer to respond was made, and two, that offer was excruciatingly long and completed with much fanfare. Further, it wasn't an invitation to community. It was extremely individualistic and private where we all bowed our heads, closed our eyes, and looked deep into our black hearts to make sure "that we knew, that we knew, that we knew" we were born again. We sang "Just As I Am" or some other mournful dirge until someone walked the aisle to repent. The invitation usually lasted longer than the actual sermon, and

sometimes I went forward to "repent" just so the whole thing would mercifully end. Jesus, however, isn't trying to get us to the mourner's bench. He is
inviting us to become real and alive in a false and dying world.

The Medicine Wheel

Robert Estienne, a French printer in the Middle Ages, is often credited with
dividing the Bible into chapter and verse. The legend goes that he did much
of this work while riding on horseback across the European continent. No
one can be certain of this, but sometimes I think that was exactly the case,
because at times dear Robert breaks up the narrative of Scripture at the most
inopportune places, as if he had been suddenly jostled from the saddle. The
Sermon on the Mount is an ideal example of this.

This sermon, or at least its context, actually begins in Matthew 4, and
that is why one cannot simply leap into the sermon without considering the
beginning of Jesus' ministry: the desert temptations, the calling of his first
disciples, and the world-shattering announcement that the Kingdom of God
was at hand. All this is prelude to the Sermon on the Mount, which is a kind
of oath of allegiance to the community of Christ. Interestingly, to become a
naturalized citizen of the United States, one must take an oath to "absolutely
and entirely renounce and abjure all allegiance and fidelity to any foreign
prince, potentate, state, or sovereignty."[2] One cannot read the Sermon on
the Mount without such thoughts going through his or her head. The disciple is being called to relinquish all other allegiances. These words are the
colors of our patriotism—not to a country or a flag but to Jesus.

The sermon begins with its most recognized section, the Beatitudes.
These make up one of the most strikingly beautiful pieces of literature one
will ever read or hear. Because of this, the Beatitudes get a large amount of
attention and discussion, and some readers remain blissfully unaware that
these are not the totality of the Sermon on the Mount. Some read the
Beatitudes and get no further while others get bogged down in the minutiae
of these verses, discussing, debating, and opining but not doing much else
with them. These are words to be *lived*, not discussed. Yet it is here that we
arrive at the challenge: These words are so demanding, so idealistic, and so
seemingly impossible to achieve. How can we possibly live them out?

I suggest we take the Beatitudes as a unit rather than treating them as a
set of individual commandments. What if we approach the Beatitudes as
spokes in a wheel, like a medicine wheel? While not as ritualistically central
to them as it is to the tribes in the American West, the Cherokee Nation also

uses a medicine wheel in various ceremonies. In the Cherokee tradition, it is an uncomplicated circle with a great fire in the middle and a number of logs extending out and away from the center. If we look at the Beatitudes using the medicine wheel as a guide, we can see them as connected to and extending out from the reign and Kingdom of God at the center.

The Kingdom is the hub of the wheel, the sacred fire, and these Beatitudes streak away from the center as characteristics of the reign of God. The Beatitudes are what the Kingdom of God, in practice, looks like in the world today. These are the personality traits of those who live within this kingdom. As we gather around the fire that is the Kingdom of God in Jesus, the sparks fly upward and outward from the center of the wheel, providing warmth, light, and identity. We can rightly call these sparks the Beatitudes.

And here is the good news: the Beatitudes are not commandments that are imposed upon us. Jesus does not command us to "Go be mournful," nor does he say, "Thou shalt be pure in heart," or "You are ordered to be poor in spirit," though this is how these verses are often explained and shackled around listener's necks. Instead, we should read these words and admit that we cannot live up to them. To attempt to do so is to undertake a superhuman struggle, a struggle that will lead to bigger failure, more guilt, the chains of legalism, and profound self-inflicted shame. Jesus isn't asking this from us.

What Jesus is declaring in the Beatitudes is the state of God's rule in the community of those who have entered the Kingdom of God. Jesus isn't issuing new laws to keep but describing the characteristics of his community. Followers of Jesus will be poor in spirit and realize their need for God. They will live humbly and hunger and thirst for justice. They will be full of mercy, have pure hearts, and work for peace and rightness, even at the expense of persecution and insult. Yet the Jesus community will be one of deep satisfaction (blessedness) where the Kingdom of God will flourish. The Beatitudes are no spiritual "to-do list" to be attempted by eager, rule-keeping disciples. Instead, they make up a spiritual "done" list of the qualities God brings to bear in the people who follow Jesus.

Glen Stassen and David Gushee, adding a useful word to our vocabulary, describe it like this: "The Kingdom of God is *performative*. What God is doing in the world is his *performance*, but we are invited to *actively participate*. As we participate we become what God desires for his world."[3] This takes the pressure off the disciple, making our biggest responsibility one of surrender. If we give up on our own abilities to bring the Kingdom of God into the world, if we loosen our grip on what we want and what we think we can do, then that space will be filled by what God can do. And what God can do in Jesus is make the Beatitudes a reality. We enter, foster, and live out the Beatitudes not by striving, trying, making promises, working harder, doing more, or aiming higher. We do it by yielding to the way of Christ; only this will lead to the kind of life and community promised by the Beatitudes.

This yielding is something we who live in the Jesus Tribe can learn from our friends the Quakers. The Quakers, the "Society of Friends" as they call themselves, developed in Great Britain in the aftermath of the Protestant Reformation. Founded by George Fox, who "may be reckoned one of the world's great mystics," their emergence was never intended to be a religious movement or an act of reformation.[4] Rather, Fox and his peers, including Pennsylvania founder William Penn, simply refused to conform to the corporate models of Christianity that surrounded them. Often persecuted and jailed for their beliefs, they sought instead to create a social order that would be a living example of God's grace, love, and compassion in the world. The goal was to be a fellowship of people who had found a better way to live, and to invite others to witness and participate in this life.

Leaning hard on Jesus' Beatitudes, Quakers often refer to their meetings and their way of life as "the Blessed Community." This is a living acknowledgment of the rule of God in the hearts of people as together they reflect and act out his peace and presence. So while Quakerism is fiercely personal, relying on God to light each individual's path, and beautifully diverse, it would be a mistake to view these Friends as enjoying anything less than a true and deep love one for another. The late Thomas Kelly, another of those Quaker mystics, described the Blessed Community as a God-filled communion that provided a home for those following Christ. He writes,

> The Holy Fellowship, the Blessed Community has always astonished those who stood without it. [But] we don't create it deliberately; we find it and we find ourselves increasingly within it as we find ourselves increasingly within Him. It is the holy matrix of "the communion of the saints," the Body of Christ which is His church . . . . Yet still more astonishing is the Holy Fellowship, the Blessed Community, to those who are within it. Yet can one be surprised at being at home?[5]

Finding a home in a Blessed Community: Isn't this what we want and need? Isn't this better than the grinding gears of the Empire? Isn't this exactly what Jesus offers?

Safe Space Is Sacred Space

In Eastern Pennsylvania there is a remarkable little village that for years seemed to be a fountain of youth. The health and longevity of the citizens of Roseto, Pennsylvania, got the attention of physicians, researchers, and scientists everywhere. In 1962, looking for that magic elixir, investigators descended on Roseto to conduct a full scientific investigation. They stayed for years, and here is a bit of what they discovered: Virtually no one under age fifty-five had ever died of heart disease in the village, and for men over age sixty-five, the death rate from heart disease was half the rate of the United States in general. The mortality rate as a whole was 35 percent better in Roseto than the average, and there was no suicide, no alcoholism, no drug addiction, no crime, no violence, and no ulcers. Everyone was dying of simple old age.

So the researchers looked at genetics. The Rosetans were all of Italian stock, descendants of immigrants from Roseto Valfortore, Italy. But genetics was not the answer to their healthy lives. Their cousins, living in other places all over the world, had morality rates just like the general population. The researchers looked at dietary habits, but the people of Roseto were cooking with lard and eating pizza every day that was loaded with sausage, meatballs, eggs, and pepperoni. They ate biscotti by the bucket full, half their calories came from fat, and there were no yoga classes, exercise groups, or jogging trails. They smoked old cigars and unfiltered cigarettes, and they drank gallons of wine. Well, maybe it was the environment. Again, no. The two closest towns just a few miles away were the same size, had the same water, same air, same diet, same dangerous jobs in the nearby slate mines, and consisted of similar European immigrants, but had heart disease and mortality rates that were triple those at Roseto.

The Rosetans broke all the "live-long-and-prosper" rules, but they lived longer. What was the answer? What made Rosetans healthy was Roseto itself. They had strong family ties with three generations often living under the same roof. There were nearly two dozen civic groups in a community of only 2,000 people. Neighbors sat on front porches together, ate together, went to Mass together, stopped and conversed with one another. The Rosetans actually cared for, respected, and valued one another. In short, the research concluded that the citizens of Roseto were living longer, healthy lives because of the community they had built together, a community that insulated them like few places in North America.

Here's an interesting footnote: Researchers in 1962 predicted that as Rosetans became more Americanized, meaning less communal, more independent, and more consumption driven, they would also become less healthy. The "Roseto" effect would wear off. Thirty years later, a 1992 survey published in the *American Journal of Public Health* confirmed this prediction.[6] The Rosetans now suffer from the same rates of mortality and heart disease as all the rest of us. The Roseto effect has vanished in a single generation, due largely to the dismantling of strong social ties and neglect of the community. When the single-family homes, fenced yards, strip malls, and country clubs were brought in, longevity and health were evicted. It is a fascinating study of the power of community; when community fails, we all are less healthy for it.[7]

We know that safe space—a place where we join fellow travelers who are on the same journey, travelers who nourish one another with strong, gracious, caring, loving relationships—is holy ground. This kind of community makes us healthier, wiser, stronger, and, yes, even better people than if we live in stubborn independence and isolation. Intuitively we know this, and the study of the village of Roseto was unnecessary to confirm it. So fundamental is this kind of community that it is the building block of God's church. The foundation of the church is Christ, and on him alone we are built, but when the movement of God's Kingdom and reign ignited with Jesus, the first spark was a new bond of community. What is more important than our doctrinal positions, our style of worship, the time and place that we gather for our meetings, the particular religious label we wear is this: living out the Blessed Community of Jesus.

While I am no dyed-in-the-wool traditionalist, not by a long shot, I still have a bit of a problem with the words we now use to describe the places where we gather together as the church. They are called "worship centers" or "multi-purpose buildings" or "auditoriums." This is unfortunate. I much prefer the word used by our grandparents: sanctuary. Anywhere the church gathers—in a storefront, a gymnasium, an auditorium, or a thousand-year-old cathedral—should be a *sanctuary*. It should be a safe place, a place where people are welcomed into a better way to live and made to feel at home. This welcome is far more substantial than saying "hello," shaking hands, or sharing coffee and doughnuts in the fellowship hall (another questionable description of a church building). Maybe English Bible translator and martyr William Tyndale got closer to the mark when with his "plowboy" English he said Christians should have a "harborous disposition."[8] To create secure harbors, a place for others to come in from the storm to be warm, safe, and healthy, is as high a calling as the church can fulfill.

I once participated in a retreat where several young people—in their twenties and early thirties—gave their unbridled, unedited assessments of the church. At times their words were immature and selfish; that much is granted. At other times their words were blisteringly accurate. They were brutally dead on, and gave everyone in the room pause. One young lady who spoke was Charis. Charis was a thirty-year-old wife and mother of two who had spent her three decades in the church. Her father is a seminary professor, and Charis herself holds a Master's degree in Biblical Studies. She was no cynical, jaded outsider. She has been a determined follower of Jesus most of her life. At one point in her talk she said to us, "I am sick of the church and what it will do to my children, what it is doing to me. I am tired of the church saying all the right things but not practicing them. It is difficult for me to come into the churches we have created at this point in history and believe any of it really matters." But Charis did not stop there. Her last remark was a hopeful prayer for blessedness. She said, "I don't want church. But I do want love, transformation, and community."

The Jesus Tribe should be synonymous with Charis's desire, not its antithesis. Comfort, mercy, communion with God, entrance into the joyful reign of heaven, open arms, open doors, open hearts—these should be the natural overflow and outcome of life together with Jesus, as natural as flowers blooming in the spring when the rain falls and the sun shines. We have spent too much collective time and energy focusing on the drivel rather than loving people. We fight and bleed over worship styles or which version of the Bible is the actually inspired one, and we draw up rules and restrictions for who can come to the Lord's Table and who can or cannot speak in a pulpit. We build all this structure and all these regulations on who is allowed in and who should be excluded, creating standards so impossibly high that Jesus Christ himself couldn't get in the door. We have endorsed and supported legalistic minutiae while neglecting the weightier issues of love, mercy, and justice. Meanwhile, people who are lonely, who are dying on the inside, who have had the absolute life beat out of them, who are racked by addiction and loss, who are burdened so low by the cares of this world that they cannot lift their heads, will not even look in the church's direction. Why? Because they feel so badly about themselves already, and they cannot imagine that the church could somehow relieve them. Those who hurt conclude that the church will not give rest for the soul; rather, the church will only pile on greater burdens.

This simply cannot be the people that Jesus describes and empowers. Out-of-balance independence, stubborn autonomy, and the captain-of-our-own-soul pride that keeps us at a distance from others cannot be the Blessed Community of Jesus. When we pretend to be familiar with others but cannot recall their names, or when we wave and smile at the one we know is having a hard time but never offer a lending hand, this cannot be following Christ. When we keep our "friendships" at arm's length and artificially professional for our own protection, this cannot be faithful to the one we call Lord. We must recognize these community-killing behaviors for what they are, name them, and by God's grace let Christ remove them. And if we will let him, remove them he will.

"There's a Wrecking Ball Outside"

Sheldon "Shel" Silverstein had one of the more extraordinary literary, music, and art careers you will ever read about, though many people will not recognize his name or his face. He was the eccentric combination of Chicago-born Jewish kid who became a country music legend, a composer, a cartoonist, the author of children's books, and a columnist for *Playboy* magazine. Quite the résumé. His two most famous works are on opposite ends of the creative spectrum. One is a country music song made famous by Johnny Cash for which Silverstein won a Grammy in 1970, a song titled "A Boy Named Sue." The other work is a children's picture book he published in the 1960s titled *The Giving Tree*. But my favorite of his children's books (and there have been many of his titles scattered around our house) is a little volume called *The Missing Piece*.

In *The Missing Piece*, a rolling circle that Silverstein has hand-drawn beautifully sloppy is missing a huge wedge of himself. The circle rolls along through life looking for his missing piece. All along, the broken, sloppy circle sings a little jingle. It goes, "Oh, I'm lookin' for my missin' piece; I'm lookin' for my missin' piece; Hi-dee-ho, here I go, lookin' for my missin' piece." And since the circle has this missing pie piece, he can't roll very fast. He travels painfully slowly. But his pace allows him to enjoy the scenery around him, to talk to the butterflies, and to look for that piece that will complete him. After many miles, he finally finds it—a triangle piece along the road—and it fits him perfectly.

Now the circle is made whole, and he zips along the road at speeds he could only imagine before. But after a while of rolling through life at break-neck speed, the circle realizes that he can't do the things he used to do. He can't enjoy the scenery. He doesn't move slowly enough to sing like he used to. He has no time to enjoy the company of the butterflies. It all moves too fast. So he removes that once missing piece, lays it aside, and goes back to the life he had, a life that was slower and where his weaknesses were obvious, but it was the life he lived best.[9]

Looking at the Beatitudes, we find words like *poverty, mourning, meek-ness, hunger, thirst, mercy, persecution,* and *suffering.* These are words of weakness and vulnerability. These reveal the gaping holes ripped out of us, holes that would seem to impede rather than empower the disciple. Yet we must embrace and take hold of these apparent weaknesses, clinging to them as the very places where Christ will enter, reveal himself, and rebuild our lives with blessedness. As long as we feel self-confident and self-sufficient, able to do God's work for him, even partially, there is no room left for the Kingdom of God to flow to and through us. The Beatitudes are about surrender and submission, the emptying of ourselves so that Christ will be in all, through all, and over all.

Jesus wants to build the kind of Blessed Community toward which the Beatitudes point, but if this is going to happen in your individual life or in your congregation of faith, one thing is certain: this community will thrive only in those who acknowledge the human impossibility of creating it. As disciples of Christ we must allow him to tear down our resistance, our stub-bornness, our false sense of wholeness, and our best efforts at living life. When we have become absolutely dependent on him, he will construct in us what is actually needed. Then we will enter the life we live best, the life Jesus lives through us. Anne Lamott said it like this:

When you ask God into your life, you think he or she is going to come into your house, look around, and see that you just need a new floor or better furniture and that everything needs just a little cleaning—and so you go along for the first six months. . . . Then you look out the window one day and see that there's a wrecking ball outside. It turns out that God actu-ally thinks your whole foundation is shot and you're going to have to start over from scratch.[10]

I have a little experience with this sort of thing. When my wife and I bought our first house together, it was a cute little ranch-style home sitting up on a ridge. We loved everything about it—except the master bathroom. It was a hideous, dark, Barney-the-Dinosaur purple. We would talk about how we needed to paint it, but we never got around to it. One Saturday, though, my sweet Cindy was gone to work, and I decided I would surprise her by painting the bathroom. I put a chair in the middle of the floor, climbed up on it to do some taping, and then one of the chair legs suddenly—inexplicably—punctured through the floor. Sometime in the distant past, a water leak, undisclosed to us by the previous owners and not found by the home inspectors, had rotted away the bathroom floor, and I discovered it when I started painting.

Well, my priorities suddenly changed. Painting wasn't very important, and I began tearing up the linoleum to get at the problem. You guessed it: the problem was much larger and more complicated than I could have anticipated. A section that measured several square feet had to be cut away. The cabinets had to be removed. Floor joists needed additional supports. The insulation had to be torn away. The leaking pipe had to be replaced. And my little painting project turned into an exercise in demolition involving three trips to Home Depot, a fair share of praying and swearing, and the assistance and tools of two of my neighbors. Cindy came home late that afternoon, and when she rounded the corner and looked into the bathroom, I was standing on the ground with my chest and arms sticking up through this four-by-four hole. Old plumbing, sawdust, ripped flooring, strange men, and destruction were everywhere. She looked at me with a mix of shock and laughter and asked the obvious: "What in the world are you doing?" I answered, "I'm painting your bathroom. The least you can say is 'thank you.'"

That's how it is with Jesus. These Beatitudes make clear that he is not interested in perpetuating our façade. He has not come to cover our ugly spots with a little soap and water or a splash of paint. He doesn't want to change light fixtures, make cosmetic changes, or do the best he can with what we have to work with. He wants to deconstruct our lives and communities of faith and rip out what does not belong. Then, in the vacancy of spiritual poverty and emptiness, Jesus will build the blessedness that flows out of the Kingdom of God. The only question left is will we let this happen? Will we move out of our lives so that Jesus the wrecking ball can swing away? Things will get out of control, of course, but things being out of our control and in his control is exactly the point.

Chapter 4

A Garden in the Wilderness

You are the salt of the earth. But what good is salt if it has lost its flavor? Can you make it salty again? It will be thrown out and trampled underfoot as worthless. You are the light of the world—like a city on a hilltop that cannot be hidden. No one lights a lamp and then puts it under a basket. Instead, a lamp is placed on a stand, where it gives light to everyone in the house. In the same way, let your good deeds shine out for all to see, so that everyone will praise your heavenly Father. (Matt 5:13-16)

When the group of Separatists rebels left England for the New World in a little boat called the *Mayflower*, they landed at Plymouth Rock in a territory that would eventually become known as the Massachusetts Bay Colony. These Pilgrims, in their simple black and white outfits and familiar muzzleloader rifles, left the comforts of home for religious freedom. They had been oppressed and persecuted by the state church and, looking for relief, they set out to create a type of religious retreat and sanctuary. The Pilgrims were not very successful. A decade later, under a new charter, they were replaced by the Puritans.

The Puritans were governed by a man who continues to have influence on the New World, Governor John Winthrop. Why did these Puritans come to America? Winthrop says they came, in paraphrase, (1) to serve the true church of God; (2) to escape the corruption of the Old World; (3) to save this continent from being wasted; and (4) to establish proper religion and government.

John Winthrop delivered his most famous sermon to this end before he even set foot on North American soil. Just off the beach on the boat that had brought the Puritans to their new home, he preached a sermon titled "A Model of Christian Charity," delivered in 1630. A portion of that sermon reads,

The Lord will be our God and . . . dwell among us, as his own people and will command a blessing upon us in all our ways, so that we shall see much more of his wisdom, power, goodness, and truth, than formerly we have been acquainted with. He shall make us a praise and glory. . . . For we must consider that we shall be as a City upon a Hill, the eyes of all people are upon us; Beloved there is now set before us life and good, death and evil. . . . Keep his commandments and his laws that the Lord our God may bless us in the land we go to possess.[1]

John Winthrop claimed that the Puritans had a new, special agreement with God. God had given them this new land to purify Christianity and serve as an example to the Old World for building a model society; almost every person running for national political office in this country since Winthrop has piggybacked upon his high idealism. That phrase, "city on a hill" or "shining light," has been used to describe the hopes and dreams for America by everyone from John Adams and Abraham Lincoln to John Kennedy and Bill Clinton, each with their own slant, but the master of this language was Ronald Reagan.

Ronald Reagan, as he finished his farewell address on January 11, 1989, said, after a few minutes of reminiscing,

The past few days when I've been at that window upstairs, I've thought a bit of the "shining city upon a hill." The phrase comes from John Winthrop, who wrote it to describe the America he imagined. . . . I've spoken of the shining city all my political life, but I don't know if I ever quite communicated what I saw when I said it. But in my mind it was a tall proud city built on rocks stronger than oceans, wind-swept, God-blessed, and teeming with people of all kinds living in harmony and peace, a city with free ports that hummed with commerce and creativity, and if there had to be city walls, the walls had doors and the doors were open to anyone with the will and the heart to get here. That's how I saw it and see it still.[2]

Beautiful, idealistic words—by Winthrop, Reagan, and so many in between—but these words have been terribly misappropriated.

The American Way ≠ The Jesus Way

"City on a hill" language is verbiage that belongs exclusively to followers of the way of Jesus, to disciples who are on the path into the Kingdom of God. No government, country, empire, or political party can ever serve as the light of the world. That is a role that belongs absolutely to the church of Jesus Christ. And no country is the "last best hope for the world." That title belongs entirely to Christ. Any organization or person that otherwise uses this language has plagiarized it and is attempting to use human power and the ways of the world to become what can only be born into the world by the power of God.

So with apologies to John Winthrop, do not expect government to be the salt of the earth or the light of the world. Do not expect this from your employer, a corporation for which you work, a social service club to which you belong, or a charity to which you give or volunteer. It can only be found in those who are following Christ on the path of becoming an alternative community in this world, a colony and outpost of the Kingdom of God that stands as a sign and symbol of how humanity can really live. Expect great and noble things from these other organizations—even demand it—but do not expect them to be salt and light. It is not within their nature to be so.

Yet this is the very nature—the supernatural nature—of the Jesus Tribe. Like the Beatitudes before, these are not qualities one possesses. This is the natural outflow of living out a life of submission to the way of Christ and the Kingdom of God. No one musters up a witness to the world: "I have to go let my light shine today; I sure hope I can. I have to be the salt of the earth— pray for me that I'm up to that." No. What is required is surrender to the identity Christ has for us. Rest in this dependence, follow his ways, and nothing can stop you from being the salt of the earth and the light of the world. But how do these metaphors speak to the identity of the Jesus Tribe?

In first-century Palestine, salt was almost priceless as it was used as a sea-soning for food, but chiefly it was a preservative. Of course there was no refrigeration in that period, so food (meat especially) had to be salted down to be cured or kept (some of us have memories of this process in our own day). Salt functioned as an indispensable commodity used to preserve and protect against contamination. So important was this seasoning that Roman soldiers were sometimes even paid with salt. They could keep it for personal use or sell it. And sometimes slaves were bought or sold using salt as cur-rency. Thus the phrase, "not worth his salt," meant someone who wasn't earning his paycheck or wasn't worth the investment put into him.

Then there is the image of light, the city on a hill that cannot be hidden. Jesus, no doubt, was thinking of Jerusalem. He compared the witness of his followers to Israel's capital city, sitting high above the Rift Valley like a jewel in the day and a neon sign at night. For weary pilgrims trying to get to the

City of God and his temple, the lights on the hill became a beacon by which to set their course. Jesus speaks of the identity of his disciples along these two lines: preservation of the world around them and light to those living in the darkness trying to find their way. Not much of these two elements are needed—just handfuls and flashbulbs here and there. But when they come in contact with a poisoned and dark world, their presence cannot be underestimated or ignored. As followers of Jesus, we get into the worst trouble when we hand over our responsibility as salt and light to others, or assume that our witness is compatible with the world of empire.

Many Christians in the United States have been operating under the fantasy, from John Winthrop forward, that this is a Christian nation. Though this is severe shorthand, the notion of a Christian nation is where our focus is on sacred buildings, a denominational or institutionalized religious organization, cooperation with power, and the demand that society serve the values of the church.[3] But a Christian nation is a delusion. No such entity exists. Living in a nation that treats us with some respect and allows us to pursue our personal ambitions does not mean the Empire and the way of Jesus are compatible. When the Empire isn't overtly persecuting the Tribe, we tend to fall into the trap of thinking it is on "our" side," shining the light and salting the earth. But this is not the case.

Eugene Peterson makes this point eloquently. He says the North American church conspicuously embraces the way of the Empire while living "in Jesus' name." The church too often "replaces the Jesus way with the American way."[4] Yes, the American way works,

> sometimes magnificently, in achieving grandly conceived ends. Wars are fought, wealth is accumulated, elections are won, victories posted. But the means by which those ends are achieved leaves a lot to be desired. In the process a lot of people are killed, a lot of people impoverished, a lot of marriages destroyed, a lot of children abandoned, a lot of congregations defrauded.[5]

We might wish things were different, that the American Empire was our partner in advancing the Kingdom of God, but it is not. All empires belong to the world of corruption and darkness, even the Empire begun with a sermon off the Massachusetts shore.

Another metaphor, beyond salt and light, comes from early American Roger Williams. Williams was a theologian, founder of Rhode Island, and champion of religious and civil liberty a hundred years before the United

States Constitution was written (incidentally, Williams was also John Winthrop's most painful thorn in the side). He said the church was like "a garden." Everything else—governments, corporations, organizations of power—were what he called "the wilderness." Williams believed those churches that gave up their unique role as witness for something else, even something that "worked," were permitting the wilderness to intrude upon the garden. As such, they would be manipulated by outside powers and policies, compromising on issues of love, justice, and mercy. Or those same churches would become the manipulators themselves, using political, economic, or religious power to force their beliefs on others. Either way, when church and state drank from the same cup, the church would be poisoned.[6]

Roger Williams's counsel to the Christian church in his day is lasting: learn to live in the world and witness to it, but do not become a part of it. Or he might say, "Plant a garden in a wilderness, but do not bring the wilderness into the garden." Thankfully, we have the right, privilege, and freedom to live out, practice, and witness to our faith in this country. But we do not have permission to use the tools of this world or the systems of this world to accomplish those ends. When we do this, planting the wild and wooly seeds of the wilderness in our garden, we compromise our witness. We lose our saltiness. We extinguish our own light.

But protecting our witness does not mean we can retreat from the world, as if we could transplant our garden from the wilderness that surrounds us. Withdrawal from our society—a society that needs us—is not an option either.

The Tale of Two Lighthouses

I read in the national papers that doomsday shelters are making a big comeback. I've never been in one of these safe havens, but I am told they were all the rage fifty years ago. At the height of the Cold War, with atomic weapons rolling like automobiles off the assembly line and a shoe-pounding Khrushchev with his hand hovering above the red button, it was not uncommon for a family to have a bomb shelter stocked with food and water in the event of a nuclear war. Now, two generations later, these things are flying off the shelves again and being installed everywhere.

One company in Texas sells fiberglass shelters that can accommodate ten to two thousand people. These lucky folks can then live underground for up to five years with power, food, water, medical care, and filtered air. You'll need to be more than lucky, though, to plant one of these things in your back yard. You'll need some serious coin. These behemoth bunkers range in price from $400,000 to $41 million. But have no fear. If you can't buy a private shelter for you and your family straight up, then you can purchase partial ownership in one of the larger facilities (I think that's called a time-share). One of these nuclear condos will set you back $50,000 for adults and $25,000 for children. And just like something out of a science-fiction movie, if you survive the initial bomb, attack, asteroid impact, plague, or pestilence and can get to your designated shelter, they will let you in as long as you have proper identification and have made all your monthly payments.

Ironically, proponents of these shelters say, "We are not paranoid. This is an investment in life." And one of the manufacturers (who conveniently has a doomsday clock on his website counting down to the end of the Mayan calendar in 2012) said, "We're not creating the fear; the fear is already out there. We are creating a solution."[7]

I wonder if this manufacturer is the chairman of the board of some churches I know, because their proposed solutions to the troubles of the world are identical: "Retreat into the safe confines of our sanctuaries and hide from the destruction on the outside." But this won't do, because shelters have a way of becoming tombs buried beneath the earth, and when we concede to the world of empire around us, we are already dead.

This is why I think Jesus chose his metaphors of salt and light most carefully. Not far from where he was speaking was the community of Qumran. Qumran flourished in the decades before Jesus' ministry and was alive and well in the first century. For all practical purposes it was a Jewish monastery. Well-meaning, devoted Jews who genuinely wanted to follow the ways of God gave up on the world and retreated to live in caves near the Dead Sea. Those at Qumran looked at the crushing, oppressive religious systems; at the unjust tax structure that was starving Jewish farmers; at the iron hand of the Roman army that for too long had occupied their holy land; at the prejudice, inequality, and collapse of all that was good and simply went to live in the desert. They resigned from living in the world around them and checked out. Jesus seems to be taking aim right at monastic communities like this one.

Residents at Qumran still had to make a living, so they mined salt from the Dead Sea, the saltiest body of water in the world. They mined the salt and sold or traded it to merchants to get the food and supplies they needed. And late at night, anyone journeying the roads of that area recognized the glow of candlelight coming from the Qumran caves high on the mountains, like stars dotting a black sky. When Jesus said, "You are the salt of the earth; the light of the world," he was saying, "You cannot keep the salt to yourself. You cannot stuff your light into a desert retreatist's cave." To serve as preserving agent and as light in the darkness requires that followers of Jesus interact with the world. Any pretense about remaining withdrawn, concentrating on a private morality, or sinking roots into a kind of spiritual reservation are obliterated here. The answer to the corruption of the world is not to withdraw from it but to enter it, and, by our very nature, to serve as both the loving subversion of the status quo and the visible community that follows Jesus.

Once, a lighthouse keeper along a dangerous coast was charged with the task of keeping the light in the tower burning. He was given enough oil every month to keep the light bright for passing ships. One day, a woman from the nearby village came to the lighthouse to ask for oil so her family could stay warm. Then a teacher came, needing oil for a lamp so she could study and instruct the children of the village. A farmer visited who needed oil for a tractor so his fields could be planted and the community fed. The keeper saw each as a worthy request and measured out just enough oil—just a little—to satisfy each request. After all, it was the helpful thing to do. Near the end of the month, the tank in the lighthouse ran dry. That night the beacon was dark and several ships crashed on the rocks. Hundreds of lives were lost. When the investigators came to the lighthouse keeper, he explained what he had done and why. But the officials responded, "You were given one task alone: Keep the light burning. Everything else was secondary."[8]

Imagine that the same lighthouse must get a new keeper. They hire a man to do the job and explain to him the past failures. "Keep the light burning," they say. So he does. He understands the importance of the light, and thus he faithfully safeguards the fuel that keeps it shining. At night he goes up in the tower and sits beside the beacon, enjoying its warmth and glow. He reads his books, writes his letters, drinks his coffee, and looks out at the rocky shoreline and stormy seas. But on one especially stormy night he notices the wind from these stormy seas causes the light to flicker. He is alarmed and asks himself, "What if the storm on the outside becomes so strong that it blows out the light?" So he comes up with a plan. He begins replacing the old, creaking windows of the lighthouse with strong, sturdy boards and shutters, for he must keep the light burning at all costs. Finally the light is enclosed in a wooden envelope, safe and sound from the world outside. He continues to enjoy the light, read his books, write his letters, and drink his coffee. But, as before, the ships pile up on the rocks in the dark.

This is what happens when we do not balance the extremes of complicity with the empire and retreat from the wilderness around us. Jesus puts it more bluntly: "But what good is salt if it has lost its flavor? Can you make it salty again? It will be thrown out and trampled underfoot as worthless" (Matt 5:13). In Greek, the English phrase "lost its flavor" is one word: *moros*. It is where we get our word "moron." If salt loses its flavor, if the people of the Way act foolishly (like morons) by giving in or retreating, then we will become useless. In Palestine in the first century, salt that had lost its composition was used as pothole filler on dirt roads. As a community, if we lose our salty spirit, we too should not be surprised when we are cast out and trampled upon, like gravel along a muddy road.

The governments of the world can lose all sense of justice and mercy and continue governing. The economic systems can lose balance, billions of dollars, and anything that resembles credibility. Still, they will be there in the morning. Militaries can lose all restraint and devolve into inhumane cruelty, but the weapons of war will continue to be stockpiled. Religious organizations can bleed out membership, money, and clergy, yet the bureaucracy will roll on under the power of its own steam as if nothing significant has occurred. But if those who bear Jesus' name lose their witness, if a local congregation no longer serves as the grace-full and Jesus-following light of a community, then there is no reason for it to remain in business. If we lose our saltiness, we have lost everything and have nothing worth saying to the world around us. We should be ignored, for that is the place we have earned.

"The Pigs Are Flying"

Bernhard Lichtenberg was a Catholic priest serving at Saint Hedwig's Cathedral in Berlin, Germany, when Adolf Hitler and the Nazi Party came to power before the outbreak of World War II. Lichtenberg, seeing the coming terror better than most, made it his ambition to help the Jewish people and other persecuted groups, and he was not afraid to use his pulpit for that purpose. While the majority of Christian churches in Germany hid their light under a bushel, complicit with the growing German Empire, Lichtenberg spoke fearlessly and acted boldly in defense of justice and mercy. His repeated protests landed on the ears of government officials and then landed him in severe trouble with the Gestapo. After a few years of uneasy tension, Lichtenberg was finally arrested for his opposition in October 1941.

During his interrogation, Lichtenberg was given the opportunity to recant his words. He would not. Rather, he said,

> I reject with my innermost the [deportation of the Jews] with all its side effects, because it is directed against the most important commandment of Christianity, "You shall love your neighbor as much as you love yourself." And I recognize the Jew too as my neighbor, who possesses an immortal soul, shaped after the likeness of God. However, since I cannot prevent this governmental measure, I have made up my mind to accompany the deported Jews and Christian Jews into exile, in order to give them spiritual aid. I wish to ask the Gestapo to give me this opportunity.[9]

Lichtenberg received a two-year jail sentence for his "crimes."

Toward the end of his prison term, friends and associates visited him with the news that the Gestapo would release him indefinitely and without further harassment if only he would stop preaching for the duration of the war. Again, Lichtenberg would not yield. Now considered irredeemable by the German authorities, Lichtenberg was condemned to the concentration camp at Dachau. Aged and in a weakened state, Bernard Lichtenberg mercifully died while waiting to be deported on November 5, 1943.

It is hard to say that Bernard Lichtenberg, almost single-handedly opposing the Nazi war machine, was acting in a reasonable manner. What could one man in a pulpit do to dismantle or otherwise deter the Third Reich? Not much, except to be persecuted, imprisoned, or executed. But the way of Jesus is not always practical. Sometimes it is insanely the opposite— madness, it appears to be. Yet practicality does not seem to be Jesus' concern. It appears he would rather have his followers pursue a path that leads us into danger than to take the course that leaves us irrelevant because we have no witness left.

If those in the Jesus Tribe submit to the peaceful, cheek-turning, treasure-abandoning, meek, and loving rule of the Kingdom of God, the powers of this world may malign, take advantage of, or abuse us. But if there is not the danger—even the expectation—that we will be taken advantage of or marginalized, even nailed to a cross, then we may not be giving witness to our Lord who endured the same. More often than not, it is in our vulnerability that we find true strength, for the people who "are to be won and saved should, as it were, always have the possibility of crucifying the witness of the gospel."[10] You can be certain that, accepted or rejected, received or rebuffed, the community of disciples will be impossible to ignore. We will be cleansing salt and shining light, bearing witness to the higher and better glory of our heavenly Father.

Again we return to that new word in our vocabulary to describe the Kingdom of God: "performative." This witness is God's performance. It is what he is doing, and we, as followers and disciples of Jesus, are invited to participate actively. Here it is: "Let your good deeds shine out for all to see, so that everyone will praise your heavenly Father" (Matt 5:16). Why are we the salt of the earth? Why are we the light of the world? Why has this responsibility been placed on the followers of Jesus? Because it is practical? No. Because it is a reasonable, logical, or safe way to live in the world? No. As we participate in this way of Jesus and the world sees it, it gives witness to the God of heaven. They will "praise our heavenly Father."

We live this way—we are these kinds of people—not because we think we can save the world; not to make our membership rolls grow; not to get more people into church on Sunday; not to gain influence over others to get what we what; not to take over or otherwise seize mastery over the Empire; not even to change people's hearts and minds. We do this as an act of devotion to our God. Light is seen but never for its own purpose. Salt is tasted but not eaten as the main course. Light and salt always point toward something else. What we point to is a better way to live. What we point to is the Kingdom of Heaven made manifest here on earth. What we point to is the Jesus we follow and the God we worship.

To conclude this chapter, I turn to another tribal group, one that I have come to know and love, living literally in my own backyard. The Muscogee Nation of Florida, only a few hundred people, is an aboriginal people group of the Americas who seeks to hold to their unique identity while surviving the culture around them. The Muscogee are led by an indomitable woman named Ann Denson Tucker. Ann directs the Tribal Council, serves as the public face and living historian of this people, and plays the role of chaplain, social worker, and attorney for her tribe. Ann has sought official recognition for the Florida Muscogee from the United States Department of Indian Affairs for many years now. She doesn't want much more than that—just an acknowledgment of their existence. But until the Muscogee bow to the economic machine of the American Empire ("Align yourself with a tribe that operates a casino and recognition will be much easier," a government official recently told Ann), that recognition will likely never come.

Yet, Ann Denson Tucker and the Muscogee do not need official recognition as a people to bear witness to something greater. Recently, when many of her people and people in the greater community were hungry, unemployed, and in need, Ann rescued an old portable schoolhouse from the county landfill to create a food pantry and community clothes closet. Critics told her it was a fool's errand. What could one little food bank in the middle of the Florida woods do to help alleviate poverty? Without official governmental recognition, how could she ever hope to sustain service? But Ann was undeterred.

On the day of the ribbon cutting, fewer than a dozen of the resilient Muscogee signed up for help. But more than two hundred from the greater community came for food, clothes, diapers, and supplies. Ann stood to speak, and said,

> What a wonderful celebration when people are able to look no farther and expect nothing more than helping each other through hard times. Creator has known that our hearts were in the right place on this project, and he has stood with us to make this possible. Imagine how strong we could be if we simply remembered that our first obligation is as caretakers of one another.
>
> We have dared to challenge those people who told us that the day we would be able to help our rural poor would be "when pigs fly." Well, the pigs are flying. And, I cannot think of a better example than this building whose destiny was one of no hope and no future. I am honored today to be able to cut this ribbon and dedicate rural relief to the working class people of [this community]. We will be here for as long as you need us.[11]

Ann's last words at the ceremony struck me like lightning: "We will be here for as long as you need us." Later I asked her why she chose to say such a thing. How, after all, could she make such a promise when her tribe was so small and the need around her so great? She answered, "Because we have no other choice. As long as there is a need in this community, someone must meet that need. It must be us."

Ann's words and example have something to teach us. As long as this world is dark and its empires corrupt, the Jesus Tribe must be there to shine the light of Christ and sprinkle the salt that is the Kingdom of God. The task may seem impossible and impractical, sometimes even dangerous, but we have no other choice. Submitting to the way and power of Jesus, it must be us.

Chapter 5

No Rules, Just Right

Don't misunderstand why I have come. I did not come to abolish the law of Moses or the writings of the prophets. No, I came to accomplish their purpose. I tell you the truth, until heaven and earth disappear, not even the smallest detail of God's law will disappear until its purpose is achieved. So if you ignore the least commandment and teach others to do the same, you will be called the least in the Kingdom of Heaven. But anyone who obeys God's laws and teaches them will be called great in the Kingdom of Heaven. But I warn you—unless your righteousness is better than the righteousness of the teachers of religious law and the Pharisees, you will never enter the Kingdom of Heaven!" (Matt 5:17-20)

In July 2001, Chief Justice Roy Moore of the Alabama Supreme Court installed a two-and-a-half-ton granite monument inscribed with the Ten Commandments in the rotunda of the Alabama State Judicial Building. The monument, you might remember, had a contentious home in that rotunda for a couple of years, and then in 2003 it was removed by court order as a violation of the separation of church and state. A few months later, Justice Moore was also removed by court order from the Alabama State Judicial Building after refusing to comply with the earlier court ruling.

Not long after these events played out across our cable television news shows, Roy Moore's Ten Commandments monument went on tour. Loaded onto the flatbed of a heavy-duty truck, it went town to town so onlookers could see for themselves the controversial work of stonemasonry. I watched the monument make its first stop after leaving Alabama in Dayton, Tennessee. This was a calculated move for the organizers of the tour. Dayton was home of the 1925 "Scopes Monkey Trial," where many feel Christian America was first besieged.[1]

An atheist was there in Dayton at that first stop, protesting the monument being placed on display, and I wondered if this man would escape with his life. Moore's supporters, about a hundred it seemed, were screaming out for the death of this single protestor. "Shoot him . . . hang him . . . put him before a firing squad!" These were all yelled from the crowd. One man speaking of the "godless" protestor said, "I'm glad I didn't bring my gun. I'd be in jail right now." The shady irony was not lost on me. Here were ardent supporters of the Ten Commandments—they had come out on a rainy day to see a stone rendering of them—wishing to violate the commandments as they called for the killing of their enemy.

Dietrich Bonhoeffer, after he "found" the Sermon on the Mount, realized that he been living the Christian life "in a very unchristian way. But then something happened, something that has changed and transformed my life," he said. "I discovered the Sermon on the Mount."[2] The change that had so great an impact on Bonhoeffer was his conclusion that followers of Jesus did not need better rules, not even those engraved in stone, for rules were powerless to change the human heart. Rather, followers of Jesus needed a "better righteousness." They needed a better way to live that transcended the religious rules altogether, even if that way of life was despised by the world and ignored by much of professing Christianity. That rule-defying, rule-exceeding way of life is the way of Jesus.

Jesus the Rebel

Jesus' contemporaries often interpreted him as a rule breaker. He "broke" the law by healing or allowing his disciples to pick grain on the Sabbath (apparently the equivalent of "working"); he did not follow the ritualistic traditions like the washing of his hands at the table; and he kept company with a questionable, unethical crowd. But his reputation as a rebel may be forever crystallized with this section of the Sermon on the Mount, beginning at Matthew 5:17 and continuing to the end of the chapter. Jesus quotes a series of well-established laws—about murder, adultery, divorce, promise-keeping, revenge, and enemies—and after each quote Jesus amends the law's meaning.

This would have been enough to get Jesus in serious trouble in most any synagogue where he would have preached. Maybe this is why he said these things outside the walls of the establishment. After all, to assail the law of God was an unforgivable crime in Jewish society, and by "law," depending on the context, it might mean (1) the Ten Commandments, (2) the first five books of the Bible, (3) the entire Old Testament canon, or (4) the oral tradition. All of these were unassailable and untouchable. Then Jesus comes along and says, essentially, "I know what you've heard about the law, but your understanding is wrong. Listen to what I have to say." This was scandalous.

Still, Jesus is quick to say that it was not his intention to undermine or to break the law. He says, "Don't misunderstand why I have come. I did not come to abolish the law of Moses or the writings of the prophets. No, I came to accomplish their purpose" (Matt 5:17). Jesus came to fulfill the law, that is, to draw out its actual meaning and to bring it to its proper completion, not to break it. There are a few ways we can begin to think about Jesus' words here.

In the spring, there are blooms on the blackberry vines in the woods that run along my house. When the blooms become berries, the flower isn't destroyed. It is fulfilled, for it has matured. When a baby is born into the world, he or she begins to grow immediately. Twenty years later, the child has not been destroyed. He or she has been fulfilled. He or she has come to maturity. When a farmer goes out to harvest his crop in the fall with scythe or combine, he is not destroying the seed. He is reaping what has come to completion. The law, at its core, was only a shadow of what was to come.

Another example: On May 14, 1804, the Corps of Discovery, led by captains Meriwether Lewis and William Clark, set out on one of the most ambitious expeditions in American history. President Thomas Jefferson, who had dreamed of just such a journey for two decades, charged the captains and their crew with the task of exploring, mapping, and traversing a portion of the North American continent that no Euro-American had ever seen. Lewis and Clark were also hopeful to discover the long illusive Northwest Passage, a waterway connecting the Atlantic and Pacific oceans. But after more than a year into their 8,000-mile journey, the Corps of Discovery had exhausted their efforts at plying the Missouri River. The river that had carried them so far and so long had become only a trickle. The Corps of Discovery would have to find a new means of transportation to complete their journey.

Lewis and Clark, with more than a little apprehension, were forced to leave their priceless boats behind, the very vessels that had carried them into the American West. Their trusted means of travel could no longer bear them across the most rugged terrain they had ever encountered. With freshly acquired horses graciously offered from the native tribes, Lewis and Clark crossed the Continental Divide into a land simply marked "Unknown" on their maps.

The Law of Moses had carried God's tribe of people along on their spiritual journey, and like Lewis and Clark's trusted boats, it was more than sufficient for travel. But to complete the journey—to move on to maturity—another means of travel was required. Jesus is the way we now journey, and he has revolutionized how we live, relate to God, and travel through life. Yes, the rules were all we had once upon a time, but now we have something better—we have Jesus himself showing us the way. Once the faithful followed religious codes to please or pursue God; that was their understanding of faith. But religious rules could not give life or spiritual freedom. While the law was instructive and useful, ultimately it could only constrict and confine. In the words of the Apostle Paul, "The letter [the rules] kills"; it can't give life (2 Cor 3:6). Now, to travel on to maturity, we must let go of what has brought us this far and live his way, that "better" way that no written law or religious rulebook can duplicate.

Going even further, Leo Tolstoy once compared religious rules to the light given off by a lamppost. It is a healthy bright light that dispels the darkness. As long as a man or woman stood in that light, he or she could see. Yet the lamppost had limitations, Tolstoy said. To remain in the light meant going nowhere; one had to stay put to remain in the light. But following Jesus, Tolstoy continued, was like carrying a light or lantern fixed to a pole. A person could carry that pole out in front of his path and travel anywhere he liked.[3] Tolstoy never held a flashlight, but we have, and we can understand his analogy that way: To remain a mere rule keeper is to remain under a street light. To follow Christ is to take a flashlight in hand and get on with it—to explore, pierce the dark, and enjoy a faith that is dynamic, not static.

Much of the church is locked into keeping the rules. Its people stand in a little circle of light, unmovable and fixed like a stone, cursing the darkness and barking at the street traffic as it moves along. The church has light, but the light does not serve it or others very well. The church might as well be chained to a post, for it is imprisoned, not growing or going anywhere.

As another parallel, once while traveling I had two sets of directions telling me which way to go. On the dashboard was a crumpled page of written notes. They were coffee stained, had scribbles all over them, and, unknown to me, did not match recent road construction changes and improvements. The other set of directions were being called out to me from a GPS system, and as I neared my destination I had a terrible conflict. When I followed my written directions to the letter, they began to fail me and I reached a point that they no longer worked. The streets those written direction told me to take weren't there—either that or their names had been changed. Meanwhile, the voice calling from the GPS was saying things like, "Prepare to make a right turn . . . When possible, make a legal U-turn . . . Recalculating route." But I kept driving according to my written directions even though it was obvious that they no longer worked. Finally, I had to take a leap of faith. I accepted the fact that my coffee-stained directions had taken me as far as they could, and now, to get to where I needed to be, I had to listen to the personal voice that was now calling me. That voice was right all along.

I know that thinking of spirituality without rules, even without the Ten Commandments, is a radical departure for many of us who have based our entire connection to God on rule keeping, "being good," measuring up, and following every bit of religious instruction. Of course, when we failed to live up to these demands—and failure was inevitable—we were swamped with guilt, fear, and shame. Still, shouldn't we cling to what is black and white, the sure and certain rule of the law? In a word, no. Now that Christ has come, there is no point in holding to the illusion of security that comes from clutching to the law. Christianity is not a heavy obligation to stagnant, inanimate rules handed down from the mountain and engraved in stone. Rather, Christianity is the free enjoyment of a relationship with a living, life-giving person.

No Leash Law Required

Thankfully, Jesus didn't arrive with more and better rules. He arrived with a transformative way to live that sets us free from the heavy burden of religion and moves us to right thinking, right feeling, right actions, and right living. Jesus came to change our hearts, for no law is capable of producing internal and outflowing love. The way of Jesus transforms us from within so that the commandment "Thou shall not murder" becomes irrelevant because hate has been removed from our hearts. The command "Thou shall not commit adultery" is unnecessary because all lust and insecurity have been obliterated within us. Work your way through them all. They are needless if the human heart has somehow been transformed. They are needless if, by the Spirit, the human heart has become the slate upon which God has inscribed himself (see Jer 31:33).

Again, here are a couple of examples to guide us further. Imagine that you go to the doctor with a collection of symptoms signaling a sickness. You are examined thoroughly by your physician: CAT scans, MRIs, X-rays, nuclear medicine, blood work, labs—everything. And in the end you get a diagnosis. The doctor calls you in and says, "We've found it. This is what you have. You have a cancerous tumor. This is the cause of all your problems." Then he props his feet up on his desk, leans back in his chair, and smiles the smile of a contented man, pleased with his diagnostic abilities.

Has that doctor really done anything for you? No. He told you what was wrong, but he has done nothing toward a cure. What you need is more than a diagnosis. You need a surgeon who will remove what is killing you. The law, even the Ten Commandments, can only diagnose our problem. These laws cannot cure us or change the pathology on the inside, but Jesus can as we submit to him and his ways. He is the surgeon who does more than diagnose and treat symptoms. He strikes with his scalpel at the root cause of the disease.

Clarence Jordan explained it like this: The law is like chaining a vicious dog to a tree. With the dog chained in such a way the owner could report, "You know, my dog has never bitten anyone. He must be a good dog." But that is wrong. The goodness of the dog is based solely upon the strength of the chain. If that dog ever got loose, he would bite everyone within the reach of his jaws. To Jesus, the law was like a leash or a chain. Make it heavy and strong enough, like interpreters and practitioners of the law could do, and it was adequate to keep the wayward human heart from hurting others and hurting itself. But Jesus' intention is to change the nature of the dog, not to manufacture a more robust chain. Jesus came to set us free from all prisons, entanglements, and bondage, even the law. Jesus, transforming the human heart, means chains are no longer needed.[4]

The Jesus Tribe is a society that "does what it pleases" because love has removed both the necessity of laws and the motivation to hurt others. Jesus taught us to love God and love our neighbor, a way of life that can change the world. But even if this does not change the world in our lifetimes, it still changes us. Jesus has fulfilled the purpose of the law and transformed its locked gates into an open doorway of freedom, grace, and love. We are changed because the nature of our relationship with God is changed. The relationship is not based on a set of laws, religious regulations, or rules. The relationship is grounded in knowing and following the person of Jesus.

This relationship does more than transform our behavior. It is a rooting out of anger, lust, self-preservation, fear, hate, and selfishness to be replaced with justice, compassion, reverence, and, above all, love. How does this happen? The only obstacle standing in the way of our transformation is us. We must give up all we have, all we have been, all we are, and all we ever hope to be so that we are empty before Christ, who wishes to fill us with himself. William Law gets to the heart of it:

> All failures of the Christian life are due to one thing: We seek to do with
> our own strength and ego what only God can do. . . . God must do all, or
> all is nothing. But God cannot do all until all is expected from Him. And

all is not expected from Him until we have no hope, trust, or longing for anything but a patient . . . humble, total resignation to God.[5]

When such resignation takes root, we are transformed.

Five hundred years ago there was a group of Christians living in Europe known as the Anabaptists. These are not to be confused with today's Baptists, though the groups do share points of common history. The more direct descendants of the Anabaptists today are the Mennonites, the Church of the Brethren, and the Amish. The name Anabaptist was not so much a description as it was a condemnation. The Anabaptists were "anti-baptizers" or "re-baptizers," scorning infant baptism and a heap of other cherished church doctrines. Because they refused to baptize babies and thus refused to accept the sacraments (and civil power) of the Roman, Lutheran, or Calvinistic churches, they were violently persecuted by governments, Catholics, and Protestants alike.

One such persecution broke out in 1569 against Anabaptists in Holland. Yes, there were some genuine fanatics in the Anabaptist tribe, but the simple, compassionate, and innocent Jesus followers were gobbled up as well, as is always the case. One such innocent was a young man named Dirk Willems. On a cold winter day, a bailiff was sent to arrest Dirk on the charge that he had been re-baptized, had been holding secret religious meetings in his home, and had allowed others to be re-baptized there. Dirk ran for his life with the bailiff right on his heels. Knowing that he would be imprisoned, tortured, interrogated, burned at the stake, or drowned ("If they insist on being re-baptized, then give them the full treatment" was the terrible logic) if he were caught, Dirk threw himself across a small lake covered with thin ice. It held his weight as he ran, and he crossed safely to the other side. But the ice did not hold for his pursuer. The bailiff chasing after Dirk crashed through the ice into the freezing water. Dirk Willems immediately turned back and rescued the struggling man from the ice. For his kindness Dirk was immediately arrested, put in prison, tortured, and, after refusing to renounce his faith, was burned at the stake May 16, 1569.

Now, here is the question asked by Mennonites, the Amish, the Brethren, and others for nearly five centuries: "Why did Dirk Willems turn back?"

Put yourself in his vulnerable shoes. You are running for your life, and while the air is so cold it can freeze rivers and lakes, the sweat is running down the small of your back. Your pursuer is so close to snatching you that you can feel his hot breath on your neck. Your heart pounds in your chest and your pulse is deafening in your ears, but from behind you still hear a crack and a splash. There in the icy water is the man who came to take you to your death. What do you do? Do you stop, and like the Israelites of old, thank God for the Red Sea that swallowed Pharaoh's army? Do you raise your praise to heaven as God has triumphed over injustice? Do you continue running into the wilderness where eventually your hands will stop shaking and there pray you will see your family again?

Dirk Willems did none of these things. He instinctively, reflexively turned and rescued his enemy, though he knew death would be the price he would pay. In the words of Joseph Liechty,

> It was not a rational choice. It was not an ethical decision. It was an *intuitive response*. No combination of mental calculations could have carried him back across the ice. . . . The only force strong enough to take Dirk back across the ice was an extraordinary outpouring of love, and the only love I know [like that] is the love taught and lived by Jesus.[6]

Dirk Willems acted as he did because he had been so spiritually shaped and formed by the words, way, and life of Jesus that his response was the only one he was capable of making. Dirk was dead long before he reached for the bailiff in the water, but not from an executioner's sentence. Dirk's life and identity had been swallowed up in the person of Jesus, and it was Christ who now lived through him. That is why Dirk Willems turned back.

Beware of the Booger Man

The kind of transformation Dirk Willems experienced is unobtainable via rule keeping and religious obligation. As Jesus said, "Unless your righteousness is better than the righteousness of the teachers of religious law and the Pharisees, you will never enter the Kingdom of Heaven" (Matt 5:20)! While the term "Pharisee" is often used today as a caricature or as an accusation against those with obvious hypocrisy, in Jesus' day the Pharisees were very real.

Emerging in the decades before the public ministry of Jesus, the Pharisees were the largest, most influential, and most vocal religious party in Palestine, referred to about a hundred times in the New Testament. The Pharisees, literally the "pious ones," ran the schools and the academies; the priests and scribes were often members of their order; and their ambition was to achieve a perfect righteousness by meticulously keeping all of God's laws through an intricate system. This rule keeping extended beyond the written

Law of Moses to their oral interpretations and traditions. (This oral tradition was eventually collected on paper as the Talmud and its cascading commentaries. It was massive and easily filled thousands of pages, swelling the shelves of any home or personal library.)

For all their legalism, nitpicking, and attention to religious detail, these Pharisees were certainly committed. They burned with a passion for the Jewish religion, a passion that the common man or woman on the street could not obtain. And that was the point: Pharisees deliberately practiced separatism and would not mix or mingle with the "people of the land" for fear of spiritual contamination. Their oral tradition prevented them from entering the homes, sharing a meal, or conducting any type of trade or business with those who were not of the Pharisee caste. Later in Jesus' ministry, when he enters the home and eats at the same table with notorious sinners, it is easy to see how offensive this act was to the committed Pharisee. This was an outlawed act that threatened personal righteousness, and personal, self-disciplined righteousness was the most important thing to the individual Pharisee.

Meanwhile, the commoners were kept on the outside. Righteousness, as defined by the Pharisees and their traditions, was simply unobtainable by the Jewish farmer, merchant, carpenter, or fisherman. The average Jew did not have access to the unending volumes of religious requirement. They did not have the time to give to rule-keeping efforts, not with livings to be made, children to rear, and oppressive taxes to be tendered. They had not been properly instructed, the Pharisees would say, and therefore were unable to meet the high and holy standards of righteousness.

To this, Jesus has the most shattering thing to say, and not at all what one would expect. He says that unless our righteousness "is better" than the righteousness of the Pharisees, then the Kingdom of God is beyond our grasp. To his first listeners (and to us) the questions must have exploded in their minds: How can my righteousness exceed that of the Pharisees, the acclaimed champions of religious rule keeping? How can I be righteous at all, being only a common man or woman, having missed the cut to play for the holy A-team? How can I reach a higher place than those who already infinitely exceed my ability?

Here is the answer: A higher righteousness is not necessarily the better righteousness. Jesus does not demand of us higher standards; he offers us himself. Jesus does not require of us super-human ability or commitments; he gives us his ability and grace. By bringing the laws of religion to their fulfillment, Jesus strikes literally at the heart of the issue—our hearts—transforming us from the inside out so that more rules and steeper requirements are no longer necessary.

A short time ago a friend of mine sent me an Internet link that pointed to an online "Discipleship Test." There were about two dozen questions on this test, and my answers determined how "discipled" I was. The test gave me a score, as if spirituality could be measured with a letter grade. After completing the test I realized that I had failed, or at the least I was informed that I had a lot of work to do to become a committed follower of Jesus. But in my defense, here is why I failed: all the questions focused on church responsibilities, allegiance to a narrow set of beliefs, and "behavior management"—questions about tobacco use, R-rated movies, how many minutes a day I prayed, how many verses of the Bible I read in a month, and how many times I went to church each week. It was nothing but a test of obligations, rules, and religious policy.

There remains only one certain, spiritual discipline: surrendering and emptying ourselves so that God, through his Son Jesus, might fill us. This is why rule keeping will never work. This is why our moral strivings are a failure and why religiosity is an abyss. These fill our hearts and lives with ourselves. The focus is always on what we can, must, or should do, and the more we fill ourselves with them, as noble as our intentions might be, the less space God has to operate until he is finally pushed out altogether and all we are left with is ourselves and our own inadequate attempts at righteousness.

So why do we stay at it, running like a hamster on a wheel, as hopeless and exhausting as it is? Because in the end, we are afraid. We are afraid of God. We think he is a cosmic rule maker, an eternally angry accountant who takes delight in auditing the records of the sinful. He shows no mercy, no grace, no flexibility, and no compassion. If you break the rules, you pay the price. We are terrified that the rule-enforcing God will obliterate us. This horrible, judgmental, angry God is everywhere I turn. People are so afraid and intimidated by him that they can't let go of the religious rule keeping that is robbing them of life. This God is a lot like the "Booger Man."

My grandmother often used the Booger Man to keep her grandchildren out of mischief. She would say to me, "You better behave or the Booger Man is going to get you." Or late at night if I had to check on the chickens or walk to the barn, she'd offer up a little giggle and say, "Don't let no Booger get you out there." I remember squirrel hunting once with one of my cousins. We kept hearing this strange noise in the woods. Trying to comfort myself, I told my cousin it was only birds. When he unsteadily replied, "But what if it's the Booger Man?" we both tore into a run, convinced our firearms would do us no good against such a creature.

Not to be confused with the Bogeyman (a European invention), my grandmother's Booger Man originated with the Cherokee Nation. The Cherokee developed a ritual known as the Booger Dance, sometimes called the Ghost Dance by the white man, to keep away evil spirits, demons, sickness, and disease. Later this dance was used symbolically to keep away the European invaders. The tribe would gather for the ritual late at night around a roaring fire, and on cue a group of pre-selected young men would come storming into the meeting house.

They were dressed in big, furry, grotesque masks and adorned with bear hide and feathers. They acted ferociously, clawing and scratching at those huddled in fear in the corners of the room. They flopped about on the floor, wailing and howling. And as the ritual went, those in the meeting house had to do the proper dance to soothe these savage beasts. This tamed each Booger Man until finally they would begin to dance with the people and then slink away into the darkness from where they came. Of course, those who might dance improperly or out of step—a young child or pretty girl— they would be snatched away, kicking and screaming, and carried into the Appalachian woods. Generations later the ritual was forgotten, but the Booger Man was not.

This is who God is to too many people. He is a lurking, spooky, otherworldly creature who waits to gobble us up when we do not perform the rituals correctly or keep the church's rules. We huddle in the corner, praying our prayers, dancing as correctly and as furiously as we can to soothe the Booger Man. But we cannot make the Booger Man/God of our imaginations reconcile with the God revealed to us in Jesus Christ. For Jesus did not come to condemn us or frighten us with rules and retribution. He came to give us a better righteousness. He came to give us life.

Chapter 6

Roundabout

"You have heard that our ancestors were told, 'You must not murder. If you commit murder, you are subject to judgment.' But I say, if you are even angry with someone, you are subject to judgment. . . . Go and be reconciled . . . .

"You have heard the commandment that says, 'You must not commit adultery.' But I say, anyone who even looks at a woman with lust has already committed adultery with her in his heart. So if your eye—even your good eye—causes you to lust, gouge it out and throw it away . . . .

"You have heard the law that says, 'A man can divorce his wife by merely giving her a written notice of divorce.' But I say that a man who divorces his wife, unless she has been unfaithful, causes her to commit adultery . . . .

"You have also heard that our ancestors were told, 'You must not break your vows; you must carry out the vows you make to the LORD.' But I say, do not make any vows. . . . Just say a simple, 'Yes, I will,' or 'No, I won't.' Anything beyond this is from the evil one." (Matt 5:21-37)

My father drove an aged blue Chevrolet station wagon that my sister and I named the "Blue Bomber." I say it was "blue," but the car was about fifteen years past its prime, so it was more rust-colored than blue, the paint having long ago oxidized. Worse, it had a hole in the muffler large enough to hold a beach ball. This resulted in a cacophony of strange, loud, guttural noises, and to add insult to injury, the windshield wipers stopped working some time before I hit puberty. So it's not hard to imagine that my begging would begin every morning on the way to school: "Dad, please drop me off at the driveway or at the far end of the parking lot." Because the last thing I wanted was to be seen in this image killer. Rain, sleet, snow, dead of night—these never troubled me. I was happy to walk through hell itself if it meant putting some distance between me and the Blue Bomber.

Sadly, my father never listened. Undeterred, he would drive that rolling junkyard right up to the front door of Gordon Central High School and force me out. After I slinked out of the backseat each morning he would stomp the gas, belching black smoke and sulfur all over me, and with his head cocked out the window he would backfire and rattle over the horizon. I hated that car and was glad to see it finally hauled away (though it mocked me while sitting on blocks in the backyard until I was in college) where I hope it was crushed, melted, and recycled into something useful.

I didn't always harbor this kind of resentment toward the Blue Bomber. There was a time when I loved that car, mainly because it didn't have any seatbelts. They had been cut out because "they got in the way," and I thought this was wonderful. My siblings and I would drop all the back seats, crawl into the cavern that was the rear of the vehicle, and pray for near misses and evasive tactics by my father. A stiff punch of the accelerator, a stomping of the breaks, or a quick swirl of the steering wheel would send us careening through the air and into each other like golf balls in a tile bathroom. It was incredible fun.

It was also tremendous fun to ride a bicycle without a helmet or elbow pads. It was fun to leave home on that bicycle on summer mornings and not return until dinner, never once checking in by cell phone. It was fun—and acceptable—to jump on a trampoline, to talk to strangers, to climb trees far too flimsy to support my weight, to play in the street, to light fire crackers without adult supervision, to go all day without using hand sanitizer, and, yes, it was fun to run with a sharp stick in my hand. But today, everything has to be safe. Safety scissors, safety vests, safety glass, safety cones, safety seats, safety ladders. It's all about safe drinking water, safe food, safe toys, safe surfing, safe sex, and safe schools. Most of these good things. Still, safety can go too far.

I took my sons to the park a few days ago to enjoy a new playground installed by the city fathers, apparently with the help of a team of safety experts and a host of litigation-preventing attorneys. Everything is right about this new playground and everything is wrong. There is no dirt, mud, or gravel at this playground. These dangers have been replaced by a synthetic, rubbery surface to cushion falls. Gone is the sharp-edged chain link fence, traded in for a short polymer-slotted wall. Even the equipment has changed. There are no domed monkey bars from which to hang upside down; no metal slides that grow hot enough in the summer sun to strip the hide from the back of your legs; no rocket-shaped climby thing; not even a seesaw. There are a few swings but—you guessed it—they have safety belts, so for the most part the new playground is just an overgrown baby bed. And I hear those aren't as safe as they should be.

There was one piece of missing playground equipment that, for all my safety raging, I am glad was removed: the merry-go-round, or as some call them, the roundabout. I haven't been on one of these things since I was ten years old and with good reason. It is basically a circular, metal whirling dervish of death. The game we played was simple and dangerously unsafe. About a thousand pounds of elementary-aged children would climb aboard while an adult (or someone's older brother) started spinning the thing with the G-force of a fighter jet. This resulted in half the kids immediately flying off or getting sucked beneath the thing, breaking arms and noses. Those who remained stuck to the handlebars usually began to spew their lunches like shaken cola cans, and the one who didn't get sick, didn't suffer a compound fracture, or could walk the straightest line when the spinning stopped was naturally the winner. I never won, and I have the scars to prove it.

Transforming Initiatives

The truth is no one ever wins on the roundabout, and we all have the scars to prove it. The roundabout I am speaking of is not a child's plaything. It is the always spinning cycle of human aggression. It is the near irrepressible need in all of us to win—to dominate, possess, and manipulate others. Viciously rotating, this game plays itself out until everyone is either flattened on the ground, holding on for dear life, or staggering about, dazed and broken. When our human emotions and desires keep us fastened to this merry-go-round of anger, lust, and pride, is there a way to get off the ride and live differently? Jesus says there is.

Approaching Matthew 5:21-37 (and much of the remaining Sermon on the Mount), Glen Stassen and David Gushee refer to Jesus' instructions here as "transforming initiatives."[1] Jesus addresses the traditional approach to doing right (prohibitions against murder, adultery, etc.), shows how this rule keeping only perpetuates the cycle of injustice and failure, and then offers a way of grace—a transforming initiative—that stops the roundabout and lets the disciple off.

The legalistic rules are plain enough and deal with murder, adultery, and promise keeping. Don't murder. Don't commit adultery. Keep your vows, in marriage and otherwise. All this seems fairly cut and dried. But Jesus strikes out against the motivations and deep emotions that drive these behaviors. Stassen and Gushee write, "Jesus was no legalist; Jesus was pointing to the breakthrough of the kingdom. . . . [These transforming initiatives] show the difference between legalistic rules and grace-based practices."[2] Jesus addresses the reasons for murder, adultery, and broken promises with early grace-based intervention long before these reasons can mature.

Before a trigger is ever pulled or a weapon ever welded, emotions have already been weaponized. Escalating anger pushes the roundabout faster and faster until everyone is dead or damaged. Before the hotel reservations are made or the romantic rendezvous carried out, adultery has already been committed in the human heart. Long before couples stand in divorce court or demonstrative oaths are taken to prop up one's compromised integrity, lies have already been told and vows already broken. By concentrating only on regulating behavior, we tend to treat the symptoms rather than the cause, and we are left only to strengthen our grip on the rails as the merry-go-round spins faster and faster.

Two things come to mind. First, when growing up it was one of my jobs, like many teenage boys, to mow the lawn. And not just at our house, but at my grandmother's and sometimes at the neighbors' houses as well. Despite all the grass cutting that had to be done, in all those years I never had a new lawnmower. We always had these mowers that were pieced together with baling wire and duct tape standing on their last legs, or we had ones that had been handed down to us after an uncle or neighbor had upgraded. So mowing was always an adventure, and if I could get through a couple of cuttings without a breakdown or without calling on my dad to come fix the mower, then it was a miracle (if you recall the Blue Bomber you see how Dad liked to hold on to old, obsolete, rusty equipment).

Once, when I was under a great deal of pressure to finish mowing because I had other stuff I wanted to do, the mower quit yet again. My father was at work and I had no patience left to wait. I took the lawnmower out back, got my dad's tools, and began working on the machine with a vengeance. I started with what I knew: I cleaned the air filter and adjusted the carburetor. When that didn't work, I started loosening bolts and screws, disassembling the thing until I was down to the mower deck itself, left with a million scattered parts. When my father got home I tried to explain myself, but to no avail. He was enraged, and rightfully so. I had made a mess.

Most of us approach our problems with our behavior with the same eagerness and ignorance that a teenager approaches a broken lawn mower. We disassemble everything, knowing that something is seriously wrong. And while we can pull it apart to assess the problem, we don't know how to put it all back together again. We don't know how to fix it. I have a modest, simple proposition to solve this problem: give Jesus a try. Jesus does far more than condemn or assess bad behavior. He offers a detour away from the dead ends to which our desires always seem to lead us.

Here's the second illustration, also about lawns: After an exceptionally cold winter, with the spring's thaw came the disappointing realization that my lawn's irrigation system was in shreds. Well, not exactly shreds—in drips, sprays, and geysers was more like it. The pipes froze sometime during the arctic that was January or February, and then burst at every turn, corner, and joint. Yes, I know I should have drained the pipes. Yes, I could have prevented all the digging madness. Yes, if I had known that April's warming temperatures would produce Old Faithful in at least a dozen places in my yard, I would have done differently. But that is water under the bridge and through the pipe now. No "woulda-coulda-shoulda" could help me with the mess I had on my hands.

Some faith leaders—entire denominations and religious systems in fact—make a living on the holes in people's lives, dug there by the shoulda-coulda-woulda. Precious little time is spent on helping people do what is best and good. Instead, all the energy and time is spent pointing out what people have done wrong. "If you would have made better choices . . . ," they condemn and criticize from their pulpits. "You could have been more prayerful, more disciplined, or more committed," they say in disaster's aftermath. "You should have listened to us! Didn't we tell you this would be the outcome!" they almost gleefully crow, as poor souls stand in the muddy and wet chill of all that has gone wrong.

Those in the church can sometimes pile on guilt, shame, and finger pointing when most people do not need to be reminded of what they have done wrong and how they shoulda-coulda-woulda lived differently. When we mess it up, we are usually the first to know. And when that recognition comes, we don't need long-winded sermons about a past we cannot change or homilies aimed at mistakes for which there is no do-over. What we need is help repairing the broken places so things work again. We need help digging the holes, bandages for our blisters, and a little glue to hold together the new pipes.

Of course, it's easy to remain disinfected and clean while standing in a pulpit or sitting comfortably in a pew. The hard work takes place on your hands and knees in the mud and muck of people's burst lives. But doing this hard work is where we belong as followers of Jesus. When our lives are full of holes, which is much of the time, I am so glad for Jesus' words when he said he "did not come to condemn the world" but to "save" it. He came to fix it.

If this world needed sermons and lectures, I figure he could have remained far from it, aloof and apathetic. Instead, Jesus put on the work clothes of human flesh and crawled onto a leaking, broken, and busted world, blistering and bloodletting his hands, hands he never used for finger pointing except to point to the "transforming initiative" of his grace.

Burning Down the House

What is Jesus' grace escape to avoid the falling dominoes of anger? It is to name, face, and resolve this anger as early as possible. "Go and be reconciled," he says. It should be noted that Jesus does not condemn what might be called "generic" anger. To do so would have been to condemn even himself, for Jesus experienced the full expression of human emotions. Neither is he speaking against rightfully admitting when someone is a fool, for sometimes it is the only appropriate word.

Jesus is calling to account the cycle of rage that lashes out at and tears apart relationships. He is diagnosing unresolved anger that leads to escalating conflict and finally violence. He is digging down to root out the seeds of anger before they have time to germinate. And the way to do this is practical: as much as it depends on the follower of Jesus, he or she must be the one to seek reconciliation and kill the anger, rather than letting the anger lead to killing. The urgency of the reconciliation is such that Jesus says one should even interrupt his or her act of worship, for communion with God is impossible when rage is harbored against another.

Appropriate anger has its purpose. It is a screaming alarm in our hearts and heads telling us that something is wrong—with the world, within ourselves, or with a relationship. Anger can then become a fuel to move us to positive redemptive action. But if that anger goes unacknowledged or unresolved, the fuel rages like a chemical fire, destroying the one who harbors the anger and most everyone he touches.

A fictional story has circulated in counseling circles for years that illustrates the danger of unresolved anger. The story involves a letter carrier and his mail route. This letter carrier loved his job, and after years of delivering mail to the same homes he came to love the people he interacted with as well. He got to know them personally, and because he daily handled their mail he knew what was going on in their lives. He knew that the widow at the end of one of the streets had been left with little income and could not pay her bills. He knew that the young man who lived in the duplex was estranged from his father and had vowed never to speak to him again. On and on, the stories mounted and developed.

So when the letter carrier found a bill or court action letter in his bag for the old widow, he would not deliver it. This was his way of protecting her from bad news. When the young man's father would write a letter, the mailman wouldn't deliver it either because he knew the words would only hurt and embitter the young man further. The letter carrier developed this habit for everyone on his route, taking home to his attic as much undelivered mail each day as what he put in the boxes. One evening flames could be seen streaming out of the mail carrier's roof and windows. Firefighters responded quickly, but the home was a total loss. Investigators soon discovered where the fire had originated. Thousands of pounds of undelivered mail, sitting on the wires in the attic, had short-circuited the house's electrical system and resulted in the terrible fire. This is precisely the destructive consequence when anger goes unresolved.

Jesus never said his followers would not become angry or would never lose our temper. He never promised us a magic button to punch to escape our rage, but he did offer a way off the vicious treadmill: the only solution is for the disciple to be the one who quickly "delivers the mail" and bears the burden of reconciliation. The disciple does not wait for peace to be initiated from the other side or the other person. Even if this other person is someone regarded as an enemy, Jesus implores those within his Tribe to be reconciled one to the other while there is still time to avoid escalating consequences. Those outside the Tribe cannot be expected to adhere to these instructions, but for those who follow Jesus, this is his way. This is the transforming initiative of grace as it concerns anger. But anger is not the only thing that burns within the heart. Jesus quickly turns to the subject of lust and adultery.

Presidential candidate Jimmy Carter jumped into the electoral fire with a daring interview with *Playboy* magazine just before the 1976 election. Carter, trying to show voters questioning his "born again" testimonial that he was a sinner too and not a spiritual perfectionist, infamously said, "I've looked on a lot of women with lust. I've committed adultery in my heart many times."[3] Some thought these words were funny. Others thought them perverse. Historical perspective, with political leaders involving themselves with blue-dress-wearing interns and South American mistresses, make these words sound harmless by comparison. But Carter was at least being honest. Lust does burn in the human heart, and this fire leads to the actual act of adultery.

As with anger, some clarification will help in understanding and apply-
ing these words. Jesus is not condemning sexual impulses. Sex is a good
thing—thanks be to God for it—but like any good thing it can be misused,
rendering it destructive. I once heard someone describe sex as a river. It is a
beautiful, flowing, life-giving thing. But if it breaks the bounds of its channel, it spills from its banks and becomes a flood, tearing down and washing
away everything in its path. This seems to be Jesus' warning. So no, Jesus is
not a prude or some religious fanatic denouncing sex or natural passions.
Nor does it appear that Jesus is equating "looking" at someone with a sinful
"lusting" after them. To lust after something is a desire to possess or own
something. It is the desire to take by force, manipulation, cunning, or deception what does not belong to us. So lusting involves looking, but looking
does not necessarily involve lusting. But once lust begins to burn in the
heart, it is only a few short steps to tragic consequences.

What is the solution? Again, it is early intervention, and in this case,
drastically so. Jesus says, "Gouge out your eye" or "Cut off your hand" if
these lead you into sin. The point is effective. If certain people are dangerous
for you to be around because of feelings you have for them, then stay away
from those people. If the Internet provides too much temptation, then go
offline. If your way home takes you by an establishment that is bad for your
spiritual or marital health, then find another way home or another job. Do
whatever it takes to avoid situations you know are too dangerous for you to
handle.

Once a young man sat in my office recounting his struggle with an
addiction to pornography. He had been exposed to the material at an early
age, and his lust had been well cultivated but well hidden until his mother
found the requisite magazines stuck under his mattress when he was a
teenager. She promptly dragged him to their pastor, who so shamed and
humiliated him that he could barely live. (The situation was complicated
further when several years later this same pastor was fired for downloading
voluminous amounts of pornography on the church's computers.) Now,
almost a decade later, with a wife and a young son, he still struggled as his
addiction ripped at his marriage. He was exhausted by this struggle, wanted
desperately to stop hurting his wife, and did not want his addiction to be a
part of his son's memory of him.

He asked me to "Pray that God will take the temptation away." This I
could not do. Temptation is not sin; it is dangerous, yes, but it is not sin.
The prayer/hope/wish that temptations might magically disappear is a delu-

sion. Jesus never promised that temptation would be removed once we begin to follow him. He did, however, give us a way off the destructive round-about. Gouge out your eye. Cut off your hand. Do what you must do to stay away from greater trouble.

Words from a Split Tongue

The Mosaic regulation for divorce grew out of "hardness of heart." (See Matt 19:8.) In the Jewish culture, as in most, there was a desire for easy dissolution of marriage, particularly if the husband had grown tired of his wife and wanted to replace her. At the time of both Moses and Jesus, Jewish society was completely male driven and controlled. Men, in fact, were the only ones who could sue for divorce, and it was easy. All the man had to do was direct the phrase "I divorce you" to his wife before witnesses and it was done, even for so slight an offense as burning the breakfast toast. In many cases the now ex-wife was abandoned, and if she did not have extended family to which she could retreat, she was reduced to beggary, prostitution, or some other indignity to stay alive. A shamed woman, she was not permitted to remarry.

Moses attempted to regulate this heartless practice by demanding that a man, in divorcing his wife, grant her a divorce certificate. This freed the woman to remarry and granted her an avenue, in the culture of the time, to recover and rebuild her life. The divorce certificate was liberation from marital limbo created by the "hardness of heart" of men who cast off their partners. So these words do not address every possible marriage/divorce situation or provide legalistic regulation of divorce, nor is this an all-in-all discourse on the subject. Jesus is commenting on a specific situation in which the dominating partner in a marriage was not simply filing for divorce but was robbing his wife of human dignity and a means to survive. These words actually go further than that; they radicalize human relationships. People cannot be treated as pieces of property, as sex objects, or as inconveniences to personal goals and ambitions, to be discarded at a whim. Jesus is reproving the abuse of power (he does this again and again) within relationships, abuses that lead to injuring and exploiting others, especially those in a weaker position.

A friend shared with me his terrible experience while coming up in a Catholic middle school. As puberty set in on him and his friends, some of those friends began tormenting one young girl who had developed physically a bit more quickly than the rest of the girls in class. Before math class each afternoon, the boys would grope and fondle her in plain view of the entire classroom and then quickly retreat to their seats just before the teacher-nun would arrive. The sister would come in, see this disheveled teenage girl, her clothing out of place, and would pronounce the same condemnation each time: "You are just like Mary Magdalene!"[4] Not once did the teacher seek further information, defend the girl, or call the young men to account. The teen girl was degraded by unjust relationships, with no recourse to correct the trouble.

This is the kind of injustice that Jesus seems to address with this particular discourse, and the jump off of this roundabout is through keeping our promises. Return to the context to which Jesus spoke: When a man took a bride he was vowing to care for her all the days of his life. As a woman, she was dependent on that promise. If he failed to keep his word, she would be left to deal with crushing misery. This kind of promise keeping goes past personal honesty and integrity, as important as these are, and protects the dignity and worth of another. Promise keeping is about how well you treat others, and it points to your willingness to let go of power to get what you want if someone else will be harmed in the process.

The transition to Jesus' next discussion is now obvious. Grandiose testimonies about our personal honesty or swearing by heaven and earth and everything in between to prove our integrity are often motivated by personal ambition, to get something we desperately want. Thus, we will make all manner of promises to put ourselves in a position of power over others. It turns out to be vain boasting. It is evil and comes directly "from the evil one" (Matt 5:37 NIV).

Remember that the evil one in the garden first deceived Adam and Eve. He did this not through simple dishonesty but through bold promises that could never be kept in the first place. He did this through deception intended to manipulate and control those who were in a vulnerable position. All such lies ever since—and all such exploitation of the weaker—have come from him who is the ultimate liar and father of lies. To avoid such deceit, Jesus says "simply let . . . 'Yes' be 'Yes,' and . . . 'No,' 'No.'" The step off this roundabout is direct, to-the-face honesty: don't let your unchecked desires convince you to hedge, negotiate, promise, and bargain your way into commitments you cannot or never intend to keep in the first place, especially when this will take advantage of the weak and vulnerable.

In the War of 1812, a mighty Cherokee warrior known to the Americans as Major Ridge joined a fire-breathing, pistol-shooting United States frontier commander in battle against a common enemy. That commander's name was Andrew Jackson. After fighting and bleeding together and winning the battle (a battle Jackson would have surely lost without Ridge and his braves), Jackson summarily tried to steal the Cherokees' land, succeeded in destroying their livestock and provisions, ran roughshod through their camps terrifying the young and old, and deprived injured Cherokee warriors of adequate medical attention. When confronted with these injustices, Jackson simply denied that they had taken place. Ridge just as promptly complained to President Madison with a written letter that read in part, "You have with you, as with us red children, those who make crooked talks; they, like the serpent, speak with a split tongue. Believe not their talks, for they are false; nor their actions, for they are deceitful."[5]

Less than two decades later, that split-tongue fire breather was president of the United States himself. Andrew Jackson would serve as commander-in-chief as the Cherokee suffered through hundreds of massacres, internment in death camps, and the breaking of treaty after treaty and promise after promise. Even when the Supreme Court ruled on behalf of the Cherokee Nation, stating that they were in fact a distinct community upon which no American state could exert force or occupation, Jackson would not enforce the law. It is rumored that he said, "John Marshall [the Supreme Court Chief Justice] has made his decision; let him enforce it now if he can."[6] Meanwhile, Jackson continued to host the Cherokee leaders, including Major Ridge, at the White House, calling them his friends and embracing them as his brothers, but he was working the entire time to bring everything they owned under the Empire's power. After Jackson left office, and even after his party lost the presidency, the trajectory for "Indian Relations" was set for the future. The only solution was removal, sometimes by force and extermination, but most of the time by simple deceit and deception, crooked talks, and words from a split tongue.

Deception is the way of the world. But it cannot be the way of the Jesus Tribe. As Chief Womankiller of the Cherokee said in the face of American lies and dishonesty, "If they act the tyrant and kill us for our lands, we shall, in a state of unoffending innocence, sleep with thousands of our departed people. I can say no more."[7] Such unoffending innocence is where Jesus in the Sermon on the Mount now leads us.

Chapter 7

Who Would Jesus Bomb?

"You have heard the law that says the punishment must match the injury: 'An eye for an eye, and a tooth for a tooth.' But I say, do not resist an evil person! If someone slaps you on the right cheek, offer the other cheek also. If you are sued in court and your shirt is taken from you, give your coat, too. If a soldier demands that you carry his gear for a mile, carry it two miles. Give to those who ask, and don't turn away from those who want to borrow.

"You have heard the law that says, 'Love your neighbor and hate your enemy.' But I say, love your enemies! Pray for those who persecute you! In that way, you will be acting as true children of your Father in heaven. For he gives his sunlight to both the evil and the good, and he sends rain on the just and the unjust alike. If you love only those who love you, what reward is there for that?" (Matt 5:38-46)

Going to bed one night, my oldest son asked me out of thin air, "Does everybody who goes to war die?" I quickly answered "No!" and gave him as much assurance as I could while he scampered up his bunk-bed ladder to bed. After I left his room, I knew my answer had been a lie. Everyone who goes to war, in fact, dies. Some die physically. Others are maimed or crippled. Still more come home suffering the lifelong ills of emotional trauma and other mental illnesses. All lose time that would have been spent with family, friends, children, and lovers. All have something taken from them: innocence, hope, optimism, or their future. So yes, all who go to war, contrary to the bedtime answer I gave my son, die.

The next day my son came rushing through the house with a beach bucket rattling around on his head and a book bag strapped to his back, his imagination obviously running wild.

"What are you doing?" I asked.

"Going to war," he said.

It stopped me cold. I took the bucket off his head, gathered him into my arms, and said, "Son, I pray you never have to go to war." With a smile and wave of his hand he said, "Oh, don't worry. That will never happen," and he returned to play. I hope he's right, but statistics aren't on his side. In the history of recorded civilization there have been less than two hundred years of actual peace among nations, tribes, and people groups. The rest of history has been engulfed in violence.

How do we counter such a dominant worldview, such a controlling theme that has dictated most of human history—this fascination and compulsion to kill our enemies? I hate simplistic answers, and while this might sound like one, it's not: we must take the words of Jesus on the matter seriously, for we have not been good at taking Jesus' words about peace and nonviolence to heart.

In all my decades of being in the church—from childhood to the pastorate, from family Bible studies to denominational leadership, from the primary Sunday school class to seminary—not once did I hear a sermon, commentary, or Bible lesson that seriously took on this text. But how could I? It would require a conflict of conscience for most of us as violence is required to maintain the security of an empire, and the church is usually very much at home in the empire.

Nowadays, as I write and speak on a wide variety of topics, this one subject—Jesus' way of nonviolence—always generates the most controversy, and blisteringly so. Why is this? It is because we believe a lie, and no one likes to think his or her belief system is erroneous. But we believe that violence can somehow save us; we believe that killing will prevent future killing; we believe that warfare will produce peace. We simply trust the way of the gun more than we trust the words and way of Jesus.

When confronted with this, well, people get angry. But I can't blame anyone for getting angry. I don't like it either—not one bit, because at the core of who I am, I am a violent, revenge-taking, retaliatory person. We all are! And I must admit that I find this section of the Sermon on the Mount the most difficult to put into practice. Even as I write these words I feel myself colliding with the dominant values around me, with parishioners, friends, and even family. (My internal conflict is heightened as I can make no guarantees that I would "turn the other cheek" if violence was brought against my person or family; I might respond with killing vengeance.) But we must do business with this man Jesus and realize that either (1) Jesus did not mean what he said, (2) he did not say what he meant, or (3) he actually said what he meant and meant what he said (it's okay to go back and read that sentence again; I had to reread it myself). Further, I see what such talk earned Jesus: a cross. If we seriously heed the words and actions of Jesus, we just might earn the same.

Counterfeit Redemption

Michael Sattler was born in Germany around 1500 and became a priest in the Catholic Church at an early age. After being exposed to the teachings of the Reformation, however, he forsook his vows, left the church, married a former nun, and moved to Switzerland. There he joined himself to a group of Swiss Anabaptists (those troublemakers keep turning up) and was instrumental in drafting one of the earliest confessions of faith that resisted rather than embraced the empire. This declaration of faith is known as the *Schleitheim Confession*, written down in 1527.

The *Schleitheim Confession* is by intention a simple document, just a few hundred words. Among other things, it addresses the refusal of infant baptism, the importance of the communion table, and the role of the pastor. But the part of the confession that was so explosive in Sattler's time is titled "The Sword." That section reads, "Violence must not be used in any circumstance. The way of nonviolence is patterned after the example of Christ who never defaulted to belligerence in the face of persecution or in punishing sin."

Michael Sattler sincerely believed these words, and when he was confronted by the empire of his day about his beliefs, those beliefs became practices. He refused to swear allegiance to the emperor and taught the members of his community not to take up arms against the enemies of the state. But his conscientious objection was not looked upon with favor. The Ottoman Turks, warring Muslims from the east, were on the verge of overrunning Austria and Europe, and all Christians were expected to enter the crusade against these infidels. Michael Sattler and many of his Anabaptist tribe, however, would not take up the sword against this enemy.

For this refusal Sattler was arrested, charged with heresy, and placed on trial. After two days of examination Sattler was condemned to death as an arch heretic, the death sentenced pronounced by the judge as if it were a favor to God. On May 20, 1525, Sattler was brought into the city marketplace where the judgment he had received at the hands of the authorities was carried out to the letter. His tongue was cut out, and he was tied down while pieces of his flesh were torn from his body with red-hot tongs. He was then thrown into the fire with a sack of gunpowder tied around his neck (his wife was forcibly drowned days later for the same heresy). The Sattlers, and countless peace-loving Anabaptists, were victimized by the very violence they resisted.[1]

Sattler's position seemed irrational in his day, and such a position seems even more so today. Today, a military invasion can be launched within minutes, a terrorist attack can be executed with a single combatant, and with the push of a button, thousands can be turned to ash. We have never held in our hands such awful destructive power, and we are convinced that if this power is used preemptively, efficiently, and "righteously," then Jesus' words can be dismissed as hopelessly unrealistic in this violent world. But it is here that we arrive at the root of the problem: the country in which we live is the greatest military power in the world—in history—and yet we claim to be the most Christian. How can these two things be compatible? They can't be. A bumper sticker I saw while sitting in traffic frames this inconsistency well: "Who Would Jesus Bomb?" The answer from many card-carrying, pew-occupying, Bible-reading Christians who often lead the Empire's march into battle and bloodshed is to bomb the hell out of anyone who threatens our national or personal security. Such violence does more than kill people. As followers of Jesus, this use of violence kills our faith.

Violence promises us something we all deeply desire, something we genuinely want—peace. Violence promises us, that in the end, when the last battle is fought, the last bomb is dropped, and the last enemy is slain, we will have what we always dreamed of—safety, a world without suffering, death, or bloodshed, a world at rest. Yet these are the very things Christ offers with the Kingdom of God. A world where the lamb will lay down with the lion, where swords are beaten into plowshares, where mercy and justice flow down like the waters, where every tear will be wiped away from our eyes, and where there will be no more death or sorrow or crying or pain. Christ and violence seem to offer the same result, the two being competitors for our allegiance. (It's worth noting that war/violence often brings out the best in some: camaraderie, unity, heroics, and bravery in a similar competitive manner the Kingdom of God.) But if we resort to violence, even to combat violence, we have left the path of Christ. We are trusting war to save and redeem us instead of Jesus. We must repent of this lack of faith.

Consider how the word "repent" was used by one of Jesus' near contemporaries, the Jewish historian Josephus. Josephus, in addition to being a recorder of historical events, was also an officer in the Roman Empire's army. He arrived in Galilee about thirty years after Jesus' crucifixion to help sort out the Jewish rebellion. When he spoke to the rebels leading the revolt, Josephus said to them, "Repent and believe in me."[2] Josephus was not giving an altar call at the end of a particular stirring sermon. He wasn't inviting the rebels to invite him into their hearts or to open themselves to a religious experience. He was inviting them to give up their rebellious agendas and trust him to guide them to peace.

When Jesus, just decades earlier than Josephus, appeared in the same Galilee proclaiming the Kingdom of God, he seemed to use the word "repent" the same way. Jesus was inviting those who heard his words to give up their lives of dependence on the empire and to trust him instead. Certainly Jesus was saying even more than this, but he could not have been saying less.[3] This kingdom, this tribe, this way of Jesus was not like anything else in the world, and Jesus realized that we could not hold to this unique counter-agendum without repentance. Repentance is about giving up our scheme for living in this world, our plans for the future, and trusting God to bring us a tomorrow not achieved with the counterfeit redemption of violence but through Jesus' way of nonviolence. This is a complete course adjustment, a detour off the path that leads to death. It is another of Jesus' rescues off the never-ending destructive roundabout.

Returning to the text, the Mosaic Law did not provide a detour away from unending violence. It did, however, put a few speed bumps in the road. "An eye for an eye and a tooth for a tooth," Moses instructed. The guidance was one of limited retaliation. We know, by looking at history and within our own hearts, that the nature of revenge is escalation. If you hit me, I will hit you harder. Maim my brother, and I will kill your father. Set off a bomb in my marketplace, and I will wipe out your entire village. Firebomb my hospital, and I will bomb your capital. It's human nature to retaliate not with equity but with greater force than what was first inflicted. The Old Testament restriction was for revenge to go no further than what the first offended person had suffered. Granted, if people, nations, armies, and litigators abided by this instruction, there certainly would be less violence in the world, but there would still be violence. As Mahatma Gandhi rightly observed, "An eye for an eye makes the whole world blind."

So Jesus changes the conversation completely not by offering more laws and restrictions but by replacing limited retaliation with unlimited love. Turn the other cheek. Go the second mile. Give more than is demanded. Love your enemy. Pray for your persecutor. Be kind to those who hate you.

So Sioux Me

The examples Jesus uses to instruct his followers in the way of nonviolence—being slapped, being forced to walk a long distance, and being dragged into court—all have a common denominator. All of these are examples of injustice inflicted on the follower of Jesus.

Beginning with the slap to the cheek, there is a subtle but important word in Jesus' command that his original hearers would have understood well. It is the word "right." If someone slaps you on the "right" cheek, offer the other one also. Being struck on the right cheek was a description of someone getting backhanded, not someone in a fistfight. A strike on the right cheek was an act intended to humiliate, used by a person in power over someone who was powerless or vulnerable (see how often Jesus concerns himself with abuse of power). It was how a master would treat a slave, a landowner would treat a sharecropper, a Roman soldier would treat a Jewish citizen, a husband would treat a wife in that chauvinistic culture. Jesus proposes neither an act of retaliation nor a humiliated cowering on the ground in submission. He offers a third way: Turn the other cheek. Rob the aggressor of his power to humiliate. By offering the other cheek the disciple says to his or her antagonist, "I refuse to be humiliated. Try again." Nonviolent, dignified resistance exposes the act as wrong and turns the humiliation back on the perpetuator of violence.

Another example: If you are being unjustly treated in the court systems—someone is taking your shirt and essentially taking your dignity—then give them your coat. Imagine what would happen if at the height of the legal deliberations the victim stood up, publicly stripped naked before the prosecutor and judge, said, "You might as well have it all," and walked out. It would shame the system that allows such injustice to prevail.

Consider a third scenario: a soldier forces someone to carry his load. In Jesus' day a Roman soldier could come along and demand a person to carry his backpack for up to a mile, no questions asked. A farmer busy on his farm or a shopkeeper in her shop or a baker at the oven—a soldier picked one of these people out of the crowd to become his personal donkey (remember how Simon was forced to carry Jesus' cross), and the individual had to comply or face the violent consequences. The good news is the compulsion was only enforceable for a mile. To this Jesus says, "Go two miles." Why? It robbed the soldier of his power and actually put his neck in the noose. Should the commanding officer arrive halfway through that second mile, how is the two-mile journey going to be explained? Further, the disciple was nonviolently showing that he would not be manipulated or controlled by abusive power.

In each case, Jesus' instruction in response to violence is the same: Do not lash out in retaliation, but do not cower in fearful compliance. Trump the power of the world with the upside-down power of the Kingdom of God. They may slap you. They may take everything you own. They may walk you to the moon and back, but do not lash out and do not let up. This is what it means to turn the other cheek and love our enemies. This is how we repent of the way of violence. Jesus, then, does not instruct his followers to be like sponges, our only response to injustice being to grin and bear it. No. When we are struck by a fist on the playground, we are not merely to take it. When sharp words lodge in our hearts at the workplace, we are not to go about our business silently. When a violent husband assaults his wife in the bedroom, she should not accept it. A nonviolent, dignified resistance says, "I will not lift a finger to hurt you in retaliation, but I will never back down from what is just and right."

A favorite class of mine when I was in middle school was physical education. In those days not many years ago, when boys my age got in trouble during class, we were not sent to in-school suspension or assigned to detention. The P.E. coach (who was also the head football coach) took us over to the water fountain. We gripped the sides of the thing, gritted our teeth, and said our prayers as he commenced in lifting our heels off the ground via our backsides with a wooden paddle. That was bad enough. But if we broke down and cried in front of our friends (or the girls), it was a humiliation worse than death.

On one particular day a fellow classmate of mine was accused of stealing an item from someone's backpack. Before we knew it he was being dragged away to the water fountain gallows to face the consequences. This kid was no angel, but we all knew he didn't do the crime—not *this* time anyway. It seemed that everybody except the coach knew he was innocent of the charges. When the boy got to the "fountain of punishment," he did something extraordinary. He dropped his gym shorts right there in front of everyone, including the girls who have such a magical power over adolescent boys, and shouted in his skivvies, "I didn't steal anything! If you're going to paddle me, it will be like this!" The coach couldn't deliver the punishment.

My classmate, unknown to him I am sure, responded as Jesus instructed. He didn't launch into a verbal tirade or take a swing at his accusers or threaten to bring his parents to the school with an attorney. Nor did he grovel on the floor and take the paddling as if he were guilty. He turned the other cheek—every cheek he had, actually. We are called to turn the other cheek not because it always works to disarm injustice or because it is always practical but because it is the way of Christ. In following this way, we give God the opportunity to act and speak, even in conflict, in ways we cannot imagine.

My final example comes from the Native American Sioux tribe. Following the American Civil War, the United States Army moved in force into the western reaches of the continent. One by one native people groups were exterminated, forcibly moved onto reservations, or starved into submission. Portions of the Sioux nation, however, led by men like Red Cloud and Sitting Bull, waged war with the Empire. This war came to a cataclysmic end in 1876 at the Battle of the Little Bighorn. This was the literal end of most of the Seventh Calvary led by George A. Custer, as they were soundly defeated. But it was also the end of the Sioux's fight for independence, as in the aftermath American public opinion about "the Indian problem" galvanized and all western tribes were subjugated.

A year after the Battle of the Little Bighorn, with gold discovered in the Black Hills of the Dakotas, the United States government broke its treaty with the Sioux and demanded these sacred lands. The tribe refused, so the land was stolen. One hundred three years later, in 1980, the Supreme Court ordered the federal government to pay $105 million to eight Sioux tribes for the land that had been taken from them. This was the original value attached to the land plus a century of interest. It was a landmark decision, but the Sioux refused this payoff. At the time of this writing, the trust fund set aside by the courts is almost $1 billion.

Why did the tribal councils refuse this payment? It is because the Sioux consider the Black Hills sacred ground to which no dollar amount can be attached. Further, to take the money would be to bless the theft. The only solution offered officially from the Sioux nation is the trust fund payment *and* the return of the land. The tribe is willing to wait—turning the other cheek, offering their clothes, and going the second mile—out of principle and justice, even while a billion dollars sits in the bank, dollars that would feed many hungry mouths and shelter many families.

"I Ain't No Mule!"

It should go without saying at this point that the Empire will not accept the nonviolent teachings of Jesus; nor should it. A person, people, or nation must fight to stay alive in the world in which we live. If you find this pragmatism to be too outrageous, it is simply a misunderstanding of unredeemed human nature. From angry little boys on the playground to heads of state with their fingers on the firing button, it is natural to want to prevail over your enemies, even kill them if you must. Violence is necessary to stay alive and is a natural part of being human. Those who think that talk or dialogue alone can end all conflict in the world have a fatalistically flawed utopian view of how things really are.

But to follow Christ is to be set free from human nature, to let go of what the world deems necessary for survival. To follow Christ means we have found a new way to live, a new way to be human, and that we are not fastened to what we once were. The old has gone and the new has come. As Christians we must oppose and resist violence of all kinds because violence is a tool of the fallen, unredeemed nature. It is of the world and does not reflect the good and gracious nature of our Father. The role of the Jesus Tribe is to be aliens and strangers, to be a counter-culture that goes against the flow of what is otherwise accepted, so Jesus followers refuse violence, even when such violence appears to be for noble ends.

This way of Jesus cannot be characterized as traditional pacifism. Traditional pacifism is a wonderful ideal, but there is no power within it actually to accomplish peace. Traditional pacifism ignores—and this is supremely important—the theological and christological motivation and power for peace. "You will be acting as true children of your Father in heaven" (Matt 5:45), Jesus says. We follow Jesus' way of nonviolence because this is how God treats his enemies. Graciousness toward others—even those who want to kill us—is like God: "You are to be perfect, even as your Father in heaven is perfect" (Matt 5:48).

The Greek word for "perfect" is *teleioi*. It was a word used to describe the appropriate sacrificial lamb that was without defect. It described a graduating student who had completed his course of study and was now ready to face the task for which he had been trained. The word was also used to describe a child or adolescent who had grown past immaturity to the place of adulthood. *Teleioi* is not functional or positional perfection. It is the realization of one's vocation and the gaining of maturity. William Barclay said, "A man is perfect (*teleioi*) if he realizes the purpose for which he was created and *sent into the world*."[4]

As followers within the Jesus Tribe, our purpose is to reflect the wholeness and identity of our Father in heaven. We are to be grace-filled manifestations of who he is as his Son shines through us. The experiences people have with us should be the experience they have with God. God is made visible and tangible not with our declarations of truth or reciting of the creeds but in us and in our world when we respond to others as he responds to them. And how does God respond to people? With grace and goodness as he sends "his sunlight to both the evil and the good, and he sends rain on the just and the unjust alike." God's love simply knows no limit: suicide bombers, serial killers, thieves, prostitutes, Wall Street pirates, dirty politicians, exploiters of the innocent. He doesn't approve of these injustices, but still he loves those in his world. "While we were still sinners, Christ died for us," and while we were God's enemies he took the necessary loving steps to reconcile us to himself.

Maybe Jesus' teachings about love and nonviolence are so startling and difficult for us because we are so unlike God. Maybe this all seems so unnatural because our way of living, our way of life, and our view of the world is such a contradiction of how God would have us live and view the world. But when, by God's power, we love without limit, we are reflecting the nature of God. What did a violent world do to God's greatest manifestation of his love for us? They ignored him. They despised him. They rejected him. They murdered him, nailing him to a cross. But the world did not overcome him. So we love not because it will work or because it is practical or because it will "change the world." We love because it is how God treats the world, and this love does much more than make us "act differently." It actually makes us different as Christ lives his life through us. Love is how we live and act. Love is how we operate.

Once again I must return to Clarence Jordan and give him the last example in this chapter (though he does not have the last word on this subject; please find other Jesus followers and engage them on this topic). Clarence spoke at the annual meeting of the Baptist Peace Fellowship in Detroit, Michigan, on May 19, 1963, and addressed these very teachings of Jesus from the Sermon on the Mount. He told the story of a man who came to Koinonia Farms to confront his peaceful ways at the height of World War II. The country was awash with patriotism and nationalism, and this particular visitor was aghast that Clarence was speaking against the war (all war, for that matter). Here's how Clarence told the story:

> The man said, "You know what I don't like about you folks?"
> I could have named quite a few things, but I asked him what. And he said, "I don't like it 'cause you won't fight."
> I said, "Buddy, you've got that wrong."
> He said, "You fight?"

"Yes sir," I said. "We'll fight."

He said, "Well, I heard you wouldn't."

"Well," I said, "we don't fight that way." And I looked out across there and saw an old mule with his head stuck out the old barn that was about to fall down, and I said to this fellow, "Suppose you walked by the barn out there right now, and that old mule reached out and bit you in the seat of the britches? Would you bite him back?"

"No, I ain't no mule!" he said.

I said, "Of course you wouldn't, and you've given the reason also why you wouldn't bite him back, because you're not a mule. What would you do?"

He said, "I'd get me a two by four, and I'd beat his brains out."

I said, "You wouldn't let the mule choose the weapons, would you? You'd fight him, but you'd do it on your terms, not his. Suppose you'd say, 'Well, old mule, I ain't scared to fight. You bare your teeth, I'll bare mine; you bite me, I'll bite you; you kick me, I'll kick you.' You'll lose! You've got to choose some weapons that a mule can't compete with. Now, we will fight, sir, but we will choose the weapons."

He said, "What kind of weapons you got?"

I said, "We'll fight with humility. But we're not going to fight with the devil's weapons, because if we do, the devil can whip us."[5]

If we refuse the Tempter's invitation on the mountain to take up the power of violence, and we refuse the Tempter's rules of engagement, he cannot "whip us." Granted, violence may eventually be used against those who won't play by the rules, but violence and death is not the end of the follower of Jesus. "Crucifixions have a way of being followed by resurrections," and resurrections cannot be defeated by any devil or killed by any empire.[6]

Chapter 8

Losing My Religion

"Watch out! Don't do your good deeds publicly, to be admired by others, for you will lose the reward from your Father in heaven. When you give to someone in need, don't do as the hypocrites do—blowing trumpets in the synagogues and streets to call attention to their acts of charity! I tell you the truth, they have received all the reward they will ever get. But when you give to someone in need, don't let your left hand know what your right hand is doing. Give your gifts in private, and your Father, who sees everything, will reward you.

When you pray, don't be like the hypocrites who love to pray publicly on street corners and in the synagogues where everyone can see them. I tell you the truth, that is all the reward they will ever get. But when you pray, go away by yourself, shut the door behind you, and pray to your Father in private. Then your Father, who sees everything, will reward you. When you pray, don't babble on and on as people of other religions do. They think their prayers are answered merely by repeating their words again and again. Don't be like them, for your Father knows exactly what you need even before you ask him!

Pray like this: 'Our Father in heaven, may your name be kept holy. May your Kingdom come soon. May your will be done on earth, as it is in heaven. Give us today the food we need, and forgive us our sins, as we have forgiven those who sin against us. And don't let us yield to temptation, but rescue us from the evil one.'

And when you fast, don't make it obvious, as the hypocrites do, for they try to look miserable and disheveled so people will admire them for their fasting. I tell you the truth, that is the only reward they will ever get. But when you fast, comb your hair and wash your face. Then no one will notice that you are fasting, except your Father, who knows what you do in private. And your Father, who sees everything, will reward you." (Matt 6:1-13, 16-18)

On my bookshelf is a tiny book that holds three great speeches by Native Americans.[1] One is by Chief Joseph, one by Chief Seattle—both leaders of tribes in the Pacific Northwest—and the third by a lesser-known man named Chief Red Jacket. Red Jacket was of the Seneca tribe, who lived in what is now New York State. Red Jacket was called to a council in 1805 by Christian missionaries from New England. The purpose of this council was to impress and impose upon the Seneca an acceptance of the Christian faith. After the missionaries had finished their lectures, Red Jacket stood to speak, and he lived up to the native name given to him by his tribe: *Sagoyewatha*. It means "He Keeps Them Awake," so great were his speaking skills. He said,

> You say that you are sent to instruct us how to worship the Great Spirit . . . . And if we do not take hold of the religion which you white people teach, we shall be unhappy hereafter. You say that you are right, and we are lost. How do you know this to be true? How shall we know what to believe, being so often deceived by the white man? You say there is but one way to worship and serve the Great Spirit. If so, why do your people differ so much about it? We do not understand these things; we never quarrel about religion.
>
> Brother: We are told that you have been preaching to the white people in this place. These people are our neighbors. We are acquainted with them. We will wait a little while, and see what effect your preaching has upon them. If we find it does them good, and makes them honest, and less disposed to cheat Indians, we will then consider again what you have to say.[2]

As the Sermon on the Mount moves into Matthew 6, we find Jesus dealing with "good deeds" or what some translations call "acts of righteousness." We might even call them "spiritual disciplines." Jesus mentions three: giving, praying, and fasting. His concern is not so much "what" we do. His concern is "why" and "how." Continuing on a theme Jesus has yet to leave alone, it's not only our behavior that matters. For those in his tribe, it is the motivation behind the behavior that counts. If all our perceived good deeds do not come from transformed, good hearts, then Red Jacket is right. There is no need for anyone, including God, to pay much attention.

Get Real

Giving, praying, and fasting were the three basic elements of Jewish holiness as understood at the time. If you were a "good" person, these were the things you did and these three acts represented the whole of spiritual relationships. God, neighbor, and self: all are involved with our individual "good deeds," and thus we see the danger. Because these are all encompassing and because these are so far reaching relationally, the temptation is to turn these good deeds into theater, a stage upon which one performs to draw attention to self. That's exactly what was happening in the synagogues of Jesus' day.

When it came to giving, some of the more religious types would wait to bring their gifts to the offering basket until they had everyone's attention, or they would find a beggar on the street and bring a whole procession to watch their generosity. They wanted everyone to see them put their money in the plate. They wanted as many people as possible to know how many zeros were filled in on their checks. They liked press releases and headlines that announced to the world how much they had helped the little people of the community.

Then there was the praying. There were three designated times of prayer in Jewish life—at nine, noon, and three. Some of the more pious members of the clergy (the Pharisees in particular pulled this trick) would make sure they were caught out in public at the designated times of prayer. At the market or outside the synagogue, the bell would sound for prayer and they would stop right where they were, bring everything around them to a screeching halt, roll out their prayer rugs, point themselves toward the temple, and babble on and on (note that "babble" is Jesus' word for such prolonged public displays, not mine).

The third good deed was fasting. Many of these same religious characters would go without food to purify body and soul. Yet they wanted everybody to know this, so nothing was purified or pure. They would disfigure their faces, sit with others who were eating but not eat themselves, and brag to others about what they were "doing for God" to get sympathy and attention. For all of this Jesus calls them "hypocrites."

"Hypocrite" is a great old word right from the Greek and Roman theaters. It means "play actor" and was a positive word when used in that context. A hypocrite was a person who played multiple roles on stage. In scene 1 he or she played one character. Later, the actor would don a mask or a costume and play another character—maybe portraying three or four different personalities on stage in a single night. Over time a hypocrite came to mean a person who changed his or her appearance depending on the circumstances or, as Jesus uses the word here, a hypocrite was an actor who played to the crowd. He or she was someone who performed for the audience.

In American literature, the biggest religious hypocrite of all time is Sinclair Lewis's Elmer Gantry, though most of us have not read the book. However, we may have seen the movie starring Burt Lancaster in an

Academy-award-winning role.[3] Elmer Gantry begins his career in the early 1900s at a Baptist Seminary in Kansas preaching at a little country church and trying to seduce the daughter of one of the deacons. Eventually he becomes a traveling evangelist who is stealing from the till, chasing skirts, and staying drunk most of the time, but his preaching is phenomenal so he always has a crowd. Through with the Baptists and the revival Pentecostals, he becomes a Methodist, rising through the ranks until he is pastor of a huge church in New York City and president of the "National Association for the Purification of Art and the Press."

Gantry preaches sensational sermons denouncing all kinds of vices. He draws larger and larger crowds and personally leads raids on the red-light districts busting brothels, bars, and speakeasies. He denounces all the other churches for their weaknesses, and meanwhile he is committing worse sins than the ones he is preaching against. He is everything a hypocrite is supposed to be, and worse. Playing to the crowd, he always put his personal interests first in order to get from the situation and the people exactly what he wants. As Lewis described him, "Everyone believed that everyone else adored him; but none of them wanted to be with him."[4]

Elmer Gantry's sin, the sin of all hypocrisy, was not that he was two-faced. His sin was that he was intentionally dishonest. He was not real. He did what he did, not out of love for God, but out of love for the applause of the crowds. He did what he did out of pride, ambition, and self-glory. The audience he was performing for was not his Maker but himself and others. That is hypocrisy. So to the hypocrites of his own day and to us today, Jesus three times gives the same warning: "They have received all the reward they will ever get" (Matt 6:2). If you play for the crowd, if your ambition is to draw attention to yourself, then you have received what you wanted. There is no further reward, no further benefit, and no other prize. God has nothing for you but an empty hand.

Again, Jesus gives us an alternative way. He says when you give, don't let your left hand know what your right hand is doing. Go to such extremes that you don't know how much you are giving. When you pray, go to a closet and shut the door. Keep it simple, between you and God. And when you fast, don't broadcast it and don't show it. Comb your hair, slap on the aftershave or lipstick (or both!), and go about business as usual. In all of these, as in all acts of righteousness, Jesus is saying the same thing: don't draw attention to yourself. In doing so, you forfeit any reward from the Father and you corrupt the good deed itself.

Earlier in the Sermon on the Mount Jesus said, "Let your good deeds shine out for all to see, so that everyone will praise your heavenly Father" (Matt 5:16). But these deeds are not for personal benefit. These good deeds are to point to our "heavenly Father," not to the doer. Selfish gain is not the way of Jesus or the Jesus Tribe. Doing good deeds is to point to Someone outside ourselves. No matter what it is—missionary work, teaching, preaching, giving, praying, singing, organizing, helping, serving—if it is to impress or to draw the attention of others, no matter how noble the act, it is wrong. Why? Because it is not driven by love for God and neighbor. Instead, it is driven by pride, self-centeredness, and ambition.

Consider the most popular type of television show on the airways today, a fairly recent genre called "reality" TV. In researching this subject, Cecil Maranville found 230 reality shows peppered across every network on television—even PBS and the Learning Channel.[5] The goal of any television show is ratings, and reality is not always interesting or entertaining enough to lure viewers. So the usual plot of any of these reality shows involves a few young girls and guys with tons of sexual tension; at least one or two people pitted against each other along religious, lifestyle, or political skirmish lines; a pile of money promised to the winners; and a season's worth of editing and re-editing, takes and retakes for a single episode. But from MTV's *Real World* to *The Apprentice*, it is not reality. It is hypocrisy.

Who, after all, are the real winners in this hypocrisy? They are the television networks and the producers of these shows who rake in millions of dollars each season built on a foundation of the trite, the trashy, and the American voyeur. I don't think Jesus would have cared much for the reality television genre. And when our acts of righteousness, worship practices, and good deeds devolve into showmanship to get ratings, entertain, draw a crowd, or pad our church coffers, then there's not much difference between what is happening behind the pulpit and what is seen on the television screen. Besides, it is now impossible to tell the difference between fictional fakers and the actual ones anyway.

This'll Get Your Goat

Lewis Smedes says there are three sources of shame in the world. These imprison us on stage as we play for the crowd's approval. Smedes names these as (1) secular culture, (2) unaccepting parents, and (3) graceless religion.[6] Secular culture (the Empire) tells us how we must look, act, smell, dress, and feel to be accepted. Tyrannically, it lays down the rules for what we

read, hear, eat, sing, and attend, and whom we befriend, love, and relate to
in order to be received. Unaccepting parents do all of this as well, along with
a healthy dose of "you'll-never-be-good-enough" indignity thrown in for
good measure. Graceless religion goes even further, building upon social and
parental pressures and adding divine displeasure. This gracelessness is thriving; more than 70 percent of Americans consider God to be unengaged or
judgmental toward his creation.[7]

Jesus words, however, aren't condemning. They are inviting. "My yoke is
easy, my burden is light," he says later in this book of Matthew. Or as
Eugene Peterson marvelously puts it in the *Message* translation,

> Are you tired? Worn out? Burned out on religion? Come to me. Get away
> with me and you'll recover your life. I'll show you how to take a real
> rest. Walk with me and work with me—watch how I do it. Learn the
> unforced rhythms of grace. I won't lay anything heavy or ill-fitting on you.
> Keep company with me and you'll learn to live freely and lightly. (Matt
> 11:28-30)

Living freely and lightly is what many of us could achieve if we could trade
in our performance-based religion for the way of Jesus. After all, how much
of what we do is based on what other people might think about us? How
binding and suffocating are the brutal expectations that others place on us?
Don't we feel an unending compulsion—out of fear, insecurity, shame, or
conditioning—to please others almost at all costs?

"You can't believe that! What will people think?"

"You can't go there! What would others say?"

"How could you ever think about or consider such a thing!"

"What would your father/pastor/spouse/professor/mother say if they
heard you?"

"Don't say or support anything that might lead to negative repercus-
sions!"

Wouldn't it be wonderful to be free from the slings and arrows of these
incarcerating sentiments? We would feel like drowning men and women
coming up for air if we could be relieved of these artificial burdens that we
both love and hate. We love them because we can't imagine living without
the sanction of the crowds, and we hate them because we know we are being
dishonest, prostituting our faith. Yet, in grace, Jesus offers us a way out. He
offers freedom from the merciless crowd, freedom from our own pride and

insecurities, freedom and confidence to be ourselves in him, to be people who no longer need the approval, flattery, or blessing of others.

This doesn't make us flippant toward the feelings of others. It redirects our actions and affections toward our heavenly Father and away from any other prospective audience. We can stop living our lives as if we are in seventh grade trying to get the girl who hit puberty over the summer to look at us (with adolescent boys in my home, I know something about this). We can stop doing and saying things we don't mean, clutching to approval we don't need, wasting time and energy we don't have. And for what? A few emotional strokes, the fleeting approval of someone who is as fractured as we are and whose approval lasts about five minutes on the stage, and then the exercise must begin again. We can let all of this go and breathe the fresh air of genuine freedom.

Here is another example from my brilliant Southern grandmother. She used a saying most every day, "Get your goat." It was one of those wonderful phrases that could be employed in any number of relevant situations. If I was misbehaving or somehow being a pest, she might say to me, "Boy, I'm gonna get your goat." That was her way of saying some heavy discipline was coming my way. Or if my brother, sister, or cousins were irritating me, she would gently counsel, "Don't let them get your goat," meaning "Find a way to let it go. Don't be so sensitive, angry, or let them get to you." And on Sundays, if the preacher sermonized passionately and sharply at the congregation, my grandmother would comment afterward at lunch, "He really got our goat, didn't he?" This usually meant he was preaching on a touchy subject or was especially lively.

So, if you "get someone's goat," you disturb or unsettle them in some significant way. The origin of the phrase apparently comes from the horseracing world. I am told that goats were sometimes put in a racehorse's stall as a calming influence, especially if the horse was nervous or high strung. If you had money on a different number, or if you wanted a particular horse to run badly, then on the night before the race you would sneakily send someone to "get his goat" out of the stall. This sabotage would upset and otherwise disquiet the horse for the night, causing him to run a bad race the following morning. I don't know if my grandmother knew the etymology behind the expression "get your goat" (probably not), but she certainly knew how to use the phrase, and it remains an appropriate slogan I continue to use for many situations.

I really had my goat got after preaching one Sunday. I waited at the door with the pastor as worshipers left the building. Many spoke of how moving and inspiring my words had been. They spoke of how freely the Spirit seemed to move. As these worshipers trickled by me, deep within my heart pride budded like a flower—or more like galloping kudzu. I quietly became self-convinced that my sermon was an oratory masterpiece that would be remembered as one of the greatest pieces of English rhetoric produced in the early twenty-first century. Sure, I coyly deflected the compliments that came my way with my "ah-shucks" boyish charm, but inside I was one smug son of a gun. The more people gushed, the more "humble" I became. And the more people gushed the more my private arrogance grew.

A lady approached me reading from the script of flattery. But then she added, "However, I must tell you something," with a dancing grin on her face, the kind of grin that said she already knew the not-yet-delivered punch line. She relayed to me her worship experience. As she sat through my illustrious sermon, she happened to glance out the huge church window positioned to her immediate left. There, just on the other side of the glass was my youngest son, Braden, playing on the gravel and the lawn. This congregation had no "children's church," so he was in his own outside world picking flowers, tossing stones, and lost in imagination. Then nature called. My son looked to the right and he looked to the left. When he was reasonably certain of solitude, he dropped his pants and relieved himself on the church wall, oblivious to the hundreds of worshipers behind the glare of the church windows.

As this parishioner cackled, told her story, and mercifully left, the loud sound that filled the now empty sanctuary was my bleating goat as he was led away to the slaughter. I was totally mortified, and I deserved it. While outside my son was lost inside his clear conscience, the inside of my heart was filled with ferocious self-importance. I had succumbed to the most common hypocrisy: this obsession with the outward show, the image-is-everything lie, where we put more stock in impressing others than serving and loving others.

Overt image-management is nothing short of sacrilege, especially when it is performed by a preacher or a people whose primary symbol is a poor, bloodied, naked man on a cross. Public showmanship that is driven by arrogance and pride is far worse a sin than raw, poor manners performed out of innocence. I am certain—absolutely certain—God was with my son that day, laughing all the time as Braden spelled his liquid name harmlessly on the church wall. And I am just as certain that God used that boy to hand me my proper reward as well.

The Fewer the Words, the Better the Prayer

The selfless way of doing good deeds is best exemplified with some of the most recited words in the English language, words we know as the Lord's Prayer. It might be better to label this the "Disciple's Prayer," for it is the model prayer that we as followers of Jesus should imitate. Certainly we pray it word for word, but that isn't necessarily the point. I don't think Jesus insisted that we pray this prayer exactly as it is recorded here in the Sermon on the Mount, but it does set the trajectory for the disciple's practice of prayer as well as his or her life. This prayer points us in a simple, humble direction that characterizes our words as well as our deeds.

Pick up religious prayer books today (they are more than legion), and simplicity is not what you will think of immediately. Popular Jewish prayer books approach nearly a thousand pages. *The Book of Common Prayer*, used by Anglicans, Methodists, and other denominations, is more than 1,000 pages in its most recent edition.[8] Hindus, Buddhists, the Orthodox, and Catholics have libraries full of prayers. And the Islamic faith revolves around prayer, requiring structured petitions five times a day. Google the word "prayer" and you'll get more than 70 million pages. Everybody has advice, it seems, on how to pray.

But when Jesus taught his disciples to pray, he used only fifty-seven words as translated in the Greek New Testament. This is an absolute revolution in terms of simplicity. Maybe this is why we pray it so often—at communion, at the dinner table, at weddings, at funerals, and when we are afraid. It is found on the lips of young children as well as dying saints. There is no reason, in our prayer lives, to look for longer invocations or more words.

The churches of my formative years convinced me that Jesus did not speak in Aramaic or Hebrew, nor did he use the stray Greek word from time to time. Nope, on the shores of the Sea of Galilee as he taught the masses, Jesus waxed as eloquently as the sonnets of Shakespeare. My pastors taught me that "the Authorized 1611 King James Version of the Bible is the only Bible, and all other versions are perversions of God's Perfect Word.™" There was even a sign attached to the pulpit to this effect, warning all would-be preachers to read from the correct translation or hell would open up and swallow them whole. Or was it "hell shall openeth up and swalloweth thee whole"?

It didn't take me long to figure out that I was being hoodwinked. If Jesus was a Jew living in the first century and King James and his Anglo accent didn't show up for the party until a dozen or so centuries later, well, I just couldn't imagine Jesus enunciating like Hamlet. It didn't make sense. Besides that, if God really wanted to communicate with humanity, why would he use a single language bound by the culture, form, and times of post-medieval England (talk about imperial arrogance)? Still, this was what my elders believed, and they proved it every time they prayed publicly.

Growing up, I never once heard the Lord's Prayer in a worship service. Never. I was told that only Catholics and Lutherans prayed like that, and that to recite it as they did, not praying from the heart, was insincere. This did not mean we couldn't be insincere in other ways. When it was time to pray, whoever was leading the public prayer—simple farmers and mill workers, most with less than a high school education—would break into an old English dialect as if that were the only language God could understand. It was awfully close to babbling (again, Jesus' word), and not the simple pattern taught in the Disciple's Prayer.

The babbling in Jesus' day was about the same. The Jews revered God's name in a way that most of us find strange. They would often say "Blessed be the Name" as a synonym for God because they wouldn't say his name for fear of misrepresenting him. In Judaism and Christianity, the name for God is Yahweh, but the scribes who wrote down the Old Testament Scriptures would not spell out this name. They intentionally left out the vowels in an effort to revere God's holy name. So a common Jewish prayer of Jesus' day began with sixteen different adjectives to describe God, but the prayer never called his name. Jesus began with the simple, audacious word "Father." This wasn't completely unheard of in Jewish literature when addressing God, but Jesus makes it normative, and this sets the tone for everything that follows in his prayer.

God, as our Father, is a transformation of status. He isn't a distant, ambivalent, or angry deity, sitting on a cloud hurling lightning bolts at us when we mess up. He loves his children like only a parent can. This is Jesus' point—not that God is male versus being female. God doesn't use the men's room. Rather, God relates to us as a compassionate parent, not a silent idol or an apathetic creator who has wound up the world and stepped away. Jesus is clear: the disciple's prayer life is best maintained by seeing God as a loving provider ("he who gives good gifts to those who ask him," Matt 7:11, NIV), not as a vindictive bully who has to be constantly placated. It is heresy to hold to the image of God as a Zeus-like character quick to take offense and even quicker to take vengeance. Sometimes I come home after being away and all three of my boys will meet me a step inside the door, shouting my name, jumping on me, grabbing my legs, and almost knocking me down. That is a better picture of prayer than all the bowed heads and folded hands in the universe.

So if God is our loving Parent and we are his children, by default we are in a position of dependence, trust, and reliance upon him. We often treat prayer, and our whole spiritual journey for that matter, as if it is all about us, what we want, what we wish to do, and what we want God to do for us. When our Father comes gladly home, we do not meet him with smiling faces and laughing joy but like self-indulged, self-centered children who yank on his shirttail demanding that he give us a prize for being especially good (see how giving-praying-fasting fit together). But prayer isn't about you or me. It is about aligning ourselves with what God is doing.

One of the greatest prayers of simplicity I ever heard was while I was pastor of a Georgia church during that summer week of Vacation Bible School (see, it's not all bad). A man named Dave was a teacher that week and had drawn the pleasure of corralling the fourth and fifth grade boys. Again, having a couple of those particular creatures around my house, anyone who takes that assignment ought to get extra points in heaven or at least a few free sins here on earth; either that or God should at least apologize to them. Dave did not have an extensive church background. He came to faith later in life, and at the time of our Bible school he was around fifty years old. I asked if he would lead the closing prayer of the VBS assembly.

Dave thought about this for a minute and finally replied, "Well, I've never done that sort of thing before, but I think I could do that." So when it came time for the prayer I said, "Children, let us all bow our heads as Mr. Dave leads us in prayer." We bowed our heads and closed our eyes in good Baptist fashion and there was a long silence. It grew so long that I had to peek to see if Dave was still in the room. He was standing there, his eyes shut tight, gripping the pew in front of him with white knuckles. When he opened his mouth to pray, he said, "God . . . [I almost expected a voice to say, "Yes, Dave?"] . . . help these children know you. And help us teach them. Amen." It was beautiful proof that sincere praying does not require an avalanche of babbling words.

Chapter 9

The Best Revenge

"Forgive us our sins, as we have forgiven those who sin against us . . . . If you forgive those who sin against you, your heavenly Father will forgive you. But if you refuse to forgive others, your Father will not forgive your sins." (Matt 6:12, 14-15)

In December 2001, the Jews of Afghanistan celebrated their first Hanukkah free of the Taliban in almost a decade. It was a small celebration, for there were only two Jews left in the entire country. And each celebrated the festival of lights alone.

At separate ends of a rundown synagogue in Kabul, Ishak Levin and Zebulon Simantov lit their candles and said their prayers. Both were happy to celebrate in freedom for the first time in many years. Both were the only living descendants of a former thriving Hebrew community in Afghanistan. Both had survived the Soviet occupation, the atrocities of the Taliban, and the American-led invasion. Both prayed to the same God and for the same things, and yet they could not share the same space or the same celebration, each worshiping alone with a heavy dark curtain dividing the room so they would not have to see each other.

Neither can remember what started the feud, but it has cost them much, including their synagogue's most treasured possession: its Torah, the ancient Hebrew scroll of sacred Scripture containing much of what we Christians call the Old Testament. The two rabbis fought over what should be done with it, each one accusing the other of wishing to steal and sell it. So it was given to the Taliban for safekeeping (those two words "Taliban" and "safe-keeping" probably should never be used in the same sentence). The scroll was never recovered.

Rabbi Levin, on the first night of Hanukah 2001, said, "For a thousand and thousand years, our forefathers have celebrated these nights, and now Jews all over the world are celebrating too." And then speaking of his antagonist on the other side of the curtain said, "But with him—it is not possible."[1]

Another Jewish rabbi said something about the impossible. Jesus said, "Forgive us our sins, as we have forgiven those who sin against us." Literally, it reads, "Forgive us in proportion to how we have forgiven others," or "Forgive us how we have forgiven others." Going even further, as a postscript to the Lord's Prayer, Jesus said, "If you forgive those who sin against you, your heavenly Father will forgive you. But if you refuse to forgive others, your Father will not forgive your sins." Forgiveness is a requirement of the disciple's life and means that the curtains of separation must be torn away.

Beyond Bumper Stickers

Traveling last year my family and I made the drive from historic Williamsburg, Virginia, to the city of Charlottesville. It is only a couple of hours drive between the two towns across Interstate 64. But on this trip it was late at night, I was tired, it was raining pitchforks, and I was behind the wheel of an unfamiliar rental car. Plus, I had a tummy full of scrambled eggs and pancakes, dulling my senses even more. So to steel my nerves and empower my driving abilities, I ordered a large cup of coffee to go from the nice waitress who had been serving our table at a nationally recognized breakfast restaurant that shall remain nameless.

Thirty minutes later, somewhere in the driving rain outside of Richmond, and near the bottom of my Styrofoam cup, my coffee began taking on a pronounced stronger, grittier taste. I kept thinking, "Wow, this will keep me awake; they must have brewed this stuff without a filter—I'm practically chewing the coffee grounds." How I wish that was what I was drinking. On my last gulp of coffee I took into my mouth what was giving my drink such a gravelly texture: a burned-out cigarette butt. I know central Virginia is still owned lock, stock, and barrel by big tobacco, and I saw plenty of their product along the way, but finding it at the bottom of my coffee cup was a bit more than I wished to discover.

These words about forgiving others (and that forgiveness serves as a requirement for our own forgiveness) when we have been so wounded, damaged, and mistreated go down about as easy as that cup of Virginia coffee. It's hard to swallow. And if you are like me (and I am certain you are on this count), you have had your fair share of hurts in this life. Betrayal, theft, injustice, abuse, dishonesty: we inflict and receive these so that no one escapes life unscathed. Sometimes the injuries are so deep and monstrous that we can't seem to get past them. For Jesus to say our spiritual health— our very communion with the Father—depends on somehow absolving these injuries is too bitter a cup to drink. It seems impossible. We would like to ignore or marginalize these words of Jesus and press ahead with a dark curtain pulled between us and our offenders. But these are not words we can disregard, for unreserved, undeserved forgiveness is the currency in which Jesus deals.

This is no isolated teaching of Jesus, and the best example of it comes later in Matthew's Gospel, in 18:21-35, with a story traditionally referred to as "The Unmerciful Servant." As a prelude to the story, Simon Peter asks Jesus a question: "How often should I forgive someone who sins against me?" This parable is Jesus' answer. A king called in all the loans he had made to his servants, updating his financial records. One loan he called in was to a debtor who owed him 10,000 talents. A talent was a denomination of money. If these were talents of gold, then by today's standards this loan was in the neighborhood of some $3 billion. Of course the man could not pay, so the king prepared to take everything the man had, sell the debtor's family into slavery, and throw the man into prison.

The debtor begged for mercy and promised to pay the debt back in its entirety. This was a lie driven by desperation, as no individual could possibly pay back this obscene amount of money. Jesus says the king was moved by all this and forgave the entire debt. He didn't give the man an extension or reconstruct the bad loan. He released the debt and set the man free.

As the newly forgiven debtor left the king's palace, literally just outside the door, he met one of his own debtors. This man owed him about $1,000. The unmerciful servant grabbed him by the throat and demanded immediate payment. Word for word, this thousand-dollar debtor begged for more time to pay his debt, but the man who was just released from a $3 billion tax lien threw the man who owed him a $1,000 gambling debt into debtor's prison. Of course, word got back to the king who reacted with rage. He called the man back in and said, "You evil servant! I forgave you that tremendous debt because you pleaded with me. Shouldn't you have mercy on your fellow servant, just as I had mercy on you?" (Matt 18:32-33). Then the king sent the man to prison until he had paid his entire debt. Jesus concludes, "That's what my heavenly Father will do to you if you refuse to forgive your brothers and sisters from your heart" (Matt 18:35).

When we hold those who "owe us" in a debtor's prison, it is a violation, but not against the individual. The person who has hurt us may deserve all the pain and suffering we can muster. However, it is a violation of the grace we have been given ourselves, for those in the Jesus Tribe cannot treat others with anything less than the grace we have received. Granted, these are hard words to hear and even harder words to practice, but these are much more than mere instruction. Jesus did more than teach us. He embodied and accomplished what he was teaching his disciples to do.

As he hung on the cross Jesus cried out, "Father, forgive them, for they don't know what they are doing." These words were not spoken in the aftermath of the resurrection after everything had worked out. Jesus spoke these words as the nails pierced his flesh and as the cross was raised on the hillside. Jesus, an innocent man wrongly condemned, undeserving of the treatment of a criminal, threw no curses toward his tormentors; instead he offered prayers of forgiveness. He prayed for the soldiers carrying out their orders. He prayed for the crowd of onlookers who easily joined in the heckling. He prayed for the religious and civil authorities who had sent him to his death. Jesus prayed for them all, and for us, releasing us all from our debts. Jesus demands from us nothing that he has not lived or experienced himself.

Len Sweet and Frank Viola have written a wonderful document called *The Jesus Manifesto*. A part of it reads,

> Jesus Christ cannot be separated from his teachings. Socrates says to his disciples, "Follow my teachings." Buddha says to his disciples, "Follow my meditations." Confucius says to his disciples, "Follow my sayings." Muhammad says to his disciples, "Follow my noble pillars." Jesus says to his disciples, "Follow me." The teachings of Jesus cannot be separated from Jesus himself. It is a profound mistake, therefore, to treat Christ as simply the founder of a set of moral, ethical, or social teachings. Christians don't follow Christianity; Christians follow Christ.[2]

If we will follow this Christ, we will do what he did. We will take into ourselves the worst that others can throw at us, and though it be a bloody, messy affair, we will pay the price, letting the offenders go free. Forgiveness isn't trite or easy. And it certainly isn't some trivial, corny bumper sticker like "Christians aren't perfect, just forgiven." Forgiveness is an infinitely costly venture that embodies the eternal words of the Apostle Paul: "Love is patient. Love is kind. Love does not demand its own way. Love keeps no record of being wronged" (see 1 Cor 13). That is the driving momentum behind any and all forgiveness; love pays the price for the wrong that has been committed.

Earlier in the Sermon on the Mount, Jesus explained that we live out this radical, revolutionary love because it is an imitation of God. He said,

"Love your enemies! Pray for those who persecute you! In that way, you will be acting as true children of your Father in heaven" (Matt 5:44-45). Little can be more God-like than the love it takes to forgive the impossible. The obvious question: Where does this kind of love come from? The answer: "Forgive us our sins, as we have forgiven those who sin against us." In praying the Disciples' Prayer we admit and acknowledge that our ability to forgive comes from Someone outside of us. The ability to forgive is rooted in God's forgiveness and grace. The kind of love it takes to forgive the worst of crimes is a love that can only come from the One who is love. If forgiveness flows out of us to others, it is because *God* is doing it.

The Monsters Can't Have the Last Word

Some wrongdoings can and should be dealt with simply and even ignored. With a smile or a nervous laugh, these small offenses can be washed away and we can move on. It's those deeper hurts we can't laugh about when we share them at a dinner party—unfaithfulness by a spouse, betrayal by a business partner, abuse by a parent or other adult when you were a child, the murder of your family member by a drunk driver. We can't dismiss these offenses with a casual wave as if they never happened. These are as horrible as any crucifixion. Acknowledging the seriousness of the injury, however, is exactly where forgiveness begins. Forgiveness does not discount that a crime has been committed. Instead, forgiveness turns and identifies wrong for what it is.

Lewis Smedes, who always has an enlightened word on the subject of forgiveness, said, "When we forgive evil we do not excuse it, we do not tolerate it, we do not smother it. We look the evil full in the face, call it what it is, let its horror shock and stun and enrage us, and only then do we forgive it."[3] This is the first planted seed of forgiveness.

In the movie *The Mission*, a group of Jesuit missionaries sets up a mission station among the tribes of South America in the late 1700s. One of the aboriginal peoples, the Guarani tribe, is won over to their gentle, peaceful ways and allows the priests to live among them. Meanwhile, there is another character loose in the jungle: Rodrigo Mendoza, a Spanish slave trader played remarkably by Robert De Niro. Mendoza makes his living not by peacefully abiding with the Guarani, but by stealing them from their homes and selling them into the plantation system.

Over the course of the story, Mendoza, in a fit of jealous rage over a shared lover, kills his own brother. In the aftermath, Mendoza enters into a crisis in which he cannot get over what he has done and what he has become. The guilt threatens to kill him, it seems, so his priest gives him an act of penance. He is to return with the Jesuits to the Guarani village pulling behind him a net filled with his armor and weapons of violence—the weapons he used to murder his brother, and the weapons he had used against these tribal people.

In the pivotal scene, Mendoza reaches the village after scaling a huge waterfall, fighting the mud and water with his heavy burden strapped to his back. The tribe is terrified that Mendoza, their enemy who has hurt so many of them and destroyed their lives, has accompanied the priests into their sanctuary. One of the young warriors of the tribe steps up to Mendoza with a long knife, and he raises it with what appears to be a death blow. Instead, he slashes the burden off Mendoza's back and kicks it clanging over the cliff, down the waterfall, and into the river below. Overwhelmed, Mendoza collapses, weeping in grief—but finally joy—as he faces the people he has harmed, receiving their grace and forgiveness.[4]

We cannot cut the burden from the back of our offender, or from our own backs for that matter, without first admitting that the burden is there. To ignore it does justice to no one. Once we acknowledge the burden, we strike it not in anger or vengeance but with grace, goodness, and what is better than the injustice deserves. Every time that kind of forgiveness takes place, the price for the offense is paid, but it is paid for by the victim rather than the wrongdoer. When forgiveness is granted, the one who has been hurt is saying, "I will live with the consequences of what has happened, without vengeance, without bitterness and without the demand of repayment. I will pay the price myself. I will absorb the loss." Again, Lewis Smedes may give the best answer. Describing those who have hurt us the worst as monsters, he says, "If we say that monsters are beyond forgiving, we give them a power they should never have. Monsters who are too evil to be forgiven sentence their victims to a lifetime of unhealed pain. [If we do not forgive] we give the monsters the last word."[5]

"God showed his great love for us by sending Christ to die for us," the Bible says, "while we were *still sinners*" (Rom 5:8, italics added). God didn't wait until we had our act together or until we showed up at his doorstep with a contrite heart. God struck preemptively and took the necessary, loving steps to reconcile us to him. When we love without limit and forgive others who have harmed us, it is not practical or natural. It is not right, fair, or justifiable; but it is love. And God's love in Christ knows no limit. God doesn't approve of serial killers, thieves, prostitutes, Wall Street pirates, dirty politicians, or exploiters of the innocent, but he has faced them all and will not allow their crimes to have the last word. It will end in forgiveness, for grace will be the last word.

So the best revenge is living this life of love that makes forgiveness possible, a love that comes from outside of us, a love that says *Your evil actions, your crimes against me will not prevail. You may have nailed me to a cross, but I will not remain this way. My forgiveness of you will be a resurrection to live life again, so help me God.* This kind of love sets both offended and offender free, and that is sweet revenge against all evil.

In modern history no one has taught the world more about the power of forgiveness than Nelson Mandela. After spending nearly three decades as a political prisoner of apartheid, he was elected president of South Africa. Rather than exercising vengeance against those who had mistreated and imprisoned him, he moved to form the Truth and Reconciliation Commission, an effort to short-circuit the deadly cycle of crime and revenge. The Truth and Reconciliation Commission met for some three years and reviewed the atrocities the white minority had inflicted upon the African majority. The commission's rules for absolution were simple: if a white policeman or army officer voluntarily faced his accusers, confessed his crime, and fully acknowledged his guilt, he could not be tried and punished for that crime. Mandela insisted that the country needed healing and forgiveness more than it needed justice, and this would be the way forward.

Philip Yancey says that at one hearing, a policeman named van de Broek recounted an incident when he and other officers shot an eighteen-year-old boy and burned the body in order to destroy the evidence. Eight years later, van de Broek returned to the same house and seized the boy's father. The wife was forced to watch as policemen bound her husband on a woodpile, poured gasoline over his body, and ignited it. The courtroom grew hushed as the elderly woman who had lost first her son and then her husband was given a chance to respond.

"What do you want from Mr. van de Broek?" the judge asked.

She said she wanted van de Broek to go to the place where they burned her husband's body and gather up the dust so she could give him a decent burial. His head down, the policeman nodded in agreement. Then she added a further request: "Mr. van de Broek took all my family away from me, and I still have a lot of love to give. Twice a month, I would like for him to come to the ghetto and spend a day with me so I can be a mother to him. And

I would like Mr. van de Broek to know that he is forgiven by God, and that I forgive him too. I would like to embrace him so he can know my forgiveness is real."

Spontaneously, some in the courtroom began singing "Amazing Grace" as this elderly woman made her way to the witness stand to embrace her former enemy, but van de Broek did not hear the hymn or receive the embrace. He had fainted, overcome by forgiveness. Yancey concludes, "Justice was not done in South Africa that day, nor in the entire country during those agonizing months. What was accomplished was grace and forgiveness. Evil is overcome by good only if the injured party absorbs it, refusing to allow it to go any further. This is the pattern of grace that Jesus showed."[6]

Gelassenheit

Moving from the "what" to the "how," the obvious question is one of appropriation: How do we get in on this kind of forgiveness? How does forgiveness become more than red-lettered words on a page, more than a stirring story, more than an example that Jesus has given us? How does it become a lived experience within our own pain and suffered injustices? In a word, the answer is *Gelassenheit*.

The word *Gelassenheit* comes from German theologian and mystic Meister Eckhart. He said, "If you do not get away from yourself, you will find trouble wherever you go. But to be empty of all things (*Gelassenheit*) is to be full of God." Literally, it is the emptying or letting go of self that God and his grace and love might fill you. Going further, Eckhart said, "It is a fair trade: To the extent that you have stripped yourself of yourself in all things, no more and no less, God enters into you with all that he is. It is here that you should begin, whatever the cost, for it is here that you will find true peace, and nowhere else."[7]

Meister Eckhart is not a name, really. It is a title. Meister is German for "master," referring to a title or rank, his being Master of Theology. Meister Eckhart was actually Eckhart von Hochheim, a German noble born in the year 1260, a time from which we have precious little information. What we do know is that as he reached adulthood, Eckhart became an accomplished preacher and theologian, a devout follower of Christ, a Christian mystic in the medieval tradition, and a troublesome agitator for the establishment. He was the only "master" of theology to be brought up on heresy charges in the Middle Ages.

When he was nearly seventy years old, the Inquisition caught up with Eckhart. The Inquisition was the religious court set up by the church to find, try, and punish those who did not line up with the church's formal teachings. This court, always led by a high-ranking church official, had imprisonment and capital punishment powers. Today, if an author writes something that is half-baked, innovative, or challenging to the church, all he or she might get is a little hate mail. If the author is considered especially dreadful, he or she might get picketed or boycotted at public appearances or have anti-websites thrown across the Internet. No one tries to execute those considered heretical thinkers . . . not yet anyway. But in those medieval centuries it was dangerous to question—even indirectly—the religious authorities. They would censure, condemn, imprison, or execute you, and then have the Pope damn your soul to hell. It was punishment now and later.

During this religious and social terror, Eckhart was called before the Inquisition to answer questions about his writings and the sermons he delivered to his little tribe of students, sermons he called "table talks." Eckhart would not stand for these accusations and appealed his case all the way to the Pope. He then walked the 500 miles to the Pope's palace to defend himself, but died after arriving and never heard the final verdict. It's just as well. While never "officially" condemning him, Pope John XXII, a year after Eckhart's death, declared seventeen articles of unorthodoxy against the old man and censured his writings, deeming his words too radical for the uneducated to read. "He sows thorns and obstacles contrary to the very clear truth of faith in the field of the Church and works to produce harmful thistles and poisonous thorn bushes," the church proclaimed.

It took many centuries for Eckhart to be rediscovered, but thank God he was, and there is now a revival of his work. Sifting through his Latin and German musings, one always finds the same subject: *Gelassenheit*. "Total letting go is the way to gain all things in the God who is the real being of all," the Meister preached. "God wants no more from you than that you should go out of yourself, and let God be God in you."[8] This is the very means of living out God's forgiveness and setting your debtors free.

I suspect this is what most of us really want. We want God to consume us and live his life through us. When we are squeezed by injustice, we don't want to react with hate, selfishness, or anger. We want God's grace to ooze out of our pores. We want to respond as Christ would respond. If you do not want to be this kind of human being and live with this degree of freedom, then stop reading now and move to the next chapter, but if this is what you want, there is a way to obtain it. Empty yourself. *Gelassenheit.*

Everything within us has to die. Our personal agendas, our selfish ambition, our greed, our pride, our ego and anger, our vengeance and hate, our feeble attempts at being good, our efforts to impress others, our running and chasing after things: all this—the very root of our being—must be exhausted and poured out until there is nothing left. Then and only then will God consume us with himself. It is the Pauline declaration of faith: "My old self has been crucified with Christ. It is no longer I who live, but Christ lives in me. So I live in this earthly body by trusting in the Son of God, who loved me and gave himself for me" (Gal 2:20).

When we are totally empty, then we are ready. God will act and pour himself into us. Until this transaction of identity takes place, it is impossible to forgive others who have hurt you. How will we know when this has occurred? Again, Meister Eckhart said, "Clearly it is not something that we will know in the same way that we know we have the flu. . . . But stand still and do not waver from your emptiness."9

Dr. Delbert Tarr has been an Assemblies of God pastor, preacher, missionary, and professor in more than seventy countries for more than fifty years. For fifteen of those years he was in West Africa in an area known as the Sahel, a swath of land 4,000 miles long just south of the Sahara Desert. In the Sahel, all the rain comes in a four-month period: May, June, July, and August. After that, not a drop of rain falls for eight months. The earth becomes a dust bowl and winds off the Sahara blow sand all across West Africa. The tribes of the region are resilient but also vulnerable, making less than $10 US dollars a month. They survived by growing sorghum in small fields during the short growing season, all the year's food having to be produced in just four months.

Recounting his experience, Tarr loved October and November in the Sahel as the granaries were full because the harvest had come. People sang and danced and ate two meals a day that consisted of what would look like Cream of Wheat to us. In December the granaries started to recede and many families went back to eating one meal a day. By January and February the one meal was cut in half. By March the elderly and the young were sick, and by April everyone was starving.

Tarr says that in the years he was there, inevitably the same thing would happen every spring. A young boy would come running to his father with sudden excitement. "Daddy! Daddy! We've got grain!" he would say. And the father would reply, "No, we haven't had grain for weeks." But the boy would not hear this. "Out in the hut where we keep the goats, there is a leather sack hanging up on the wall. I put my hand down in there and there's grain in there! Give it to Mommy to cook so tonight our stomachs will sleep!" The father gently explains, "We can't do that. That is next year's seed grain. It's the only thing that will feed us later."

Then, when the rains do arrive, the little boy and his entire family must watch their father do the most ridiculous thing possible: he pours out the seed—the only grain they have—into the dirt. For the child with a growling stomach, his father is throwing the last of their food and security away.[10] Was the father throwing away what he had while his family starved? Of course not. He believed the harvest would come and that his granary would once again be full, but to get there his bag, his stomach, and his storage bins had to be empty. He could hold nothing back.

Some of us have held on to our unforgiveness and resentments for so long that we can't imagine life without them. We keep fighting, digging in for the thousandth time, nibbling on the last crumbs of bitterness and thinking these will keep us alive. We are afraid of actually letting go of it all and learning to live a different way. It can be an ugly and agonizing proposition, yes, but getting to the end of yourself is necessary to truly know the grace of God and grant it to others. Once we are empty, the harvest of God's presence and grace can explode from the dry, cracked soil and give us what we truly need, doing for us what we cannot do on our own.

I cannot say this any more intensely: human nature is strong, sometimes it appears infinitely so, and to empty ourselves of all things is nothing less than a death, but nothing less will do. Those who will give themselves over to this death of self will find a hope, peace, and way of life that otherwise they could have never experienced. They will find grace—for themselves and for those who have hurt them—and grace will always have the last word.

Chapter 10

Gotta Serve Somebody

"Don't store up treasures here on earth, where moths eat them and rust destroys them, and where thieves break in and steal. Store your treasures in heaven, where moths and rust cannot destroy, and thieves do not break in and steal. Wherever your treasure is, there the desires of your heart will also be.

Your eye is a lamp that provides light for your body. When your eye is good, your whole body is filled with light. But when your eye is bad, your whole body is filled with darkness. And if the light you think you have is actually darkness, how deep that darkness is!

No one can serve two masters. For you will hate one and love the other; you will be devoted to one and despise the other. You cannot serve both God and money." (Matt 6:19-24)

On September 7, 2008, the United States government seized mortgage makers Fannie Mae and Freddie Mac as the two organizations collapsed under $5 trillion of over-leveraged mortgages. It marked the beginning of what economist Paul Krugman coined as "The Great Recession," an economic crisis that will profoundly affect a generation of Americans. Four days later, in a prelude of things to come, Lehman Brothers Investment Bank announced that it was looking for a buyer, and on word of that news, Lehman's worth in the stock market dropped almost 50 percent in a single day.

Before the month ended, financial institutions with formerly sterling names—Merrill Lynch, Bank of America, AIG, Goldman Sachs, Morgan Stanley, Citigroup—had either merged, collapsed, filed bankruptcy, changed their status, or been granted emergency funding from the federal government. With the financial system of the Empire in tatters, on the last business day of September 2008, the Dow Jones Index fell a record 777 points in a single day, the largest one-day point loss in its history.

In the weeks that followed, phrases like "government bail-out" and "rescue plans" became common exchanges on news programs and at breakroom water coolers. There were Senate hearings, House debates, desperate appeals from automobile manufacturers, and plenty of Federal Reserve testimonies. All the while the common citizen was dealing with the terrible fall-out: unemployment rates that soared to double digits; millions of homes going into foreclosure; and the value of the United States stock market dropping by almost 50 percent, a decline only exceeded by the economic collapse of the Great Depression. Consider how that 50 percent drop translates for investors, college savings accounts, and retirees. Reports indicate that the 2008 stock market losses amounted to about $7 trillion.[1]

One trillion dollars, a meager sum tossed about by economists these days, is an almost impossible figure for us to imagine. If you piled $1,000 bills one on top of the other, a stack of them worth a trillion dollars would be sixty-seven miles high. Or put another way, if you earned $1 dollar for every second you were alive, you would have $1 million after just two months. You would have $1 billion after thirty-two years. You would not have $1 trillion until the passing of 32,000 years. It takes the United States Bureau of Engraving and Printing about five years to print $1 trillion. It takes multiple lifetimes and millions of people to make that kind of money. And it can all be lost in a single day.

If Jesus were preaching the Sermon on the Mount today, in a globalized, multi-layered, geo-political economy, I imagine he might say something like this: "Don't store up your treasures in the commodities market, in off-shore accounts, in questionable hedge funds where inflation erodes them away, where market volatility destroys them, and where people like Bernie Madoff can break in and embezzle them, Bank of America can mismanage them, or Lehman Brothers can lose them. Rather, treasure the eternal things of God, those things that are not endangered by corporate layoffs, those things that the empire cannot destroy, and those things that cannot be hidden under a mattress or subjected to bank foreclosure. It is impossible to walk in opposite directions at the same time. So stop trying to serve both God and your financial security."

The Seven Generations

In striking at our love for and addiction to money, Jesus has struck at the very heart of what it means to be an American. Success within our current empire is almost always measured by the size of one's paycheck, the corporate bottom line, or the quarterly dividend report. The "American Dream" is related directly to prosperity, so when Jesus addresses our materialism, our "way of life" (an interesting phrase that few of its users take time to ponder) comes under siege. Yet Jesus' intent is not simply to tear us down or back us into a corner. His words are meant to set us free from depending on this money-oriented, greedy world in order to pursue a life and treasure of far greater value. Yes, our hearts need something to chase after; our hearts need something to long for and to love. The challenge is to seek what is right and best, to seek what will actually fulfill that search, but the illusion of wealth and security that the world offers cannot satisfy. It can only imprison.

The imprisonment comes not from the ownership of things. The constant threat is that things will own us. This is a condition that David Gushee calls "affluenza": materialism, commercialism, and consumerism drive us to get the latest and greatest with no thought for the least of these, no thought for what it does to our own souls, and no thought for what it does to God's good world.[2] Left untreated, "affluenza" is a terminal condition for those in poverty, for those of us who store up our accumulated wealth, and for our planet. While we may be able to afford the monthly payment on a lot of different luxuries, treasuring the treasure of the world makes us unfaithful to the way of Jesus and costs us much more than dollars. So these are not verses about greed, per se; ultimately, these are verses about Lordship and a forgotten concept in the Christian cosmos: stewardship.

In Genesis 2 God's newly created world is called a "garden." The word for "garden" was often used in Hebrew as a euphemism for sexual satisfaction. The Hebrews were modest people, so they might refer to an evening foray as a "walk in the garden" (wink, wink). Don't miss the point. The garden, God's creation in its original state, provided and provides everything human beings need for contentment. Here is this beautiful, magnificent, fantastic world that needs nothing from us to improve or better it. Human beings were implanted into this living biosphere with a divine assignment: Take care of it. Cultivate it. Serve and protect it.

As Christians, we have allowed rhetoric, activism, and radical extremism—on all sides—to take from us this responsibility, a responsibility that we should be leading, for cultivating, protecting, and loving creation is a deeply primal, spiritual act. God made us in his image and gave us the mandate to protect and preserve the life-giving order around us, not abuse it for our own selfish gain. Today's extreme materialism is a result of seeing creation not as something to which we belong, but as something we should conquer. Then we wring out every drop of its resources. "God gave it to us to use," we say, seeing it as theological permission to do violence against nature.

With this disregard for God's world is a baptized ideology that functions as its twin. As it goes, the highest goal of the Christian life, even its final end, is to leave this creation behind in ashes. I grew up under the tutelage of a strand of apocalyptic theology that taught me that one day soon Jesus would return to take his own, and those left behind would perish, along with the planet and the known universe, in a great cosmic atomic explosion. Thus, the only real spiritual ambition was to make sure you caught the heavenly bus for the other side. This particular interpretation of the Scriptures—one of many and a fairly recent interpretation—has done much more harm than it has good. After all, if it's all going down the toilet anyway, why bother? Why not exploit creation? This kind of thinking has empowered Christians to abuse our world and conveniently divorce the material from the spiritual, something Jesus unquestionably does not do here in Matthew 6.

Do I believe Jesus will return to establish his kingdom? Absolutely. But my reading of the Scriptures informs me that his return will be one of renewal and restoration. He will make things right and complete the divine task to make all things new. It will be a return to the simplicity, beauty, romance, and majesty of the garden, not a kick into the cosmic trash barrel. The question I grew up with was always, "What if Jesus came back today?" That is a good question. But questions just as challenging are "What if Jesus does not come back today . . . or tomorrow . . . or next year . . . or next decade . . . or next century? What kind of world do we want to leave for our descendants?"

Let us allow two more tribal societies to inform us here. First, the Iroquois nation instructed their leaders to consider the impact of their decisions on the seven generations around them. These seven generations included themselves, the three generations that preceded them, and the three generations that would follow them. Their great-grandparents, grandparents, parents, children, grandchildren, and great-grandchildren were their active participants in this life, good or bad. Each tribal member was bound by honor to care for these seven generations.

We who live in the Jesus Tribe should be bound by a similar ethic. We know that the grotesque consumption rate of the current Empire is unsustainable—economically and materially (if everyone consumed at the rate of the average American, it would take multiple planet Earths to support the current human population). We have lived long enough to see Paul's words realized here in North America: "This world as we know it will soon pass away" (1 Cor 7:31). It will collapse, and disciples of Jesus, rather than attempting to prop up its dying remains, must choose a path of less materialism, less greed, and less chasing after the treasures of this current age. We do this to be a kind of people who revere the eternal things within the temporary and to provide witness to a watching world.

Second, several years ago I was in Honduras on a mission trip. At the conclusion of the week the locals came to us to thank us for our work and we shared a wonderful meal together. After the meal many of the children, dressed in bright, beautiful costumes, began to dance a traditional Lenca tribal dance. The Lencas are an aboriginal people group who live in and around a village called La Esperanza in western Honduras. I appreciated the dance and enjoyed it very much. But when some of my fellow Anglos began to join in the dancing with them, I kept my seat. Why? Well, not because I'm a terrible dancer, though I am; and not because I was taught that a "dancin' foot can't be attached to a prayin' knee." I refused to join the dance because I am not Lencan. The colorful dress, the words sung, and the hand and head movements of the dance all told a story. It was the story of the Lencan people: their emergence, colonization, and continued struggle for survival. As much as I would have liked to jump in, their story was not my story to tell.

The temptation before the church will always be the same: we will always be invited to join a way of life or participate in a story that is not ours; to dance to a tune our Lord did not compose; to adapt to the rules and reality of the world, not the rule and reality of Jesus; to pursue the American dream and not the dream of God's now present and still coming kingdom. Yet I fear that we have all become converts to the most dangerous of American convictions: it is a faith that has multi-million-dollar shopping malls as its places of worship, salespersons and game-show hosts as its clergy, sales reports and budget projections as the daily devotional readings, and possessions as its god. We long and pray for the advent of a messiah who will one day come to save us and our money, bearing the banner of a 50 percent off sale, with coupons and discounts for all, and no-interest payments until next year. This is the good tidings of great joy for which we now trust and hope.

What Would Jesus Drive?

We will always be tempted to settle for less than God has for us. To avoid this and stay on track requires a single devotion, a good eye. The frequently overlooked verses of this particular teaching of Jesus are Matthew 6:22-23, sandwiched between the more familiar words about treasure and serving two masters. Jesus says, "Your eye is a lamp that provides light for your body.

When your eye is good, your whole body is filled with light. But when your
eye is bad, your whole body is filled with darkness. And if the light you think
you have is actually darkness, how deep that darkness is!"

If you can see clearly, you can live well. You can see the signs. You can
read the directions. You can stay on track. But if you cannot see clearly—if
you are blind—you can only stumble around recklessly in the darkness. And
what is worse, if you are blind but think you can see, it is twice as bad. When
we chase after the things of this world and the temporal priorities and
rewards it offers, we think we can achieve a place of safety and security. If we
can just get enough money in the bank; if we can just get the right piece of
property; if we can just reach that next rung on the security ladder; if we can
just make our monthly payments; if we can just shape the right fiscal policy
or elect the right official, then we will be able to relax. We will be able to
have some peace of mind and will no longer worry about being left out in
the cold. But this is blind-man talk.

Trusting the security the Empire offers attaches to mere personal possessions more weight than they can bear. Our security cannot be bound up in
our financial portfolios. It is impossible to measure the worth of human
beings by the outcome of the bottom line. The size of our house, the price
tag on our automobile, the number of properties we own—none of these
will satisfy. We can enjoy these, but they will never be enough to help us
sleep at night. When these become our obsessive goals, we are demanding
that they play the role of God in our lives, and they simply aren't able to bear
that kind of weight. Jesus has come to rip the blindfolds from our eyes, to
shine light on that darkness, and say to us, "If you are looking for better
treasure, something that will really last, you've come to the right place. Come
to me. Leave all this other junk behind."

More than a decade ago I made a couple of trips to Alaska. Driving from
Anchorage to Fairbanks, I stopped with friends to take pictures of Mt.
McKinley, or Denali, the tallest peak in North America. It was a bit cloudy,
as the Denali range is so massive it creates its own weather, so it wasn't the
best day to view the mountain. Still, we took in the sight and snapped some
good pictures. In Fairbanks the next day we had the pictures developed
(there was not much digital photography "back in the day"), and I was showing them to a friend who lived in Fairbanks at the time. He was quick to
correct me. The pictures I held in my hand were not of Mt. McKinley, but of
a smaller mountain, properly named Mount Deception.

Mount Deception earned its tragic name in September 1944 when a United States Air Force C-47 transport plane crashed into the side of the mountain in bad weather. The pilot was flying blind, using only instruments, and could not see where he was going—thus the name. Deception has lived up to its name ever since, but for a different reason. It continues to fool tourists like me because from certain angles the mountain looks just like Denali. The next day the weather was clear and my friend took me back to see Denali. There in the distance was Mount Deception at 11,500 feet. Looming behind it was what I could not see earlier—Denali at more than 20,000 feet, terrifyingly large. It was so large that what I thought were clouds the day before were actually the slopes of that massive mountain. I simply failed to see the peak. My friend showed me where and how to look for it.

Too many of us are looking at a mountain we think is the real thing, but it is Deception. We are blind to the greater reality that a bigger mountain has materialized on the horizon. We fail to see that we have fixed our eyes on the wrong goal. As a result, we will never arrive at the right place because what we begin with is where we end up. Our sights are set too low and we are blindly crashing our lives against this mountain. We have chosen to be enslaved by the god of Mammon.

Most modern English Bibles use the contemporary word "money" over the archaic "Mammon" when referring to riches. But I think Mammon, with a capital "M," is a better translation. Harmlessly, Mammon originally referred to possessions or money that was put into trust. Mammon was what was given to a banker or a trustee as collateral or as an investment. Over time, the meaning of Mammon transitioned sinisterly from resources *that were entrusted* to resources in which a person *put his or her trust.* Jewish rabbis eventually capitalized the word, regarding it as nothing less than a competing god. George Watts captures this false idol best in his oil painting where Mammon is portrayed as a fat, ugly creature grotesquely sitting on his throne, nursing his money bags, and crushing poor souls with his weight.[3]

Jesus makes it clear that Mammon is a god you can serve. You can bow the knee and worship at the altar of Mammon, but you can't do that and follow Jesus at the same time. No one can be a slave to two masters. This isn't a shame-inducing strategy by Jesus to make us feel bad about our decisions. It is the honest truth. You are not able to be married to one while keeping the other as a mistress; it is impossible. Sometimes the anxiety we feel about our financial security happens because we are in a tug-of-war trying to follow

Jesus, while under the power and spell of Mammon (a rival god who ruthlessly demands everything but delivers nothing).

I will hurry to say this: Jesus does not declare money itself to be evil. Money is not evil, but it is dangerous—extremely so—like a loaded gun; and it is as dangerous as liquor to an alcoholic or crack to an addict. One has to be careful with it because, unlike anything else in the world, it has the power to steal our souls, and not just rich souls. One can be as poor as a dirt farmer and still be serving Mammon, enslaved to that horrible god with barely two nickels to rub together. So no, money is not the root of all evil as we have been told. The Hebrew parable tells us *love* of money is the root of all evil.

In regard to this, Tony Campolo asked a tricky question a few years ago: "Would Jesus drive a BMW?" Here is his answer:

> This is a car designed to do 200 miles per hour on the German autobahn and corner at 150 miles per hour. Why would anybody in the United States, where the speed limit is 55, need a BMW? The answer's simple: The BMW is not a car. It is a statement, a symbol of an individual's status. The question for a Christian is this: In a world where there are such incredible needs, can I spend [this kind of money] on a status symbol? In the face of hunger and need and suffering, would Jesus say, "Hey, more important for me is buying a BMW"? If he were living today, I'd have a hard time believing he would do that. The point is not whether you should have a BMW. The point is, what is it about you that makes you want this car? The issue is why you get pleasure out of that instead of getting your pleasure out of [the Kingdom of God].[4]

Mortgaging the Ministry

The Roman poet Ovid could have easily been describing American society when he told the story of a young woman named Echo who fell in love with an exceptionally beautiful boy. In fact, everyone was in love with this boy. By the time he was a young man, every girl and half the boys in his village were infatuated with him, but he was viciously cruel and thought no one worthy of himself. He spurned everyone who chased after him. This young man's name was Narcissus. One day Narcissus was out on a hunting trip when Echo found him. She rushed to him to express her love, but he pulled away and spurned her. Narcissus left Echo with a broken heart, and she spent the rest of her life longing for the love she would never know. Her spirit died within her until only her voice remained.

As punishment for his cruelty, the gods arranged for Narcissus to come across a deep still pool in the forest. He bent down to take a drink, and as he did he saw his reflection for the first time in his life. He fell in love with the beautiful boy mirrored in the water. When he realized that the image he saw in the pool was his reflection and that he could never act upon this love, he sorrowfully took his own life. The myth is told that today Narcissus is still in love with himself, gazing at his own image in the waters of the river Styx.

The Empire in which we live maintains and promotes a culture of extravagance, self-indulgence, and self-centeredness; we know this. If this egotism were confined just to the American Empire, that would be one thing, but the church has not been immune to this disease, and I'm not just talking about televangelists. With declining numbers, greater competition, and the constant danger that those in the congregation are not "being fed" or "having their needs met," more and more congregations and church leaders are becoming obsessed with branding and marketing their church's image. Pastors and church leaders have become trademark specialists who are excruciatingly sensitive to what their target market demands, and congregations across the land are vesting their legitimacy and witness in the fickle audience of the Mammon-bowing, image-is-everything consumer. And if that consumer wants an *American Idol*-like stage presence, an army of specialized pastors to run their spiritual spa and pour lattes, hipsters behind the pulpit who know more about social networking than they do about Jesus, and a Disney-World-qualified children's ministry, then by God that's what the consumer will get—even if we have to spend (or borrow) a gazillion dollars to make that happen.

This kind of corporate narcissism, concealed as it has been by a legion of fog machines and ministerial doubletalk, is now on perfect display for all to see in these hard financial times. Giving has shrunken. Expansion plans are delayed. Ministerial staffs are reduced, and yes, some congregations even have a hard time hanging on to their property. Wall Street tycoons, credit card holders, and shyster speculators are not the only ones who suffer the guilt of their greed: pastors, church boards, and church building committees are guilty too. "Come, let's build a great building to the glory of God" can be pretty close to the same words spoken at Babel, especially when there's a seven-figure mortgage attached to that building. Of course, the mortgage may be more than seven figures. As I write these words, the bankruptcy filing of the famed Crystal Cathedral is still in the news; the congregation's total

debt could approach $100 million. That's a long way from the simple con-
verted drive-in that Robert Schuller began with.[5]

While not at the Crystal Cathedral (I don't see that invitation material-
izing any time in the near future), I was invited to speak to a congregation
that had fallen on hard times. When I arrived, I found a beautiful campus
with all the expected embellishments. The auditorium was enormous. There
were thousands of dollars invested in multiple projection screens and in
sound, video, smoke, and lighting equipment. There was a stage larger than
most middle-class homes, and it had more greenery and floral arrangements
than you would find at a Home Depot garden center. Outside were acres of
black-topped asphalt. The only thing that distinguished this place from a
performance arts center or a theater was the conspicuous acrylic pulpit at
center stage and the twenty-foot cross hanging on the back wall.

But for all its grandeur, this church was now hemorrhaging members
and attendees so that on the warm, sunny Sunday morning I was there, they
had barely fifty people in attendance. Half of those were in the worship band
or positioned behind tripod cameras (to whom were they broadcasting?) or
massive sound boards (for so few of us?). The two dozen or so who made up
the rest of the congregation . . . well, we sort of rolled around inside all that
empty space like BBs in a barrel. When it came time to pass the plate, the
pastor was especially earnest. It seemed it was getting more and more difficult to pay the church's bills. In fact, the mortgage payment was late. The
pastor's appeal was direct: without the "help of God's people," he pleaded,
the church was in danger of defaulting. It made me wonder if these were the
same people of God who had signed for the loan in the first place.

Consider this: the first Christians did not own church property, and it
remained so for centuries. The majority of the world's Christians who gather
for worship each week do so in homes, in open fields, or in ramshackle shelters—not in elaborate, mortgaged supercenters. Even our own forefathers
understood moderation in such things. The old houses of worship built generations ago were built by the hands of the parishioners, typically on donated
land, and hoisted into place in classic Amish barn-raising style. Buying the
most strategically centered piece of property in town didn't seem to be an
objective. After all, they were building a church, not a Walmart. And having
a multi-million-dollar mortgage on the church? Such a thought was inconceivable. It should be inconceivable still, even as American churches spend
$19 billion a year (every year) on building construction and maintenance.
That much money spent every year on food and on education programs

could eliminate global starvation and malnutrition in less than a decade. In these crushing financial times, wouldn't it be better for those of us in the church to have to concentrate on and pray about how we are going to keep up our feeding programs, our donations to missions, paying our teachers in the tutoring programs we run, and taking care of the widows and the orphans rather than paying interest on lumber, two-by-fours, and real estate?

Granted, this is just the beginning of what it means to live out these words of Jesus, and the beginning is filled with questions: Should we sell all of our homes and belongings and give the proceeds to the poor? Because we balance our checkbooks and keep an eye on our retirement accounts or church reserve funds, does this mean we have bowed our knee to Mammon? Are most of us driving the "wrong" cars? Are we worshiping in the "wrong" buildings? Would Jesus have us give away our savings accounts? Can our businesses or churches financially survive within the Empire if we practice Jesus' instructions about money and possessions?

There are no easy, boilerplate answers to these questions; it is left to those of us in the Tribe to "work it out." We must begin to make decisions and engage in actions that empower, not inhibit, our ability to pursue the Kingdom of God. We must find creative ways—individually and corporately—to open ourselves to change. And change we will if we stop mimicking the style, ways, and means of the world, and stop merely reading the words of Jesus. Change will be the consequence of actually doing and becoming, of putting Jesus' instructions into practice. There is no other way. What will it look like? Maybe this: An American pastor was preparing to return from a Chinese mission trip. Having witnessed the simplicity and substance of these people, he asked how we in America could pray for them. The Chinese pastors answered, "Pray that we can one day own buildings and become like you." The wise pastor responded, "I cannot do that. Instead, pray for us, that we might become more like you."

Amen.

Chapter 11

A Leap of Faith

"That is why I tell you not to worry about everyday life—whether you have enough food and drink, or enough clothes to wear. Isn't life more than food, and your body more than clothing? Look at the birds. They don't plant or harvest or store food in barns, for your heavenly Father feeds them. And aren't you far more valuable to him than they are? Can all your worries add a single moment to your life?

And why worry about your clothing? Look at the lilies of the field and how they grow. They don't work or make their clothing, yet Solomon in all his glory was not dressed as beautifully as they are. And if God cares so wonderfully for wildflowers that are here today and thrown into the fire tomorrow, he will certainly care for you. Why do you have so little faith?

So don't worry about these things, saying, "What will we eat? What will we drink? What will we wear?" These things dominate the thoughts of unbelievers, but your heavenly Father already knows all your needs. Seek the Kingdom of God above all else, and live righteously, and he will give you everything you need." (Matt 6:25-33)

The emergency landing of US Airways Flight 1549 in January 2009 was one of the most incredible things many of us have seen. After multiple bird strikes to the engines, the heroic captain and crew conducted a successful splashdown right in the middle of the Hudson River. Every time I get on an airplane, either by video or intercom, a flight attendant tells me what to do "in the event of a water landing." I always look at *Sky Mall* magazine or read during this portion of the program because, while I have flown many times, my flights rarely take me across large bodies of water. Plus, I like to distract myself from thinking about everything that can go wrong while in the air (more about that later). I think I'll pay closer attention next time. A few people on Flight 1549 must have been paying attention; all one hundred fifty-five people on the flight survived with only a few minor injuries.

Those survivors all have a similar tale to tell. Everything went from normal to circling the toilet bowl in less than four minutes. One of the reasons people remained so calm, aside from the pilot's training and the flight attendants' leadership, was the speed of the entire event. They didn't have time to panic. And because of the nature of the crash, with water rising just outside the windows and seeping into the tail of the plane, everyone escaped quickly with no thought for what they were leaving behind. Some passengers stopped to grab their bags from the overhead bins, but they were quickly—and properly—shooed away by those with clearer thinking.

Experts say that when an airline crash takes place and there are survivors on board, those survivors normally have about ninety seconds to escape. Those same experts reveal that evacuation is often slowed, if not crippled entirely, because a passenger or two reaches up to retrieve a suitcase or a precious laptop out of the overhead bin. But if you pay attention to that pre-flight speech—and now I really listen—what you should do is clear: unfasten your seatbelts, proceed to an emergency exit, and do not take anything with you. That's what those survivors did, and it made all the difference. Suitcases can hold some of our most important valuables, but they are in no way as valuable as breathing. Laptops are now almost indispensable (I can't imagine life without mine), but I do not want to trade my life for it. We travel with some essential stuff, but no stuff is worth clinging to when the rivets are bursting their seams, the plane is in the drink, and time is running out. There is only time to let it all go.

When we become more concerned with our citizenship on earth or in the empire—clinging to and protecting our stuff—than we are with Christ's rule over our lives, the natural outcome is anxiety. Why? Because Jesus followers do not belong to the world; our citizenship lies elsewhere. So allegiances that pull us away from seeking "the Kingdom of God above all else" conflict and entangle us, ripping us away from the Source of our peace. But when the disciple rejects the gods of this present age—materialism, greed, self-indulgence, and consumerism—he can be free from the mind-racing, palm-sweating, turf-defending, paralyzing worries of the world. He can let go of all the things that would pull him down and destroy him. He can stay safe in the crash.

Competing Commitments

To paraphrase Karl Barth, we must preach and speak with the Bible in one hand and the newspaper in the other.[1] Use the ancient Scriptures, Barth would say, to speak to the issues that are ruthlessly current. When I read the newspapers today, I come to this conclusion: Christians are afraid and torn with worry at a level I have never witnessed. We live in the most technologically advanced, health-conscious, scientifically enlightened, warning-labeled, intervention-driven, tamper-proof-packaged society in the history of humanity, and we likely are more afraid today than our Neanderthal ancestors who had to fight saber-toothed tigers for every meal. We have been consumed by fear. Such anxiety is nothing less than a sin, particularly when the most repeated command in the Bible is "Fear not."

Here is the source of our fear, I think. We have deeply invested ourselves in the economic, political, social, and religious systems of the world at the expense of the Kingdom of God, and being thus invested, we have something—at times, everything—to lose. The Empire around us has its hooks in us so deeply and in a way that when things get shaky (not *if* but *when*), our only response is fear. We have bought into the lie that says we can follow Jesus and be comfortable in the world around us at the same time. We are not trusting and behaving as "believers"—as those who have faith in Christ. We have forgotten our place in the world as the community of Christ. When we forget who we are, or, more accurately, betray who we are, there will be more than enough fear and confusion to go around.

Once again, I return to the words of Clarence Jordan, who properly observed, "We are nourished from the system to which we have committed ourselves."[2] In committing to the systems of the empire around us, we find that these cannot nourish us, and we are terrified. For example, in the economic collapse of recent times many Christians were wringing their hands in despair. I didn't lose a single minute of sleep. Why? Because I have great faith? No. It was because I did not have anything in the market to lose. If you aren't invested, there are no worries. (I don't share that as financial planning advice. I'm just broke.) So while many were agonizing, a whole demographic of the American population slept just fine because we had nothing at risk. We had nothing committed to the system and therefore nothing to lose.

Here is another practical example: Recently I received a letter from my local municipality inviting me to connect to their water utility at a tremendously discounted rate. Times being what they are, they need a broader customer base, so finally the water lines have made it to the boonies where I live. But thus far, I have declined to take them up on their offer. My reason is simple, and it is not because I distrust the city fathers. I have an artesian well that provides water to me and my family that tastes better than anything I can buy in the store, in a municipality's pipe, or in a bottle. It is water that is nearly perfect, without additives, chemicals, or impurities. My well and my municipality are two different systems, two different sources of water, two different pipelines. I have chosen my source because it is better for me and my family, so whatever the local water works wants to do or not do is their business, not mine. I am not hooked up to their supply and therefore not dependent on that supply. I don't have to worry about their rules, policies, prices, or dependability.

The amount of worry in our lives will depend upon the pipeline to which we are connected. The level of anxiety we experience will be related directly to our investment, and we simply will not worry about things in which we have no vested interest. If the source of our security, our identity, and our well-being is this current empire and all its systems, we should hire better money managers, take more medication, and stuff gold coins under our mattresses because difficult days are here to stay. But if our pipeline is Christ and the Kingdom of God he incarnates, then, no, life will not be easy, but the strength and security he offers are endless.

Jesus provided a couple of practical examples in the text of Matthew 6: the birds of the air and the lilies of the field. Jesus said, "Look at the birds of the air; they do not sow or reap or store away in barns, and yet your heavenly Father feeds them. . . . See how the lilies of the field grow. They do not labor or spin. Yet I tell you that not even Solomon in all his splendor was dressed like one of these" (Matt 6:26-29).

The "birds of the air" Jesus refers to are obvious. The lilies of the field, however, were most likely the Palestinian poppies that bloomed brightly for only a day or so and then died away. But while they bloomed, Jesus said they were more beautiful than the greatest and richest king in Jewish history. Small birds and blooming poppies: neither of these have natural defenses. They are at the mercy of the elements. They have no way of storing up supplies for a rainy day. They have to greet each morning with no guarantee of their survival. Yet they do not worry (and it's not because of their lack of emotional capacity; Jesus' metaphor isn't that complete). They do not worry because the system that sustains them is governed and maintained by our heavenly Father. They are dependent on him, as he has given all of nature the gift of faithful resignation and trust. The challenge before us is to live the same way.

"Aren't you far more valuable to him than they are? Why do you have so little faith?" (Matt 6:26, 30). The question is not, "Do you have enough faith?" The question is, "In whom or in what are you placing your faith?" If we have placed our faith in the economic machinery of the empire, we will worry. If we have placed our faith in the political structure of the empire—

regardless of affiliation—we will worry. If we have placed our faith in the religious institutions of this current age, we will worry. If our personal happiness, security, and peace of mind must be maintained by the culture around us, then the fear, anger, and paralysis will be more than we can bear. As followers of Jesus, we are not designed to live in this type of prison.

Suppose I came home one evening and found my three boys in tears and huddling together in the driveway. Of course I would leap from the car and begin a vigorous inquiry: "What is wrong? What has happened? Why are you crying?" Suppose then that they begin telling me their fears. My oldest says, "I was at the neighbor's house, and it was time for dinner. But they wouldn't feed me. They told me to get out because there wasn't enough to go around. So here I am, not knowing where my next meal is coming from. I just know we are going to starve to death." I turn to my middle son and through his tears he tells a similar story: "I don't own a house. I don't have a car. I don't know where I'm going to sleep tonight. This winter, I'm going to freeze to death!" And finally the youngest speaks: "No one loves me. I don't have anyone to read me a goodnight story. I don't have anyone to wake me up in the morning. I just don't know if I can make it much longer." What would my reaction to such an experience be?

I would probably say something like, "You silly, foolish children! Dry your tears and come inside! The neighbor's house isn't where you get fed. We have plenty to eat in our cupboard. Why are you crying about nowhere to sleep? You have your own beds just inside the door. How can you say you are not loved? Don't I tell you that every day? Don't I show you my love in a multitude of ways? How have you lost your faith in me? Why are you chasing after these other things to give you the comfort you are looking for? Get up and dry it up! Wash your faces and hands and come on inside." My boys are not alone; they are sustained by their father, and so are we.

Pagans and Porcupines

In Matthew 6:32 Jesus says, "These things [striving after the treasures of this earth] dominate the thoughts of unbelievers." The NIV is even more direct and more accurate. It reads, "For the *pagans* run after all these things" (italics added). We might think of pagans as wild, animalistic people who live on a remote island, boil severed heads in a pot, and eat human flesh. I guess that definition would apply. However, that is not how Jesus uses the word. In a broader sense, a pagan was literally a "country dweller." A pagan was a foreigner or someone who lived outside a particular civilization or outside the communal village. The word translated "pagan" in the NIV (*ethnos*) is tribal language. A pagan was someone not yet a part of the family.

Thus, when Jesus used the word "pagan," it was not necessarily a judgment statement about morality or religion or even who was right or wrong. It was a statement about the home tribe or village to which certain people belonged or did not belong. Pagans were those living outside the Kingdom of God. Those within the Jesus Tribe, conversely, follow a different path and therefore have an entirely different way of looking at and acting in the world. Pagans find their satisfaction and hope in things, but it cannot be this way with those following after Jesus. The danger in letting the pagan way of the empire into our hearts is clear: It will lure us away from home. It will pull us away from the Father. It will trick us into pursuing a way of life that is not ours.

Giving up the pagan life has serious implications. It might mean changing our consumption habits, how we buy or sell goods, or the way we pay for a home. It might mean looking for legitimate sustainable ways of living that are not dependent on the systems of the empire. It might mean being more "unplugged" from the scheme of things. When I have brought up these implications to individual or groups of Christians, there is almost always stern objection. Those objections go something like this: "If everyone who was a follower of Jesus unplugged from the systems of the empire, everything would crash! What would happen to our economy, our political system, and our social structures? Wouldn't these all implode? Isn't it irresponsible to do something like this?"

I respond to these objections with a change in pronouns. These systems of the world and empire are not "ours." They are "theirs." It is not the disciple's responsibility to prop up, condone, or otherwise perpetuate the systems to which we do not belong. Again, the way of Jesus must have our primary allegiance. This is a return to, or maybe a first understanding of living out the radical, alternative community of Jesus. It is a community in which we do not simply work to make the world and its systems better. We don't concentrate on a privatized, inward faith. Instead, we follow Jesus in all things and at all costs, even if the stars fall. This is the genuine responsibility of citizens of the Kingdom of God.

Similar to these objections, sometimes a well-meaning Christian (or a whole horde of them) will protest that the church has an obligation to the empire by quoting Jesus' words in Mark 12:17: "Give to Caesar what is Caesar's and to God what is God's" (NIV). Yet Jesus' words in the Gospel of

Mark are not about our earthly citizenship or what the disciple owes to the kingdoms of this world. In that referenced passage, Jesus takes a coin and rhetorically asks whose image it carries—Caesar's, of course. To the Jews of Jesus' day this was much more than a coin of the empire. It was nothing short of an idolatrous graven image, an image that marked Rome's territory and ownership (remember, the empire's money was no good at the temple). Jesus, it appears, was using his trademark wit to show that his followers were living a different life within the territory and under the ownership of a different lord than Caesar. He had not come to create a synthesized union of the Kingdom with the world. He had come to bring the reign of God to earth, evidenced in the alternative, redemptive life and choices made by his followers.

Jacque Ellul says it succinctly and boldly: "'Render unto Caesar' in no way divides the exercise of authority into two realms. The mark on the coin is that of Caesar; it is the mark of his property. Therefore give Caesar this money; it is his. . . . It means that Caesar, having created money, is its master. That's all. Let us not forget that money, for Jesus, is the domain of Mammon, a satanic domain."[3]

This response is similar in tone to that of Methodist bishop William H. Willimon. Once in an interview he was criticized for holding opinions that seemed to lead Christians to shirk their social and citizenry responsibilities. He responded that such a conclusion was incorrect. Rather, he said Christians should influence the culture but it "should be done like porcupines making love . . . very carefully." He and his partner in subversion, Stanley Hauerwas, go on to say,

> If you believe the Gospel, you feel yourself in collision with the most widely held and deeply affirmed values of this society. . . . American Christians need to stop feeling at home. We . . . ought to feel like missionaries in the very culture we thought we had devised. American Christians thought that we had created a culture in which people were at last safe to be Christians. That was a mistake. . . . By being adopted to be part of a journey called discipleship, Christians are permanently ill at ease in the world.[4]

So we refuse to collaborate with the power systems of the world not because we hate the world (Jesus has forbidden that) and not because we reject the world; rather, we invite all who will to join us. We are rejecting the world's power over us and within us, and rejecting all the anxious worries that accompany such power.

I am calling for a whole-hearted, leap of faith without reservation, where we throw ourselves on the way of Jesus and let all other options go. If we are going to bear his name, let us bear it with all our hearts, souls, minds, and bodies, even if it makes us feel out of place and uncomfortable in this world we used to call home. The biggest indication, in fact, that Jesus is truly becoming our Lord is the sensation that we no longer fit in with what is usual and expected. Then Jesus is becoming more real than ever. Then we will be a people who live out his way and words in the Sermon on the Mount—God's righteousness—where we humble ourselves at the feet of our Master. Then we will be found with those described in the Beatitudes. We will reject the legalism of dead religion. We will tell the truth, remain faithful in our relationships, turn the other cheek, and walk the second mile. We will love our enemies, pray for those who abuse us, practice our faith in quiet, peaceful rest, and refuse to bow our knee to Mammon, Caesar, nationalism, or anything else that gets in the way of our commitment to the way of Jesus. We will let our lights so shine before humanity that they will see our good deeds and glorify our Father who is in heaven.

So no, do not retreat from the world. Go be a banker, a surgeon, a musician, a business owner, a waitress, a pilot, a teacher, a citizen—almost anything. But do this work in the world as a loving, peaceful, justice-seeking follower of Christ whose very life is a contradiction of the world around you and calls the way of the world into question. Seek first the Kingdom of God and his righteousness, trusting Christ no matter what. Or, as Eugene Peterson has translated the verse, "Give your entire attention to what God is doing right now, and don't get worked up about what may or may not happen tomorrow. God will help you deal with whatever hard things come up when the time comes" (Matt 6:33-34, *The Message*). We must shirk our unbelief that God is not as qualified as the empire to sustain us.

The Universe Is Sideways

Philip Yancey tells about an editorial that first appeared in the *Wittenburg Door* more than two decades ago. A pack of Cub Scouts went camping in the mountains of northern California. Late one night they sat around the fire telling ghost stories and tales of forest creatures who would come out of the woods and eat Cub Scouts in their sleep. Well after midnight, and very much afraid, the whole pack crawled into a single tent. One boy awoke a couple of hours later with a full bladder. He fumbled his way to the door but was too scared to go outside. The entire population of the tent awoke the next morning to soggy sleeping bags. The boy was so scared of what might be on the outside that he made of mess of everything on the inside.[5]

Little could better describe the mindset of so many of us today when it comes to trusting Jesus and his way for us. I say this not only about the immediate text we have explored in this single chapter but about the entire Sermon on the Mount. When Jesus says, "Turn the other cheek," we are afraid Jesus is wrong and we will not be able to bear the humiliation of such an act. When he says, "Blessed are you when you are persecuted," we don't believe him, denying that anything resembling blessedness could come as a result of persecution. When he says, "Don't worry about the things of this world," we have precious little faith in Christ to provide, care for, and protect us. We look out our tent flap at the world—a world that is dark, terrifying, and disorienting—and we cannot push ourselves out there to follow Jesus in it. So we stay where we are, unmoved, unchanged, and paralyzed by fear.

I know this fear, and like so many reading this page, I sometimes find it challenging to maintain any level of real trust in following Christ or to believe him. There is so little of which we can be certain, so few things we actually can control, so much about this way of Jesus that seems absurd. How do we do it? We must take the leap of faith. Returning to Eckhart, it is *Gelassenheit*; we must empty ourselves of all things. That is faith. No, we will never understand all there is about Christian spirituality, about following Jesus, or how to best live as disciples in the land of the empire. But we do not have to understand it all. For in leaping/trusting/emptying, we begin the lifelong, eternity-long free fall toward understanding. I know we want to understand everything before we start. We want certainty. We want ironclad answers and real assurances that this way of Jesus will "work" for us. Those things may come to us, but they may not. The way of Christ does not begin with confidence and move toward faith. That is getting caught with the cart in front of the horse. It begins with faith and moves toward confidence. This jump into the way of Christ will eventually land us beyond our fears and beyond the absurd to the life God has for us.

With just such a landing in mind, I'll end this chapter where it began: in the cockpit. Every time my wife sits in an airplane, she looks around at her fellow travelers and asks herself, or asks aloud if I am traveling with her, "I wonder if these are the people I am going to die with?" This delightfully optimistic retort is fun and games for my wife. She loves to fly and is as comfortable in the flight cabin as she is stretched out on a sofa. She buckles up, slaps on her earphones, settles down with a book or magazine, and is good to go. It's not so easy for me. I think my sweet spouse uses her preflight question intentionally to stoke my very real flying fears.

I travel and fly much more than I used to, but I still get the jitters—serious jitters—every time I leave the ground. The only way I can tumble down the runway (the takeoff is the worst) is by much prayer and fasting, a dose of Ativan, and a visit to an airport bartender. Even then, I never relax once I'm in the air. I feel every bump, grow suspicious of every unusual sound, and nearly grind my teeth to dust each time the plane sways or banks. Flying with my youngest son once during one of those banking moves, I heard him blurt out in excitement, "It's so much fun when the universe is sideways!" No, it is not; and yes, he is obviously his mother's son.

I was on a sideways flight a few years ago from Washington, DC, to Atlanta, Georgia. It was a cold, stormy night and my flight had escaped Reagan National Airport just before a blizzard shut down the entire eastern seaboard. But escape from the nation's capital was not an escape from my fears. The homeward flight was turbulent and choppy, and we were swallowed by clouds as thick as bricks. The cloud cover was so dense that as we entered our holding pattern over Atlanta, I could not even see the lights below—not a single highway, not a single landmark, nary a porch light. As we circled and circled (and circled), we lurched and jerked, accelerated and dropped. I dug my fingernails deeper and deeper into the arm rests, pulled the seatbelt as tight around my waist as possible, wiped the pools of sweat off my face and forehead, and prayed like a dying man.

Then, without warning, I felt the hardened thud of striking the runway. Safe and sound, we coasted to the terminal. Incredibly, the pilot had landed the plane not only in the dead of night but also in absolute zero visibility. As I disembarked from the plane, the pilot was standing at the door—sort of like the preacher at the end of Sunday worship—shaking hands, thanking us for our patronage, and wishing us a fine evening. I stopped, thanked him for his skill, and, pointing out the window, asked him, "How did you land this plane in that?" He answered, "It was no sweat. I just trust the instruments." I am certain that if this pilot, as capable as he was, had tried to feel his way toward Atlanta using his senses for some glimpse of certainty, none of us would have ever made it home. We would have missed the city completely or, worse, have attempted a landing on Interstate 85 somewhere. To fail to trust the instruments pointing us along on the journey would have been a disaster.

Most of the time we can't see what waits for us on our way to that home whose builder and maker is God. The clouds are too thick; the view too obscured; our fears too many. We can't even see where our next footstep will land. But in the absence of certainty, we leap forward in faith as we follow Jesus. He has given us his words, his way, his Spirit, his very self—these are the instruments that will lead us in the right direction. The pilot who answered me so confidently as I left the plane that evening, while not as fearful as me, had his own anxieties about flying blind. He didn't say anything about it, but he could not hide the circles of sweat that bled through the underarms of his suit coat. Still, sweating bullets or not, his trust in the instruments had gotten us home. That kind of trust always will.

Chapter 12

Two Moons in His Moccasins

"Do not judge others, and you will not be judged. For you will be treated as you treat others. The standard you use in judging is the standard by which you will be judged.

And why worry about a speck in your friend's eye when you have a log in your own? How can you think of saying to your friend, "Let me help you get rid of that speck in your eye," when you can't see past the log in your own eye? Hypocrite! First get rid of the log in your own eye; then you will see well enough to deal with the speck in your friend's eye.

Don't waste what is holy on people who are unholy. Don't throw your pearls to pigs! They will trample the pearls, then turn and attack you." (Matt 7:1-6)

Gary Hamel and C. K. Prahalad tell about a science experiment involving four monkeys in a room (no, this is not a bad joke). In the center of the room, researchers placed a tall pole with a bunch of bananas suspended at the top. One particularly hungry monkey eagerly scampered up the pole intent on retrieving a banana. Just as he reached out to take hold of the treat, he was hit in the face with a gush of cold water from an overhead shower. Squealing and crying, the monkey ran down the pole. Each monkey, in turn, attempted to get a banana. Each received a cold shower, and each scampered down without a meal. After repeated treatment like this, the monkeys finally gave up on the bananas. With the monkeys thus conditioned, one of the original four was removed from the experiment and a new monkey was added to the room.

The first thing the new monkey did was (you might have guessed it) start up the pole to get a banana. The other three monkeys in the room quickly reached up and yanked their new comrade back down the pole. Later, if the new monkey tried again, he would be snatched down again. After a few of these aborted attempts, the new monkey got the message loud and clear: don't climb the pole. Even after all four of the original test subjects were replaced and the shower head was removed, not a single monkey ever ventured up the pole again.[1]

Many people, too many people, have given up on church, God, or anything that sounds like Jesus' Kingdom or Tribe. They won't even attempt to "climb the pole" because they have been pulled down for so long by the others in the room that there's not even a reason to try. And some of us in the room have been so hardwired by our Puritanism, our fundamentalism, our Catholicism, or a hundred other "isms" that we think certain people are welcomed by God and others are not. God accepts some people, but there are others who are simply disqualified because of their gender, their race, their nationality, their religion, their socioeconomic status, their denominational alliance, their place in society, their past failures, or their sexual behavior. So some of us in the room feel compelled to police the pole and keep these people away.

We violate the Native American proverb, "Do not judge a man until you have walked two moons in his moccasins." Since we can never duplicate the experiences and heart of another, our feet will never fill those moccasins. For the disciple, as usual, the way of Jesus is best: "Do not judge others."

Go to Hell

The better translation of Jesus' prohibition against judging others is "Do not condemn others," as the word "judge" can be ambiguous. The Greek word used here, *krinō* (think "critic"), can mean two different things depending on the context. First, "to judge" can mean to distinguish or to differentiate. Second, "to judge" can mean to punish or to damn. Certainly Jesus wants his disciples to be discerning, choosing between right and wrong, the dark and the light. The context of this Sermon, particularly the verses that follow about choosing the right path, staying clear of false prophets in sheep's clothing, and making correct life-building selections, precludes Jesus speaking of whole and healthy discernment. Granted, this type of discernment can still get the disciple up to his or her ears in controversy, but Jesus isn't speaking about discernment.

Jesus is using that second meaning of *krinō*: It is not the place of the disciple to condemn others. Those in Jesus' Tribe are not qualified to sit in enlightened judgment over another person, meting out punishment or reward. Jesus isn't teaching us to refuse to make ethical decisions. He isn't saying we should dismiss all principles or that it is impossible to determine what is right or wrong, just or unjust. He is saying that Christians should not be in the business of convicting people for their perceived crimes. That is not the role of the follower of Jesus.

In some regards, Jesus is telling us the same thing our parents and grandparents taught us: "If you can't say something nice about someone, then don't say anything at all." Keep your criticism and condemnation to yourself. Leave things in the hands of the Father, the only one competent enough to judge justly. But does the church heed these words of Jesus? Hardly.

Turn on your television or radio, read much of what is printed by Christian publishers, listen to what is repeated in church pulpits, or spend time perusing the Christian blogosphere. It is an exhaustive collection of condemnation and angry finger pointing at what everyone else is doing wrong. Yes, there is always room for correction, but there is never room for condemnation. It is arrogance when we condemn others and a failure on our part to let God's grace have its way in our lives. We should be characterized by meekness, mercy, peace, and love, not by judgmentalism, spiritual snobbery, self-righteousness, and criticism.

There is more than enough anger, hate, separation, and polarization in the world: Christian versus Muslim, white versus black, male versus female, North versus South, East versus West, haves versus have-nots, Protestant versus Catholic. But the church is called to a different kind of existence. The church is united not by race, color, creed, nationality, ethnicity, or socioeconomic standards. We are united by the body and blood of a crucified and risen Jesus. The New Testament church was (and remains) the only society in which people can come together as equals. It is a tribe that does not identify others based on the town of their birth, the accent with which they speak, or the shape of their house of worship. It's no utopia, mind you. There will always be those, on the way with Jesus and off the way, with whom we will passionately disagree. There will always be squabbles, controversies, and at times little to hold in common. But these disagreements should not—they cannot—be allowed to grow hatred in our hearts. When hate is allowed to grow, it clouds our vision and makes us see others as inferior. Once they are less than we are, they can easily be condemned, written off as unimportant to God (for God is on *our* side), and quickly assigned to hell.

Let there be no doubt: condemnation is a death sentence. When we condemn, we are wishing those who are the object of our wrath to be flushed away to some final destination of the damned. We are telling them, "God loves you and has a wonderful plan for your life; of course, if you do not see things our way, you can go to hell right now."

Maybe this inclination to judge others is why Matthew places these words of Jesus where he does in the Sermon on the Mount. After all this vigorous teaching of Jesus, the disciple might be lured into the trap of thinking we have it together. "We are followers of Jesus. We are different. We are special. We are separate and apart. Don't you wish you were as good as we are?" Shame on us for such thinking, such preaching, and such living! These words serve as a radical but necessary course correction. The church is not permitted to be a judgment-making society whose only voice to a watching world is that of a crotchety old man, angry that the neighborhood kids won't stay off his lawn. Our role is to follow Jesus, and for the most part to remain quiet. This doesn't mean we don't have Jesus-informed opinions. This doesn't mean we don't give a verbal witness to our faith. But it does mean we refuse— absolutely refuse—to say the final word over a person or his actions. That role belongs only to God.

There is an old folk tale about an elderly man who lived in a tiny village. Although he was poor, he was the envy of all his neighbors because he owned a beautiful white stallion. People offered amazing prices for the horse, and certainly he could have used the money, but the old man always refused. "This horse is not a horse to me," he would tell them. "He is my friend. How could I sell a friend?"

One morning he found that the horse was not in his stable. All the villagers came to see him. "You old fool," they said. "We knew someone would steal your horse. How could you ever protect such a valuable animal? It would have been better to have sold him. Now the horse is gone and you have nothing." The old man responded, "Don't judge so quickly. Say only that the horse is not in the stable. The rest we do not know. Only God knows." The people of the village laughed. They knew he was a fool.

After several days the prized horse returned. He had not been stolen at all. He had merely run away into the forest. Not only did he return but he brought a dozen beautiful wild horses with him. The village people gathered around again. "Old man, you were right and we were wrong. What we thought was a curse was a blessing. Please forgive us." The man responded, "Once again, you go too far. Say only that the horse is back and a dozen horses returned with him, but do not judge. Unless you know the whole story, how can you judge? No one knows but God."

The old man had a son, an only son. The young man began to break the wild horses. After a few days, he fell from one of the horses and broke both legs. Once again the villagers gathered around the old man and cast their judgments. "You were right," they said. "Those wild horses are no blessing after all. Your only son has broken both his legs, and now in your old age you have no one to help you. You are poorer and more pitiful than ever." The old man spoke again. "You people are obsessed with judging. Say only that my son broke his legs. Who knows if it is a blessing or a curse? God knows, but no one else does."

A few weeks later, the village's king declared war against a neighboring country. All the young men of the village were drafted and pressed into service in the army. Only the son of the old man was excluded because he was injured. Once again the people gathered around the old man, crying and grieving because their sons had been taken from them with little chance that they would ever return. Once again they spoke: "You were right, old man," they wailed. "This proves it. Your son's accident was a blessing. His legs may be broken, but at least he is with you. Our sons are gone forever." The old man spoke a final time. "It is impossible to talk with any of you. You are always drawing premature conclusions. Say only this: 'Your sons had to go to war, and mine did not.' No one knows if it is a blessing or a curse. No one knows but God."

The Prejudice of Love

I had the distinct pleasure the other morning of telling a sheriff deputy that my radar detector had been stolen from my car. "Awkward" does not even begin to describe my discomfort. The burglary itself could have been much worse, I suppose. My family and I have lived in the same small town for years now. It is the kind of town where everyone knows everyone, people look after each other's kids, and when your neighbor waves "hello," he or she is actually being friendly.

Having grown so comfortable with our surroundings, we have never locked a door on anything we own. In fact, on the night of the break-in, our home and both our vehicles were unlocked, and the keys to both cars were safely tucked in the ignitions. But the thieves, it appears, were not interested in committing grand theft auto. They only wanted our CDs, the change in the consoles, our phone chargers, and those two radar detectors—yes, two; there was one in each car. So as the deputy sat in my living room taking my statement and cataloging my missing goods, I felt like a stinking, hypocritical fraud.

There I was, reporting what had been taken from me, and yet every time I climbed behind the wheel of my car, I was intentionally breaking the law and using the now absent electronics to evade the penalty for my transgression. Granted, clicking down the road with a radar detector is no huge crime. In my state it's not even illegal. And no, my deception was not on the scale of a slimy Elmer Gantry, but I sure didn't feel any better about it. A few days later when a detective called to tell me that officers had arrested the alleged bandits, it didn't please me. They were just kids, but they had done some damage in the community, committing more than a hundred car-hopping smash-and-grabs. With so much already stacked against them, I told the detective to let my report find its way to the shredder.

This whole duplicitous affair reminded me of one of the great British writers of the twentieth century: G. K. Chesterton. Chesterton was a 300-pound mountain of a man whose intellect, honesty, and savvy were even larger. He authored thousands of literary works from simple newspaper articles and short stories to complex novels and poetry. A committed follower of Jesus, he often faced skeptics, agnostics, or atheists in public debate. He would proceed in taking them to pieces with his humor and brains, and then with grace and civility treat his vanquished foes at the pub, drinking, debating, and laughing with them as friends.

When Chesterton was at his peak of popularity and wit, a London paper, *The Times*, solicited responses from its readership by asking this question: "What is wrong with the world?" You can imagine the result. Hundreds of long, detailed letters poured in to the editor. Then *The Times* asked a number of leading thinkers of the day to respond with full essays answering the question. Again, the essays poured in, verbose and long winded. The shortest and most powerful response came from Chesterton. Here is Chesterton's answer to what is wrong with the world. He wrote, "Dear Sirs, I am. Yours truly, G. K. Chesterton."

Chesterton's actions serve as commentary on one of Jesus' most recognizable metaphors. Jesus said, "And why worry about a speck in your friend's eye when you have a log in your own? How can you think of saying to your friend, 'Let me help you get rid of that speck in your eye,' when you can't see past the log in your own eye? Hypocrite! First get rid of the log in your own eye; then you will see well enough to deal with the speck in your friend's eye" (Matt 7:3-5).

Imagine that you wake with a little dust under your eyelid, and try as you might, you cannot remove it. So you go to the optometrist to get help. You think maybe she can flush it out with saline or somehow pick it out. You make your appointment and they lead you back to the little dark room with the lettered chart and the comfy chair. The doctor comes in and you think, "Finally, I'm going to get some relief." But holy cow, your optometrist has a 2-x-6 laminated beam sticking out of one of her eyes. She says, "Good morning! My assistant tells me you have a little something under your eyelid. We'll get rid of that right away. It'll be a lot easier than that cataract surgery I performed earlier this morning, let me tell you."

So she goes to work assembling her tools for the procedure (as you suddenly see clearly for the first time in a long while), and as she turns to her assistant, the beam knocks him down. She's knocking the charts off the wall and banging around on the optometry machine. She reaches for the tweezers but picks up the scalpel instead. And God help you when she finally positions herself in a way that she can actually get to your head. Before it is over she's bloodied your nose, put both your eyes out, and cut most of your forehead off. She's killing you because she's not fit to perform such a delicate operation when she needs that stick pulled out of her own head.

When we make decisions about people or situations, about most anything, we make them with biases firmly in place. We all use prejudice based on our life experiences. For example, if you have been harmed in a relationship, your bias in your next relationship (we might call it baggage) might be distrust. You can hardly help it. If you had a bad experience as a child or teenager in a particular religious denomination, it is likely you will be suspicious every time you encounter that denomination. Our families, our business dealings, the mistakes we have made, our successes—our entire environment—hardwire us to pre-judge others.

The change of nature that Jesus is producing in us is to be biased and slanted in the direction of love, not experiencing the warm and fuzzy feelings of emotionalism but treating all others as neighbors and not as enemies. The role of a judge is to hand down punishment to others based on the rule of law. But we are not in the punishment-issuing business. We are not judges. We are lovers and servants of Christ and of others. That is our bias. As Christians, it would be glorious to be rightly accused of prejudice, to be narrow-minded in the direction of a love that looks to clear one's own biases before seeking to correct someone else.

The prejudice and bias of love demands that we turn our attention to our own hearts and examine our own lives, not the lives of others, because our own failures, shortcomings, and blurred vision disqualify us from working on others. Again, this does not mean we do not exercise discernment; it means we approach every situation and person with deep humility, knowing that we are all fractured. Bonhoeffer said it like this: "Jesus is the only standard by which disciples should live, but he is not a standard we can apply to others. He is a standard we can only apply to ourselves."[2] So when we as Christians get blisteringly angry with those who sin differently than we do, we should remember to mind our own business. That business is to love, not condemn.

This isn't always easy, especially for pastors, Christian leaders, and those with any type of public platform. I often feel the pressure from my peers and others to "take a stand" on a moral or social issue. Typically, I refuse to do so, or at least I refuse to do so in a way that will please my critics. On many of the hard and divisive issues of our times, I don't close my eyes. I do stand for something: I stand for love. For if Jesus came not to condemn the world but to redeem it, how can we who bear the Name respond any differently?

Without a doubt, what I believe about all these moral and social issues matters. But these beliefs mean nothing if my first and consuming conviction is not love for those who are different and believe differently than me. We have a choice: we can choose to show how "right" we are or we can choose to love. Sometimes it is impossible to do both at the same time.

The Rabbi's Gift

Jesus ends this section of the Sermon on the Mount by quoting an old Jewish proverb, one not as well known as the "plank in the eye" one. He says, "Do not give dogs what is sacred; do not throw your pearls to pigs" (Matt 7:6 NIV).

Dogs and pigs were animals for which Jews had little regard. They came to represent Gentiles, outsiders, and those who did not abide by God's way. In the Gospel of Luke, for example, a sick, crippled man named Lazarus lies begging outside a rich man's gate. The dogs, Jesus says, came and licked the sores on Lazarus's body. These were mangy, nasty street animals that represented all that was dirty (see Luke 16:19-31). Once, Jesus was asked by a Canaanite woman to heal her daughter (Matt 15:21-28). He winsomely referred to the request as coming from a dog (of course, Jesus healed the girl). In Philippians 3 the Apostle Paul warns the Christians there to "beware of dogs"—those who are conniving evildoers. And in the book of Revelation John sees a vision of the heavenly city and outside its walls he sees the dogs (22:15)—they are once again outcasts.

The pig theme is just as striking. In the Gospel of Matthew, Jesus casts the demons out of two afflicted men (see 8:28-34). The demons possess a herd of pigs—those nasty, forbidden animals—and the herd plunges into the sea. In the great story of the prodigal son, the prodigal's demise is powerfully illustrated when he ends up as a pig farmer, hanging on to the lowest rung of society's ladder (see Luke 15:11-32). So dogs and pigs, used by a Jewish rabbi, had a clear meaning; Jesus wasn't talking about actual animals. He was talking about those who were outside the community. Further, they were not merely outsiders, they were the disciple's antagonists.

What is the disciple's relationship with these outside antagonists, with those who so easy become our enemies? Jesus' instruction is not to cast our pearls to the swine. Don't give what is sacred to the dogs. In other words, don't engage them. Don't take the good and holy way of life you are living and, in using it as a standard to judge others, bring unnecessary trouble back on yourself. Some will not listen, learn, or participate in a profitable conversation of any sort. Some will never respect divergent opinions. So use discretion. Don't get into a street fight with an alley dog. Don't get down in the mud and wrestle a pig in the pigpen. You're not going to win. You're only going to get dirty and get hurt and lose what is holy.

When it comes to some who live far differently than we do, who are outsiders to our way of life, Jesus is teaching us to keep our distance entirely. Some people are better loved and respected with a sense of detachment rather than engagement. Do not bring shame to the way and name of Christ by using him as a weapon of judgment against others. You would do better to string a pearl necklace around a pig's neck, for what is good and beautiful will not be received or appreciated. Yet this distance does not imply hatred or apathy. We commit ourselves to quietly, peacefully, and humbly loving others with the love of Christ. Fundamentalist, homosexual, Arabian, liberal, undocumented worker, political demagogue, fear monger, Wall Street banker: whatever label is attached to whomever we find repulsive cannot stand in the way of our seeing every person—*every person*—as an individual God loves and for whom Jesus died.

To help us think about these words of Jesus on many different levels, I wrap up this chapter with a retelling of a story called "The Rabbi's Gift."[3] It seems a famous monastery had fallen on hard times. Once it was a thriving order, but over the years it had become so decimated that only a few old monks were left living in an even older house. People no longer came there to be nourished spiritually, and only a handful of aged monks shuffled through the cloisters with heavy hearts.

Deep in the monastery woods was a little cabin that an old rabbi occasionally used as a retreat to fast and pray. No one ever spoke with him, but whenever he appeared the word would be passed from monk to monk: "The rabbi walks in the woods." For as long as he was there, the monks would feel blessed by his presence. One day the abbot decided to visit the rabbi and open his heavy heart to him. After the morning Eucharist, he set out through the woods. As he approached the hut, the abbot saw the rabbi in the doorway. It was as if he had been awaiting the abbot's arrival. The rabbi stood with his arms outstretched in welcome. Though they had never spoken, the two embraced like brothers. They entered the hut. In the middle of the room stood a wooden table with the Scriptures open on it.

They sat in the stillness of the hut for a few moments without saying a word. Then the rabbi began to weep. The abbot could not contain himself. He covered his face with his hands and began to cry too. The two old men sat there like lost children, crying their hearts out, filling the hut with their shared pain and tears. When the tears ceased and all was quiet, the rabbi lifted his head and spoke. "You and your brothers are serving God with heavy hearts," he said. "You have come to ask a teaching of me. But it is the same in my town. Almost no one comes to the synagogue anymore." Little else was said.

When the time came for the abbot to leave, he embraced the rabbi once again and said, "It has been a wonderful thing that we should talk after all these years. But is there nothing you can tell us, no piece of advice you can give us that would help us save our dying order?" The rabbi paused and said quietly to the old abbot standing in his cabin, "Well, there is one thing I have to tell you: One of you is the Messiah." The abbot left without a word and without ever looking back. The next morning, the abbot called his monks together. He told them he had spoken to the old rabbi from the woods, and then he looked at his assembled brothers and said bluntly, "The rabbi said that one of us is the Messiah."

In the days and weeks that followed, the old monks began to think about the rabbi's words and wondered whether they could actually be true.

"The Messiah is one of us?"

"Could he possibly have meant one of us, here at the monastery?"

"If that's the case, who is it? Do you suppose he meant the abbot?"

"On the other hand, he might have meant Brother Thomas. He couldn't have meant Brother Jonathan, but maybe the rabbi did mean Brother Jonathan."

"But surely not Brother Philip. Could Philip be the Messiah?"

"Of course, the rabbi didn't mean me. He couldn't possibly have meant me. I'm just an ordinary person. Yet supposing he did? Oh God, not me?"

As they thought like this, the old monks began to treat each other with extraordinary respect on the off chance that one of them might actually be the Messiah. And on the off, off chance that each monk himself might be the Messiah, they began to treat themselves with extraordinary respect. A gentle, warm-hearted, concern began to grow among them that was hard to describe but easy to notice. Over time, as people visited the beautiful forest in which the monastery was home, they sensed the extraordinary respect that now began to surround the old monks and seemed to radiate out from them. There was something strangely attractive, even compelling, about it. Hardly knowing why, people began to come back to the monastery more frequently to picnic, to play, to meditate, and to pray. They began to bring their friends to show them this special place, and their friends brought their friends.

Then it happened that some of the younger men who came to visit the monastery started to talk more and more with the old monks. After a while one asked if he could join them. Then another. And another. And it happened that within a few years the monastery once again became a thriving order and light to the community, thanks to the rabbi's gift that taught them to look at and love others expecting the very best.

Chapter 13

Asleep in the Storm

"You can enter God's Kingdom only through the narrow gate. The highway to hell is broad, and its gate is wide for the many who choose that way. But the gateway to life is very narrow and the road is difficult, and only a few ever find it.

A good tree produces good fruit, and a bad tree produces bad fruit. A good tree can't produce bad fruit, and a bad tree can't produce good fruit. So every tree that does not produce good fruit is chopped down and thrown into the fire. Yes, just as you can identify a tree by its fruit, so you can identify people by their actions.

Anyone who listens to my teaching and follows it is wise, like a person who builds a house on solid rock. Though the rain comes in torrents and the floodwaters rise and the winds beat against that house, it won't collapse because it is built on bedrock. But anyone who hears my teaching and doesn't obey it is foolish, like a person who builds a house on sand. When the rains and floods come and the winds beat against that house, it will collapse with a mighty crash." (Matt 7:13-14, 17-20, 24-27)

It began in 1980 when the executives of one of the largest companies in the world secretly commissioned a scheme titled "Project Kansas." The commission had the most daunting task any group of business people could be given: reengineer and repackage a product, and then successfully market it to regain the falling market share of the last thirty years. The commission got to work. They completely redesigned their product and its packaging, performed field tests, assembled focus groups, piloted sample marketing, and conducted surveys. The results were strong. The new product was favored by consumers nine to one over the old one. So with great anticipation, on April 23, 1985, the company stopped production of its now antiquated product and unveiled to the world its new creation: New Coke.

I grew up a couple of hours away from the Atlanta headquarters of Coca-Cola. The company and drink have been so influential in that neck of the woods that every carbonated drink in existence is simply referred to as "a Coke." It's not "pop" or "soda" or "cola." It's not Root Beer, Sprite, Pepsi, or Dr. Pepper. It is Coke. But not in 1985. New Coke was a disaster, especially in the Southeast. The small minority that didn't like the new product not only didn't like it, they felt deeply betrayed by the Coca-Cola Company. In the words of the venerable Lewis Grizzard, "The only way that I could figure they could improve upon Coca-Cola, one of life's most delightful elixirs, which studies prove will heal the sick and occasionally raise the dead, is to put rum or bourbon in it."[1]

Lobbying organizations were formed and public protests were staged. Coke had to hire additional staff to respond to complaints, and their signs were booed at major sporting events. Even Fidel Castro complained. Three months after its launch, the company made the announcement that old Coke, "Coca-Cola Classic," would return to the marketplace—an announcement so important that Peter Jennings interrupted *General Hospital* to tell the nation. And by the end of the year, just eight months after the fiasco had begun, the Classic formula was outselling every cola product on the market, a position it has not given up to this day.

Barrels of ink have been poured out over this topic. How could this have happened? Why were Coke's marketing studies so flawed? Did the executives do this on purpose? On and on it goes with no consensus. But there is agreement about one thing: Coca-Cola's continued success is due largely to the fact that its leadership admitted their mistake and had the courage to return to its original formula. They succeeded not because of product transformation or innovation or because of anything "new." They succeeded because of product restoration. Maybe the church should do the same.

A lot has changed in the church over the years: renewals, reformations, and changes in style, music, administration, and architecture. Many of these changes have been cosmetic and cultural, but I think much of what is at the core of who we are has been reformulated. I don't think it is as simple as saying, "If we just did church like the first Christians, everything would be perfect." It wouldn't be, because things weren't perfect for them, and they were people of their own time. But I do think there is an "original formula," to use Coca-Cola language, for the Christian life. It is simply following the person and way of Jesus, articulated best in the Sermon on the Mount. It's not anything new. It's classically old, and to it we must return.

If I Were a Carpenter

Jesus ends the Sermon on the Mount with a series of contrasts, making it clear that we all have a decision to make about what we have heard. We can choose the narrow gate of his words and way, or we can choose the path of least resistance and let that path wash us down the wide gate. We can embrace his words and bear good fruit, or we can reject them and allow our lives to be overrun with briars, thorns, and kudzu. We can heed the words of this true shepherd who has come to lead us, or we can follow the siren song of the false shepherds who will lead us to destruction. We can become wise builders, constructing our lives on his solid foundation, or we can build on locations of our own foolish choosing.

This building theme is a common one with Jesus. It should be, for his occupation as a carpenter was well established. This does not mean Jesus was an accomplished industrial engineer. He was more like the village handy man, the one who arrived in his ladder-covered work van and overalls when you needed to finish a fix-it-up project. Jesus' use of language betrays the work he did, for he speaks with repeated references to and examples from the world of construction.

How did he teach his disciples not to judge others? Having rubbed more than one wood chip from his own watering eye, he told them to be sure to remove the beam lodged in their own cornea before attempting to point out the speck under someone else's eyelid. And the life of discipleship? He compared the decision to follow him to building a tower; it was a costly enterprise that should only be initiated by those with the resources and resolve to finish building. And once while Jesus was teaching and healing, a group of men came to him carrying their sick friend on a stretcher. The press of the crowd was too great, so they tore the roof off the house above Jesus. Then they lowered their friend by rope to where Jesus was. Jesus never protested their demolition project, and I have often wondered if he stayed afterward to repair the damage. He certainly knew how.

But Jesus is not the only carpenter. We all are. Our lives are like houses under construction. Some of us build on sand. When the storms of adversity come—and they are certain to come with driving rain, rising floods, and hurricane-force winds—our lives collapse in a great disastrous heap, the foundation upon which we have built being unable to bear the strain. But those who build upon the rock—that rock being the words and way of Christ—survive the hard times. The windows may get knocked out. A blue tarp may have to cover the shingle-less roof. Some sheetrock and carpet may have to be replaced, but the house remains firmly on its foundation.

The construction of these two buildings is never brought into question. No doubt, they are both sturdy and well built. The point of contrast is in the groundwork. One is built to last. The other will wash away with the next flash flood (a common scene for Jesus' first listeners when flash floods rolled into Palestine). Both houses experience the same storm, but the aftermath is radically different, and not because one's construction is faultless or because certain builders are more accomplished. The home that survives does so only because it is resting on solid ground.

Following the way of Jesus and building upon the teachings and words of Christ will not prevent the storms from making landfall at your front door. Having Jesus in your life doesn't put up a geo-dome or a force field over your life, your family, and your circumstances, keeping all the bad stuff on the outside. If you follow Christ, you will face the same storms, adversities, and pressures as everyone else—and, based on the Sermon on the Mount, sometimes even more so—but the foundation of your building is different. In these red-letter words of Jesus that we embrace (and often resist), we find what it takes to withstand the storms and adversities of life within this world of empires. There is no other lasting substitute.

Nevertheless, building our lives on "his wonderful words of life" is not as obvious a proposition as it appears. A lot of good things can get between Jesus and the disciple, things that cannot bear the weight of living in this world. We cannot build our lives on any church. We cannot build our lives on creeds, as helpful as these may be in articulating our faith, or on what some bishop, pastor, writer (including me), or denominational leader says. The foundation of the Christian life is not built on any of these things. The foundation can only rest on Jesus.

I have found that it is easy even for the Bible to distract us from following Jesus. We make the Bible our unassailable authority on all things (or at least our interpretations become unassailable), and then we begin to generate doctrines, confessions of faith, creeds, and so forth. These things can turn the Bible into a giant fact-filled encyclopedia so that we end up with a lot of information but actually miss the point. When someone asks us what we believe, we point to a religious resolution or a paper voted on by an ecumenical gathering rather than speak of a living relationship with Christ.

Yet our faith is not built on the Bible, nor is the church built on the Bible. There is only one foundation that is already laid: Jesus Christ. On him our faith rests. On him the church is built. The Bible is not the end. It is a God-breathed directional arrow on life's road pointing us to Christ. As N. T. Wright put it, "The risen Jesus, at the end of Matthew's gospel, does not say, 'All authority in heaven and on earth is given to the books you are all going to write,' but 'All authority in heaven and on earth is given to me' . . . .

Scripture itself points away from itself and to the fact that final and true authority belongs . . . to Jesus Christ."[2]

We must hold to Christ as the authority and chieftain of our Tribe, casting everything else away as worthless in sustaining us. "Because nothing else is as satisfying as knowing and following Jesus our Lord; thus, we give up everything else, counting it all as garbage, wanting nothing more than Christ and the enjoyment of belonging to him" (Phil 3:7-8, author's paraphrase).

For example, imagine a friend comes to your home one day after a vacation. While on her trip, she acquired the most beautiful, stunning, and incredible piece of artwork you have ever seen. It is so dramatic you cannot take your eyes away from it. As you try to take in its beauty, your friend says to you, "I want you to have it. It is yours." You are astounded and begin to resist such an offer. There is no way you could receive something so priceless (of course, in your heart you are beyond ecstatic). After your friend leaves, you begin searching your home for the right place to showcase your new treasure. This piece of art will be what your entire home hinges upon, so it must have the supreme location. But everywhere you put it, it's wrong. The light is too dim. The rooms are too small. It cannot be seen from the kitchen. When you sit to eat your meals or wake in the morning, it's not there before you.

You decide that, to do the gift justice, you must commit to the unthinkable: you tear down your house. It's not a remodel, not a renovation, not an additional room to house the gift you have received; you level your home and start over. You build a new house to exhibit the gift you have received, no matter the cost, so that from every room in the house, to every visitor that enters your home, it is obvious that the house was built around this priceless gift. That is what it means to follow Jesus. Take the priceless gift he has given you—himself—and build your life on and around him, even though this means tearing away everything else.

Break the Case

Yet Jesus—his person and his words—is no static gift to be gawked at as if on display in a gallery. If we are going to enter the Jesus Tribe and truly build our lives on Christ, there is only one way forward: we must live out his instructions. The Sermon on the Mount is not intended for debate or analysis. It is intended to be lived. As challenging as these words are, they are not mere ideals. They are not suggestions. They are concrete, real, workable solutions for living in this world as the followers of Jesus. He calls us to do something with what we have heard and to get on with it.

To illustrate, consider Antonio Stradivari, the master instrument maker of the last five hundred years. Stradivari built a number of stringed masterpieces including harps, cellos, and guitars. But his name is most closely associated with his violins, which are unsurpassed in beauty and legendary sound. A Stradivarius violin blooms beneath the musician's ear, I am told, like few others. It has the ability to warm a small room or fill an enormous concert hall. One classical musician has said, "Playing a Stradivarius is like driving a high-performance automobile. It responds to the slightest touch, but always has power in reserve."[3]

Stradivari made more than a thousand of these sports-car violins over his career, and several hundred survive. But if you want to get your hands on one of them, you'd better liquidate your savings account. It will cost you several fortunes. The top five world record prices paid for any musical instrument are for Stradivarius violins. For example, in 2006, Christie's auctioned a Stradivarius called "The Hammer" for a record $3.5 million. It's a tidy sum, but even that cannot touch the worth of Stradivari's most priceless violin, a work of art called "The Messiah."

"The Messiah" was supposedly discovered in Stradivari's workshop after his death. It changed hands a few times and earned its name because one of its owners would always talk about the beauty and perfection of the instrument, but he would never let anyone see it. One of his critics sarcastically responded, "Then your violin is like the Messiah: one always expects to see him, but he never appears." The name stuck, and so has its elusive character.

The final owners of "The Messiah" considered the instrument to be such a precious piece that they bestowed it to a British museum where it remains in safekeeping even today. As a condition of the bequest, however, the museum can never allow the instrument to be played. "The Messiah" may be the world's most perfect and expensive instrument, but it sits inside a glass box, untouched by musicians and unheard by lovers of music. Honestly, if someone could get their hands on "The Messiah" to play it, it would likely sound terrible. Violins, like most stringed instruments, have to be played in order to retain their sound. The more they are played, the better they get. In fact, the easiest way to destroy an instrument—even a masterpiece—is not by playing it but by locking it away.

Those who follow Jesus have a similar challenge and opportunity. The one we accept as our Messiah was born into the world not purely to be worshiped and talked about. He means for us to follow him. All the same, this invaluable gift of God can be locked away in an observational case. Religious disputes, angry arguments with our theological enemies, points and counter points: these are used to debate the validity of our faith at the expense of practicing that faith. Some of us behave as if exposing our faith to the real world will somehow contaminate it. Those outside the sterile container in which we have placed our faith have hands dirty with questions, objections, and contradictions. Surely they will damage what has been entrusted to us.

No, the Kingdom of God is not that fragile.

Possessing and professing faith in Christ is absolutely no good unless we let him loose in our lives and in our world. This doesn't mean we enter the world with an answer for every question, a proof text for every objection, or a black-and-white set-in-stone conviction for every issue. It means we enter the world to put Jesus into play with our lives. I'm not saying that serious religious exploration is not a worthy exercise. What we believe matters, but only if our first and consuming conviction is practicing the love of God as revealed to us in Jesus. As one of those early followers of Jesus said, "If I understand everything and have faith that moves mountains, but do not have love, I am nothing" (1 Cor 13:1-3, author's paraphrase). So we have a choice: we can use all our energy fighting, defending, and struggling to protect what we have been given, or we can give it and ourselves away to the world in a labor of love. I think you know what Jesus asks of us. Only by surrendering to and then practicing the life of Jesus will he become the "true and living way" (John 14:6, BBE) for our lives.

When we Christians speak of Jesus as "the way," we sometimes have in mind (or at least it appears so) that he is standing *in* the way. Our perspective is not of Jesus as an open door that leads to life but of Jesus as a roadblock. "Do you want the abundant life? Do you want to get to God? Sorry, you have to go through Jesus." Jesus becomes an irate troll living under a bridge, ready to jump out and devour anyone traveling along the road. But Jesus hasn't padlocked himself behind some barricade waiting for those with the secret security password to get through. He calls to all who will follow him into the Kingdom of God to come and discover what life can really be.

Most every day I cross the beautiful Choctawhatchee Bay. Birds, dolphins, jumping fish, boaters, and kayakers are usual sights along the way. But to cross the bay, I have to use the Clyde Wells Memorial Bridge. A mile and a half long and hanging there in the Florida sky, it is the only way to get my vehicle to the other side. What if I arrived at the foot of the bridge and treated it like a roadblock instead of a bridge? What if I reacted by asking, "Who put this bridge in my way? I'm trying to get to the other side. What am I going to do now? My car doesn't float, you know. I guess I'll just turn around and go home." How stupid! The bridge is not *in* the way. It *is* the way. So it is with Jesus.

He invites us to travel with him and through him on the journey to know and experience God. This is much more than getting to the other side (going to heaven when you die). Following Jesus is a way of radical living for today. The Sermon on the Mount does not answer the hypothetical question, "If you were to die tonight, would you go to heaven?" It answers far more practical questions than that:

What kind of person and human being do you want to become?

Will you reflect the joy, patience, and peace of Jesus with your life?

What kind of life do you want to lead in the time you have on earth?

Can you become a person who graciously defies the expectations of the world and the empire around you?

Are you building your life on the foundation of Christ?

The answers to these questions depend on whether these words of Jesus remain ink stains on paper or become life-shaping, Christ-pursuing instructions to which we give ourselves above everything else.

From Robin and the Reb

Mitch Albom has written a superb book titled *Have a Little Faith*. It contains a story from his beloved rabbi Albert Lewis, to whom he affectionately refers as "The Reb." Reb's story, from a 1975 sermon, goes like this:

A man seeks employment on a farm. He hands his letter of recommendation to his new employer. It reads simply, "He sleeps in a storm."

The owner is desperate for help, so he hires the man.

Several weeks pass, and suddenly, in the middle of the night, a powerful storm rips through the valley.

Awakened by the swirling rain and howling wind, the owner leaps out of bed. He calls for his new hired hand, but the man is sleeping soundly.

So he dashes off to the barn. He sees, to his amazement, that the animals are secure with plenty of feed.

He runs out to the field. He sees the bales of wheat have been bound and are wrapped in tarpaulins.

He races to the silo. The doors are latched, and the grain is dry.

And then he understands. "He sleeps in the storm."

My friends, if we tend to the things that are important in life, if we are right with those we love and behave in line with our faith, our lives will not be cursed with the aching throb of unfulfilled business. . . . We will never wallow in the agony of "I could have, I should have." We can sleep in the storm.[4]

As I write these words, the wife of my best friend is dying of cancer, and by the time you read this page, she will be gone. Her name is Robin. She is thirty-nine years old, the mother of four beautiful school-aged children, and one of the most undeserving cancer patients in the history of the world. Seven years ago Robin beat back breast cancer with a double mastectomy, radiation, and chemotherapy. Three years ago the cancer returned on her liver, spine, a rib, and her vocal chords. Again, the treatments began and she seemed to beat the odds. Then came the devastating news that the disease had metastasized to her brain.

Her husband, Chad, has been my friend since we were fifteen years old. We sat side by side on the night of our high school graduation and took our senior trip together. I stood up for him at his wedding. I sat in on his ordination service. I held all his newborn babies and he held mine. When we were living closer together, some fifty miles apart, we would meet at this little drug store café in Fairmount, Georgia, and have a "Judy Burger" (I don't know who Judy is but she makes a great burger, especially when it's covered with her chili). There we would discuss everything from dispensationalism and John Calvin to the Southern Baptist Convention and what deacons in our church we would like to see swallowed up by the earth. We didn't always see eye to eye. We still don't. But he is the best friend I have had for more than twenty years, and over those years, especially the last few, I have watched him and Robin sleep soundly through the storm around them.

There is a strain of preaching and teaching that says people like Chad and Robin are somehow defective in their faith. Practitioners of this brand of snake oil claim that no harm could ever befall those who are living right. The good and holy live the divinely charmed life with no worries about the future as they have been written a cosmic blank check on the endless resources of God's heavenly bank. The spiritual mathematics of this kind of confidence say, "If I am godly, then this will equal never being in need or having trouble." The corollary is also true: "If you are not very godly, you will not always have what you need, and you will suffer in this life." To hear some tell it, those who please God always land on top of the heap. Their cupboards are always full, their gas tanks are never empty, their cup is always running over, their checks never bounce, sickness never invades their lives, and they are forever insulated from tragedy. But this scheme that righteous, kingdom living, and building on the way of Jesus always leads to the good life won't hold up for long.

Countless numbers of good and godly people have suffered, have gone without, have lived in abject poverty, have been chained in prison, have suffered inexplicable injustice, and even worse. Why? Because they possessed an inferior faith, a faith not big or strong enough to get them out of trouble? No. They suffered because of their good and great faith, not because of an absence of it. The writer of the book of Hebrews concludes that those who suffer this way are "too good for this world . . . and earn a good reputation because of their faith" (Heb 11:38). Or, as C. S. Lewis put it, "'Why do the godly suffer?' Why not? They are the only ones who can handle it."[5]

Following Jesus and embracing life within his Tribe does not mean the healing of every cancer, the restoration of every marriage, the bringing home of every prodigal, or the stopping of every foreclosure. And it certainly doesn't mean the promise of a 5,000-square-foot home, an 800 credit score, a new Escalade in the four-car garage, and a perpetual six-figure salary. So much of this thinking isn't Christian at all. It is thinly disguised American greed and consumerism masquerading as the gospel of Christ. When Jesus spoke of lives that will not collapse in the storm, he was speaking of the lasting genuine reign of God, for our most pressing needs cannot be measured by our financial bottom line, by our medical charts, or within our few days full of trouble. Our greatest need is renewal, redemption, and re-creation. In Christ, God has begun that work in the lives of those who come to him. So much of what it means to live within the Jesus Tribe (and to live alternatively in the world) is to live as a reflection of this renewal that will one day be made complete.

There is a day coming when God will take up residence on a renewed earth, and we will be his newborn people beneath a renewed heaven. The desert ravines will fill with water, the barren landscapes will bloom, wine will drip from the hillsides, milk and honey and all that is good will be spread across the tables. The lion will lay down with the lamb, our swords will be beat into plowshares, and our weapons of war will be converted to flower baskets. A day is coming when the door will always be open, the table will always be spread, the dance music will always be playing, and everything will be as it should be.

There will be no more starving Africans, no more cancer patients, no more abused children, no more AIDS orphans, no more grieving families, no more unanswered questions, no more broken relationships, no more abuses of power, and no more empires except for the eternal Kingdom of God. The Father himself will "wipe every tear from our eyes, and there will be no more death or mourning or crying or pain, for the old order of things will have passed away" (see Rev 21:4).

Has God given my friends who are suffering because of cancer what they need? From my limited perspective, I am tempted to say, "No." I don't believe for a minute that God is responsible for Robin's cancer, but God and I sure have been wrestling over this. I have shaken my fist, finger, and prayers at him about it. And that's okay. He's not intimidated by me. I throw all my frustrations at him because I can't take it—not sitting down, anyway—and he can take it. And I know I'm not going to get an explanation in this current life as to how such a tragedy could befall someone as wonderful and precious as this woman and her family. It's a huge question mark. But finally, I must relinquish all my frustrations and questions and accept the conclusion that living a life that is centered on the kingdom, not on the things of this world, means there is something that lasts much longer than what I can currently see and perceive.

Robin seems to understand this better than most, certainly better than I do. While the storm rages, she sleeps easy in the storm, for her life is built on the only foundation that will bear the strain.

Conclusion

"We are on the eve of leaving that country that gave us birth . . . we bid farewell to it and all we hold dear." (Charles Hicks, vice chief of the Cherokee, embarking on the Trail of Tears, 1838)

"A little child shall lead them," the prophet Isaiah said (Isa 11:6). If that is true, then my youngest son, Braden, has a leash around my neck. And if you have read far enough to get to this conclusion, you know that he and his brothers are my best teachers. I've learned more from the three children who live in my home than from all the sacred books and theological studies in the world, as it should be in the Kingdom of God.

Braden is a particularly good leader/teacher because he is such a curious seeker himself. He is always investigating, exploring, and questioning things, especially when it comes to things about Jesus. When he was a bit younger he and I were talking and he asked me, "Does Jesus really know what we are thinking inside our heads?" I told him "Yes," and as he walked away I heard him mumble, "Dang, I knew it." A couple days later he came to me with another query: "What is a Christian?" That's a good question, no doubt.

I tried to shape an answer that a six-year-old could appreciate, so I said, "Braden, it's just like playing 'Follow the Leader.' A Christian is someone who follows Jesus." I was proud of my answer, but before I could get smug about it the boy smirked back at me and said, "Well, I'm not going to be a Christian."

Willing to take the bait, I asked him, "Why not?" He answered with his usual wisdom: "I'm not going to follow Jesus. I don't even know where that will take me." Amen, my son, amen.

Yet, if we have heeded these words from the Sermon on the Mount at all, we do know where following Jesus will take us. It will take us into the teeth of the empire. It will lead us upstream and against the grain of the world around us because the way and power of Jesus is in conflict with human ways and power. As this great sermon ended, the listeners were astounded by all they had heard. Matthew reports, "When Jesus had finished saying these things, the crowds were amazed at his teaching, for he taught with *real authority*" (Matt 7:28-29).

Real authority. The Empire with its economic, religious, political, and military power is living a rebellious sham. It is a usurper whose authority, while fierce, does not flow from the risen Christ. So when disciples of Jesus enter the world living in graceful, peaceful submission to the way of the one true Lord, those disciples become living contradictions. They become people who will not conform because they have been transformed by the power of Christ, and non-conforming, transformed people smash against the status quo.

Honestly, I wish it weren't this way. I wish that following Jesus were without so much internal and external conflict. But it's not. We won't wake up one morning and have all our prickly problems solved. We won't reach a place where all the tension of belonging to the Kingdom of God while living in the empires of the world will be marvelously defused. We will not enjoy a state of complete and total harmony this side of the final return of Christ, but this does not keep us from following him. Where else can we go? Only he has real authority. Only he leads us to *Qualla*—not a physical location, but a way of faithfulness as we make our journey. Only he has the words that lead to life, even when his leading leaves us wondering where we are going, and even when his words sometimes leave us with more questions than answers.

This call to *Qualla*, to become a unique Tribe in the land we once called home, is a crisis in the full sense of the word. In the West we often use the word "crisis" as a synonym for disaster. A crisis is a problem to solve or a tragedy to avoid. So once we are in a crisis, we don't take the time to listen, learn, or grow from it. We only want to get out of it as quickly as possible. The Chinese, as you may know, speak of a crisis as a fork in the road. It is a point of decision. Our response can lead to disaster, yes, or the response can lead to incredible achievement. But in Hebrew, crisis is the same word used to describe the birthing stool upon which a woman sits while giving birth. Thus, a crisis is the stage, quite literally, for something new and wonderful to be born into the world. Of course, this birth cannot be successful without some pain and pushing.

No, we cannot avoid the pain or the pressure that will sometimes accompany the life of discipleship. We cannot always find the definitive answers for which we are looking (sorry, Braden), but we can seek to ask the right questions while living within the crisis that is the American Empire. For it is when we ask the right questions that we are pushed away from the false powers that surround us and drawn closer to the One we follow. Drawing closer to him is our only recourse, but he is more than recourse enough; "For the living Christ still has two hands, one to point the way, and the other held out to help us along."[1]

A final metaphor from the Cherokee people seems appropriate here: In 1828, just a few rolling hills away from my childhood home, a few shiny rocks were discovered in a mountain stream. They were gold. Whatever tenuous hold the Cherokee had on their ancestral home was now broken. Greedy prospectors came pouring over the hills with picks, shovels, dreams of wealth, and a new Georgia folksong on their lips: "All I ask in this creation is a pretty little wife and big plantation, way up yonder in the Cherokee Nation."[2] The empire let these colonizers have what they wanted.

So it was that a decade later, the United States Army and the Georgia Militia began assembling the remaining Cherokee for the thousand-mile forced march across the Mississippi River to what is now the state of Oklahoma. "Build a fire under them," Andrew Jackson had instructed a Georgia congressman. "When it gets hot enough, they'll move."[3] And the Empire's fire burned hot as any hell: farms were stolen; homes were burned; violence was normal; Christian missionaries living among the Cherokee were forced to take oaths of allegiance to the state of Georgia or be imprisoned (some were). Once assembled, hundreds of Cherokee died in the stockades, held as they were like caged animals for months. Those deaths were just the start; of the 16,000 Cherokee put on the Trail of Tears, more than a quarter died of starvation, exposure, and disease.

By the time of the Trail of Tears, many of the Cherokee had become followers of Jesus. "Jesus has risen from the dead. Only the greatest shaman could do that," some of their chiefs had encouraged.[4] So in spite of the fact that many proclaiming Christians had been instrumental in their sufferings, they placed their faith in Christ and called upon it as they marched across the continent, asking Jesus to help them. Alongside their traditional songs and chants, the Cherokee lifted their spirits by singing their adaptations of Wesleyan and frontier hymns.[5]

One such hymn, "Guide Me, Oh Great Jehovah," was lifted as a prayer for the trail. I offer a portion of it here as the same, and as a fitting conclusion to this book. It is my hope that we in the Jesus Tribe will sing this together on our journey through the land of the Empire:

Guide me, O Thou great Jehovah; Pilgrim through this barren land.
I am weak, but Thou art mighty; Hold me with Thy powerful hand.

Lord, I trust Thy mighty power; Wondrous are Thy works of old;

Thou deliver Thine from bondage; Who for naught themselves had sold.

Musing on my habitation; Musing on my heavenly home,
Fills my soul with holy longings: Come, my Jesus, quickly come.[6]

Questions for Reflection

Chapter 1: A Three-legged Stool

1. Consider the following statement from chapter 1: "Every empire, from Babel to the current nation-state, operates under the same unifying principle: to commandeer heaven; to depose the Creator and play the role of God in the world." Do you agree? Why or why not?

2. Living as an alternative society can quickly devolve into withdrawal and "retreatism." How can followers of Jesus prevent this from happening?

3. I interpret the temptations of Jesus in the wilderness as directly related to the allure of power. Do you accept this as a reasonable interpretation? Why or why not?

4. When it comes to living in the current Empire, how can Christians in North America best participate (or not participate) with the powers that be?

5. Is it possible to hold power in this world without violence or exploitation? Explain your answer.

Chapter 2: Abandon Ship

1. Is it "overblown" for me to warn about the church keeping its distance from power? Why or why not?

2. Can you imagine a situation in which the church and the state could be partners? If so, what would such a partnership look like?

3. What is the difference between "inviting Jesus into our hearts" and responding to Jesus' message that the "Kingdom of God is near"?

4. What are the practical ways that Jesus "knows the ropes" and can show us how to live today?

5. Would you consider Clarence Jordan's effort at building a "demonstration plot for the Kingdom of God" practical? Why or why not?

Chapter 3: The Blessed Community

1. How does the comparison of the Sermon on the Mount with an oath of allegiance strike you?

2. What is the difference between the Beatitudes being a "state of God's rule" versus being commandments that Jesus' disciples should follow?

3. How can local congregations create a safe and sacred space for seekers and those wishing to learn more about following Jesus?

4. Why is it so difficult for us, as followers of Jesus, to embrace our weaknesses?

5. What are some of the hardest or most difficult things for us to let go of or to let Christ tear out of our lives?

Chapter 4: A Garden in the Wilderness

1. I state that "city on the hill" language should not be applied to a nation or a government. Explain why you agree or disagree with this conclusion.

2. "A Christian nation is a delusion." How would you support or critique this statement?

3. Have you ever been part of a congregation that operated like it was a "doomsday shelter"? What was life like within such a community? What would it take for such churches to change?

4. What does a church that has lost its "saltiness" look like?

5. What other organizations, people, and institutions do Christians often endorse as light and salt for the world?

Chapter 5: No Rules, Just Right

1. Was Jesus a rebel? Why or why not? Would he be perceived as a rebel if he were living on earth today?

2. Why is it impossible to move on to spiritual maturity while remaining a keeper of the Law?

3. How does love remove "both the necessity of laws and the motivation to hurt others"?

4. Read again the true story of Dirk Willems. What would such an act of "intuitive response" look like by a follower of Jesus today?

5. Why are people afraid of God? Should people be afraid of God? Why or why not?

Chapter 6: Roundabout

1. How would you describe the "transforming initiatives" of Jesus in the Sermon on the Mount? What is the source of their power to change us?

2. In what ways can disciples follow Jesus into the world with a ministry of redemption rather than condemnation?

3. When is anger appropriate? How do we know when we have "crossed the line" with our anger?

4. Was Jesus' instruction to "gouge out your eye" or "cut off your hand" literal? Why or why not?

5. What leads us into deceiving others, even when our original intentions were never to do so?

Chapter 7: Who Would Jesus Bomb?

1. Does war and violence really kill everyone it touches? How or how not?

2. How do we reconcile Jesus' words about nonviolence while living in (and sometimes actively supporting) the largest military power in the world?

3. I make the point that the Kingdom of God and the way of violence are in competition one with another. Do you agree or disagree with this? Explain your answer.

4. What are some practical ways followers of Jesus can walk the extra mile, give away our coats, and turn the other cheek?

5. "Violence is . . . a natural part of being human . . . but to follow Christ is to be set free from human nature." Is this really a practical statement? If so, how does it work itself out? If not, why is it impractical?

Chapter 8: Losing My Religion

1. Giving, praying, and fasting are not such prominent "good deeds" as they once were. To what "acts of righteousness" do we attach a great deal of weight today?

2. How have churches become "shows to get ratings"? How can this be changed?

3. What are the long-term effects of living your life obsessed with what other people say or think?

4. Why have prayer books become so prolific, especially in light of the simple prayer that Jesus taught to his disciples?

5. Having been taught to address God as "Father," why is there often a move away from this inviting, spontaneous type of prayer toward a more formal, prescribed use of language?

Chapter 9: The Best Revenge

1. Why would Jesus say, "If you refuse to forgive others, your Father will not forgive your sins"?

2. Is it really possible to forgive others, especially those who have hurt us so deeply? If so, how?

3. Read again and react to this word from Lewis Smedes: "If we say that monsters are beyond forgiving, we give them a power they should never have."

4. How do we empty ourselves that God might fill us with himself?

5. Even when we know that forgiving others will give us fresh life and forgiveness ourselves, why do we hold on to our grudges and resentment?

Chapter 10: Gotta Serve Somebody

1. How have prosperity and money become synonymous with what it means to succeed in America?

2. Is stewardship of the earth acceptable as a "Christian responsibility"? Why or why not?

3. Why have we put so much trust in our financial security? What will it take to reverse this trust in *things*?

4. Tony Campolo asks, "Would Jesus drive a BMW?" What is your answer and why?

5. How do our congregations' ways of spending, sharing, and borrowing inhibit or aid our pursuit of the Kingdom of God?

Chapter 11: A Leap of Faith

1. How would you describe the current fear level of Christians living in the United States?

2. Can followers of Jesus participate in the economic systems of the Empire without relying on them? Explain.

3. When we feel like we are dependent on the system of the Empire for our security, how can we "unplug"?

4. Willimon and Hauerwas say, "American Christians need to stop feeling at home." What is your reaction to their statement?

5. I define the way of Christ as beginning "with faith and moving toward confidence," not vice versa. In what ways does this work out in your life?

Chapter 12: Two Moons in His Moccasins

1. It is not unusual for the church to be described as "judgmental." Is this description fair or unfair? Why?

2. In what ways are we guilty of going after the speck in another's eye while ignoring the log in our own eye?

3. How would you describe the "prejudice of love"?

4. Jesus seems to be telling us to keep our distance from situations and people that are antagonistic toward our message. Do you agree or disagree with this interpretation? Why?

5. How would our personal lives, communities, and congregations change if we "looked at and loved others expecting the very best"?

Chapter 13: Asleep in the Storm

1. Is the Sermon on the Mount the "original formula" for practically following the person and way of Jesus? Why or why not?

2. Jesus said some of us would build our "house upon the sand." What are some of the sandy surfaces upon which we unfortunately build our lives?

3. I say "our faith is not built on the Bible." How could this statement be misunderstood or misapplied?

4. In what ways do we encase our faith rather than letting it loose to serve the world? How can we further free our faith?

5. My last story involves my friend Robin, diagnosed with cancer. What would you say to those who conclude that her sickness is a lack of genuine faith?

Endnotes

Introduction

1. Edward J. Gallagher, "The Literature of Justification," *Requerimiento (1510)*, http://users.dickinson.edu/~borges/Resources-Requerimiento.htm (accessed 12 November 2010).

2. Vernard Eller, *Christian Anarchy: Jesus' Primacy over the Powers*, chapter 1, online at http://www.hccentral.com/eller12/part1.html (accessed 15 October 2009).

3. This union of state and religious powers is traditionally referred to as "Christendom" and can be traced to the Roman emperor Constantine, who used the growing Christian faith to hold his crumbling empire together.

4. Seth Godin, *Tribes* (New York: Portfolio, 2008) 1.

5. Mike Yaconelli, quoted by Becky Garrison, *Jesus Died for This?* (Grand Rapids MI: Zondervan, 2010) 11.

6. Karl Barth, *Church Dogmatics* (Edinburgh: T. and T. Clark Publishers, 1961) 4.3.2.

7. My ancestors were John Jackson Welch Jr. and Sarah Brown (Cherokee). The shamans gave Welch the name *Wodigi Asgoli*, literally meaning "Brown Head" or "Head of the Brown Family," when he and Sarah married.

8. John Ehle, *Trail of Tears: The Rise and Fall of the Cherokee Nation* (New York: Anchor Books, 1988) 156.

9. Ben Witherington III, *Matthew*, Smyth & Helwys Bible Commentary (Macon GA: Smyth & Helwys, 2006) 113.

Chapter 1

1. Unless otherwise noted, all Scripture references are from the New Living Translation.

2. Darrell J. Fasching and Dell Dechant, *Comparative Religious Ethics* (Malden MA: Blackwell, 2001) 300.

3. Hendrik Berkhok, *Christ and the Powers* (Scottdale: Herald, 1977) 43.

4. Donald B. Kraybill, *The Upside Down Kingdom*, 25th anniversary ed. (Scottdale PA: Herald, 2003) 33.

5. John Dominic Crossan, *The Historical Jesus*, paperback ed. (New York: HarperCollins, 1992) 220–24.

6. Elizabeth Williamson, "Some Americans Lack Food, but UDSA Won't Call Them Hungry," *The Washington Post*, 16 November, 2006, online at http://www.washingtonpost.com/wp-dyn/content/article/2006/11/15/AR2006111501621.html (accessed 10 March 2007).

7. Spanish physician Josep Brugada Terradellas determined in 1992 that "Sudden Unexplained Nocturnal Death Syndrome" was actually a chromosomal disorder that led to arrhythmia of the heart. The syndrome is now referred to as Brugada Syndrome.

8. Shelley Adler, "Sudden Unexplained Nocturnal Death Syndrome" *Journal of American Folklore* 104/411 (1991): 54–71.

9. Tony Campolo quoted by Shane Claiborne, *Jesus for President* (Grand Rapids MI: Zondervan, 2008) 151.

10. Stanley Hauerwas and William H. Willimon, *Resident Aliens* (Nashville: Abingdon, 1989) 74.

11. Barack H. Obama, "Remarks by the President at the Acceptance of the Nobel Peace Prize," delivered at Oslo City Hall, Oslo, Norway, 10 December 2009. Available online at <http://www.whitehouse.gov/the-press-office/remarks-president-acceptance-nobel-peace-prize>.

12. Alan Hirsch, via Twitter, 13 December 2009. Alan Hirsch is an author, speaker, and Founding Director of Forge Mission Training Network.

Chapter 2

1. John 1:14 from Eugene Peterson, *The Message* (Colorado Springs: Navpress, 1995).

2. Donald B. Kraybill, *The Upside Down Kingdom*, 25th anniversary ed. (Scottdale PA: Herald, 2003) 25.

3. Clarence Jordan, quoted by J. Randall O'Brien in "The Church: A Non-Prophet Organization?" *Prophetic Ethics* (Waco: Baylor University, 2003) 37.

4. A brief but informative book about the life of Clarence Jordan is from Joyce Hollyday, *Clarence Jordan, Essential Writings* (Maryknoll NY: Orbis, 2003) *passim*.

Chapter 3

1. *The Truman Show*, directed by Peter Weir, written by Andrew Niccol, Paramount Pictures, 1998.

2. *Oath of Allegiance for Naturalized Citizens*, Citizenship and Immigration Services, U.S. Department of Homeland Security.

3. Glen H. Stassen and David P. Gushee, *Kingdom Ethics; Following Jesus in Contemporary Context* (Downers Grove IL: Intervarsity Press, 2003) 21. Emphasis added.

4. David S. Noss and John B. Noss, *A History of the World's Religions*, 9th ed. (New York: Macmillan, 1994) 560.

5. Thomas R. Kelly, *A Testament of Devotion* (New York: HarperCollins, 1992) 53–55.

6. Brenda Egolif, Judith Lasker, Steward Wolf, and Louise Potvin, "The Roseto Effect: A 50-Year Comparison of Mortality Rates," *American Journal of Public Health* 82 (1992): 1089–1092. Available online at http://ajph.apha-publications.org/cgi/reprint/82/81089.pdf.

7. Based on Malcolm Gladwell, *Outliers* (New York: Little, Brown and Co., 2008) 3–11.

8. This is William Tyndale's translation of the common word "hospitality" in Romans 12:13.

9. Shel Silverstein, *The Missing Piece* (New York: HarperCollins, 1976).

10. Anne Lamott, *Bird by Bird: Some Instructions on Writing and Life* (New York: Anchor, 1995) 167.

Chapter 4

1. John Winthrop, "A Model of Christian Charity," on board the Arbella, 1630, online at http://religiousfreedom.lib.virginia.edu/sacred/charity.html (accessed 25 May 2010).

2. Ronald W. Reagan, "Farewell Address to the Nation," 11 January 1989.

3. Michael Frost and Alan Hirsch, *The Shaping of Things to Come* (Peabody MA: Hendrickson, 2003) 226–27.

4. Eugene H. Peterson, *The Jesus Way* (Grand Rapids: Eerdmans, 2007) 1, 5.

5. Ibid., 9.

6. Adapted from Ethan Fishman, "Unto Caesar," in *American Scholar* 76/4 (22 September 2007): 36–39.

7. Keith Matheny, "Doomsday Shelters Making a Comeback," USA Today, 28 June 2010. Available online at http://www.usatoday.com/news/nation/2010-07-28-doomsday28_ST_N.htm.

8. Adapted from Max Lucado, *Just Like Jesus* (Nashville: Word, 1998) 97.

9. One of the better articles about Lichtenberg is found at Yad Vashem's "The Righteous Among the Nations." Available online at <http://www1. yadvashem.org/yv/en/righteous/stories/lichtenberg.asp.>

10. David Bosch, *Transforming Mission* (New York: Orbis Books, 1991) 485.

11. Author's recording and notes from Ann Denson Tucker, untitled speech, 17 April 2010. See <http://mnof.org/?page_id=35>.

Chapter 5

1. Formerly known as *The State of Tennessee v. Scopes*, this trial involved a biology teacher who taught evolution, violating state law at the time.

2. Geffrey B. Kelly and F. Burton Nelson, eds., *A Testament of Freedom: The Essential Writings of Dietrich Bonhoeffer* (rev. ed., New York: HarperSanFrancisco, 1995) 424.

3. Leo Nikolayevich Tolstoy, *Epilogue to the Kreutzer Sonata,* 1890, online at http://www.ccel.org/ccel/tolstoy/kreutzer.ii.html (accessed 10 January 2010).

4. Clarence Jordan, *Sermon on the Mount,* Koinonia Edition (Valley Forge: Judson, 1970) 32.

5. William Law, *Freedom from a Self-Centered Life/Dying to Self* (Minneapolis: Bethany House, 1977) 75 and 97.

6. Joseph Liechty, *Why Did Dirk Willems Turn Back?* Online at the Anabaptist Network, http://www.anabaptistnetwork.com/node/175 (accessed 20 January 2010).

Chapter 6

1. Glen H. Stassen and David P. Gushee, *Kingdom Ethics; Following Jesus in Contemporary Context* (Downers Grove IL: Intervarsity Press, 2003) 133.

2. Ibid., 144.

3. Robert Scheer, "The Playboy Interview: Jimmy Carter" *Playboy* 23/11 (November 1976): 63–86.

4. Mary Magdalene is often identified as a repentant prostitute, though this identity cannot be (and should not be) confirmed.

5. John Ehle, *Trail of Tears: The Rise and Fall of the Cherokee Nation* (New York: Anchor Books, 1988) 128.

6. Ibid., 255.

7. Chief Womankiller quoted by Hezekiah Niles, *Niles Weekly Register* 1/1 (4th series; 29 August 1829): 235.

Chapter 7

1. The best retelling of Sattler's life is Myron Augsburger's historical novel *Pilgrim Aflame* (Scottdale PA: Herald Press, 2005).

2. N.T. Wright, *The Challenge of Jesus* (Downers Grove IL: Intervarsity Press, 1999) 44.

3. Ibid.

4. William Barclay, *The Gospel of Matthew*, vol. 1, rev. ed. (Philadelphia: Westminster Press, 1975) 177, italics added.

5. Clarence told this story on numerous occasions. My retelling is adapted from Henlee H. Barnette, *Clarence Jordan: Turning Dreams into Deeds* (Macon GA: Smyth and Helwys, 1992) 27–28.

6. Joyce Hollyday, *Clarence Jordan, Essential Writings* (Maryknoll NY: Orbis, 2003) 125.

Chapter 8

1. Kent Nerburn, Compiler, *The Wisdom of the Great Chiefs: The Classic Speeches of Chief Red Jacket, Chief Joseph, and Chief Seattle* (Novato CA: New World, 1999).

2. Ibid., 141–45.

3. Sinclair Lewis, *Elmer Gantry* (New York: Harcourt, 1927); and *Elmer Gantry*, directed by Richard Brooks, MGM, 1960.

4. Lewis, *Elmer Gantry*, 14.

5. Cecil Maranville, "Reality TV—NOT!" *World News and Prophecy* 8/2 (February 2005): 5–7.

6. Lewis Smedes quoted by Philip Yancey, *What's So Amazing about Grace?* (Grand Rapids MI: Zondervan, 1997) 32.

7. This is a subject I hope to return to in the future. For now see the book by Paul Froese and Christopher Bader, *America's Four Gods; What We Say About God—And What That Says About Us* (New York: Oxford, 2010).

8. *The Book of Common Prayer*, readers' ed. (New York: Oxford, 2008).

Chapter 9

1. Laura King, "Afghanistan's Two Jews in a Poignant and Solitary Hanukka," *The Associated Press*, 10 December 2001.

2. Leonard Sweet and Frank Viola's original essay is now in expanded book form as *The Jesus Manifesto: Restoring the Supremacy and Sovereignty of Jesus Christ* (Nashville: Thomas Nelson, 2010).

3. Lewis B. Smedes, *Forgive and Forget: Healing the Hurts We Don't Deserve* (San Francisco: HarperSanFrancisco, 1996) 79.

4. *The Mission*, directed by Roland Joffé, written by Robert Bolt, Warner Brothers, 1986.

5. Smedes, *Forgive and Forget*, 79.

6. Philip Yancey, *Rumors of Another World* (Grand Rapids MI: Zondervan, 2003) 223–24.

7. Meister Eckhart, *Selected Writings*, trans. Oliver Davies (New York: Penguin, 1994) 7.

8. Meister Eckhart, *Meister Eckhart: The Essential Sermons, Commentaries, Treatises and Defense*, trans. Bernard McGinn (Mahwah: Paulist Press, 1981) 184.

9. Meister Eckhart, *The Complete Mystical Works of Meister Eckhart*, trans. Maurice O'C Walshe (New York: Crossroad, 2008) sermon 4.

10. Delbert Tarr Jr., "Making Truth Memorable," *Leadership*, Spring 1983, online at http://www.christianitytoday.com/le/1983/spring/83l2066.html (accessed 21 March 2010).

Chapter 10

1. Renae Merle, "Wall Street's Final '08 Toll: $6.9 Trillion Wiped Out," *The Washington Post*, 1 January 2009.

2. Glen H. Stassen and David P. Gushee, *Kingdom Ethics; Following Jesus in Contemporary Context* (Downers Grove IL: Intervarsity Press, 2003) 426.

3. George Frederic Watts, *Mammon: Dedicated to his Worshippers*, 1884–1885. See <http://darkclassics.blogspot.com/2011/02/george-frederic-watts-mammon-dedicated.html>.

4. Tony Campolo, "The Urgency of the Call," delivered at Urbana 87, Urbana IL, 29 December 1987. "Urbana" is a periodical missions conference sponsored by Intervarsity. See <http://www.urbana.org/home>.

5. Nicole Santa Cruz, "Crystal Cathedral Files for Bankruptcy Protection," *Los Angeles Times*, 19 October 2010.

Chapter 11

1. "Theologians: Barth in Retirement," *Time Magazine*, 31 May 1963, online at http://www.time.com/time/magazine/article/0,9171,896838,00.html, accessed 19 July 2010.

2. Clarence Jordan, *Sermon on the Mount*, Koinonia Edition (Valley Forge: Judson, 1970) 71.

3. Jacques Ellul, *Anarchy and Christianity* (Grand Rapids: Eerdmans, 1988) 20.

4. Stanley Hauerwas and William H, Willimon, *Where Resident Aliens Live* (Nashville: Abingdon Press, 1996) 24–25 and 113–14.

5. Philip Yancey, "The Church's New McCarthyism," in *Christianity Today*, 18 July 1994, online at http://www.christianitytoday.com/ct/1994/july18/4t8072.html?start=1 (accessed 15 May 2010).

Chapter 12

1. Gary Hamel and C.K. Prahalad, *Competing for the Future* (Boston: Harvard Business School Press, 1994) 51–52.

2. Dietrich Bonhoeffer, *The Cost of Discipleship*, rev. ed. (New York: Macmillan, 1963) 205.

3. Based on William R. White, *Stories for the Journey, A Sourcebook for Christian Storytellers* (Minneapolis: Augsburg, 1988) 108–109.

Chapter 13

1. Lewis Grizzard quoted by William E. Schmidt, "Home of Coke Laments Change in Winning Formula," *The New York Times*, 26 April 1985, A15.

2. N.T. Wright, *The Last Word* (New York: HarperSanFrancisco, 2005) xi, 24, italics added.

3. Miles Hoffman, *The Sweet Sound of a Stradivarius*, NPR Morning Edition, Washington, DC, 24 June 2004.

4. Mitch Albom, *Have a Little Faith* (New York: Hyperion 2009) 93.

5. C.S. Lewis quoted by Skip Heitzig, "In the Midst of Pain," *The Connection Devotional*, 4 June 2010, online at http://www.christianity.com/devotionals/connection/11632638/ (accessed 3 August 2010).

Conclusion

1. T. W. Manson quoted by Thomas G. Long and Cornelius Plantinga, Jr., eds., *A Chorus of Witnesses: Model Sermons for Today's Preacher* (Grand Rapids MI: Eerdmans, 1994) 168.

2. John Ehle, *Trail of Tears: The Rise and Fall of the Cherokee Nation* (New York: Anchor Books, 1988) 213.

3. Ibid., 220.

4. Ibid., 116.

5. *We Shall Remain: America through Native Eyes*, "Trail of Tears," directed by Chris Eyre, written by Mark Zwonitzer, Apograph Productions for PBS American Experience, 2009.

6. William Williams Pantycelyn, "Guide Me, Oh Great Jehovah," (Originally in Welsh: Arglwydd, arwain trwy'r anialwch) 1745; English translation by Peter Williams, 1771.

Other available titles from

Baptimergent
Baptist Stories from the Emergent Frontier

Zach Roberts, ed.

Emergent Christians are those who believe there is more to God, Jesus, and God's kingdom than modern Christianity and its denominational categories have been able to define. Emergent Baptists believe it is incumbent upon them to participate in—and write—the narrative for their time and place. 978-1-57312-551-2 192 pages/pb **$17.00**

Beyond the American Dream

Millard Fuller

In 1968, Millard finished the story of his journey from pauper to millionaire to home builder. His wife, Linda, occasionally would ask him about getting it published, but Millard would reply, "Not now. I'm too busy." This is that story. 978-1-57312-563-5 272 pages/pb **$20.00**

The Black Church
Relevant or Irrelevant in the 21st Century?

Reginald F. Davis

The Black Church emerges from the author's great love, admiration, and deep concern for the future of the black community and the black church. Davis contends that a relevant church struggles to correct oppression, not maintain it. How can the black church focus on the liberation of the black community, thereby reclaiming the loyalty and respect of the black community? 978-1-57312-557-4 144 pages/pb **$15.00**

Bottom Line Beliefs
Twelve Doctrines All Christians Hold in Common (Sort of)

Michael B. Brown

Despite our differences, there are principles that are bedrock to the Christian faith. These are the subject of Michael Brown's *Bottom Line Beliefs*. 978-1-57312-520-8 112 pages/pb **$15.00**

By My Own Reckoning
Cecil Sherman

By My Own Reckoning is Cecil Sherman's gift of memory to those whose lives he has touched through his many years of ministry and service. In this rare autobiography, Dr. Sherman reflects on his life as a pastor, as a husband and father, and as a key figure in the SBC political controversy of the 1980s.   *978-1-57312-502-4 288 pages/hc* **$24.00**

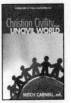

Christian Civility in an Uncivil World
Mitch Carnell, ed.

When we encounter a Christian who thinks and believes differently, we often experience that difference as an attack on the principles upon which we have built our lives and as a betrayal to the faith. However, it is possible for Christians to retain their differences and yet unite in respect for each other. It is possible to love one another and at the same time retain our individual beliefs.   *978-1-57312-537-6 160 pages/pb* **$17.00**

The Disturbing Galilean
Essays About Jesus
Malcolm Tolbert

In this captivating collection of essays, Dr. Malcolm Tolbert reflects on nearly two dozen stories taken largely from the Synoptic Gospels. Those stories range from Jesus' birth, temptation, teaching, anguish at Gethsemane, and crucifixion.   *978-1-57312-530-7 140 pages/pb* **$15.00**

The Enoch Factor
The Sacred Art of Knowing God
Stephen McSwain

The Enoch Factor is a persuasive argument for a more enlightened religious dialogue in America, one that affirms the goals of all religions—guiding followers in self-awareness, finding serenity and happiness, and discovering what the author describes as "the sacred art of knowing God."   *978-1-57312-556-7 256 pages/pb* **$21.00**

Facing Life's Ups and Downs
The Struggle to be Whole
William Powell Tuck

William Tuck makes the important connection between religion and daily living. Our faith can help us deal with circumstances that try to twist and distort our perspective, bearing us safely over the angry current to the shore on the other side.   *978-1-57312-561-1 190 pages/pb* **$17.00**

Faith Postures
Cultivating Christian Mindfulness
Holly Sprink

Sprink guides readers through her own growing awareness of God's desire for relationship and of developing the emotional, physical, spiritual postures that enable us to learn to be still, to listen, to be mindful of the One outside ourselves. *1-978-57312-547-5 160 pages/pb* **$16.00**

The Good News According to Jesus
A New Kind of Christianity for a New Kind of Christian
Chuck Queen

In *The Good News According to Jesus*, Chuck Queen contends that when we broaden our study of Jesus, the result is a richer, deeper, healthier, more relevant and holistic gospel, a Christianity that can transform this world into God's new world.

978-1-57312-528-4 216 pages/pb **$18.00**

Hope for the Thinking Christian
Seeking a Path of Faith through Everyday Life
Stephen Reese

Readers who want to confront their faith more directly, to think it through and be open to God in an individual, authentic, spiritual encounter will find a resonant voice in Stephen Reese.

978-1-57312-553-6 160 pages/pb **$16.00**

Hoping Liberia
Stories of Civil War from Africa's First Republic
John Michael Helms

Through historical narrative, theological ponderings, personal confession, and thoughtful questions, Helms immerses readers into a period of political turmoil and violence, a devastating civil war, and the immeasurable suffering experienced by the Liberian people.

978-1-57312-544-4 208 pages/pb **$18.00**

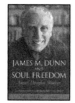

James M. Dunn and Soul Freedom
Aaron Douglas Weaver

A self-described "Texas-bred, Spirit-led, Bible-teaching, revival-preaching, recovering Southern Baptist," James Milton Dunn, over the last fifty years, has been the most aggressive Baptist proponent for religious liberty in the United States. Soul freedom—voluntary uncoerced faith and an unfettered individual conscience before God—is the basis of his understanding of church-state separation and the historic Baptist basis of religious liberty. *978-1-57312-590-1 224 pages/pb* **$18.00**

Joint Venture
Jeanie Miley

Joint Venture is a memoir of the author's journey to find and express her inner, authentic self, not as an egotistical venture, but as a sacred responsibility and partnership with God. Miley's quest for Christian wholeness is a rich resource for other seekers.

978-1-57312-581-9 224 pages/pb **$17.00**

Leaving Religion, Following Jesus
Essays About Jesus
Ronnie McBrayer

This is a book about running after Jesus, about a journey with the Christ—his journey and ours. It is a book about looking and listening to the unexpected. It is a book about opening our eyes, unstopping our ears, and soaking up the gracious wonder that God is.

978-1-57312-531-4 216 pages/pb **$17.00**

Let Me More of Their Beauty See
Reading Familiar Verses in Context
Diane G. Chen

When we turn to God's Word for encouragement, guidance, and instruction, familiar verses often come to mind. Our associations with these verses are nearly automatic, and they comfort us.

How do we know, though, if we are using these verses to mean what they meant to their original audiences? *Let Me More of Their Beauty See* offers eight examples of how attention to the historical and literary settings can safeguard against taking a text out of context, bring out its transforming power in greater dimension, and help us apply Scripture appropriately in our daily lives.

978-1-57312-564-2 160 pages/pb **$17.00**

Looking Around for God
The Strangely Reverent Observations of an Unconventional Christian
James A. Autry

Looking Around for God, Autry's tenth book, is in many ways his most personal. In it he considers his unique life of faith and belief in God. Autry is a former Fortune 500 executive, author, poet, and consultant whose work has had a significant influence on leadership thinking.

978-157312-484-3 144 pages/pb **$16.00**

Mark (Smyth & Helwys Annual Bible Study series)
Finding Ourselves in the Story
Brett & Carol Younger

The stories of Jesus are familiar to most of us. We have walked the paths of his life with him and his disciples over and over again. We could easily think that we are finished gleaning any new wisdom from these stories. The good news for those of us who have already read Mark's Gospel, the first testament to the life of Jesus Christ, is that this living story, with its living characters, is never finished with us.

Teaching Guide 1-978-57312-566-6 192 pages/pb **$14.00**

Study Guide 1-978-57312-569-7 96 pages/pb **$6.00**

Overcoming Adolescence
Growing Beyond Childhood into Maturity
Marion D. Aldridge

In *Overcoming Adolescence*, Marion Aldridge poses questions for adults of all ages to consider. His challenge to readers is one he has personally worked to confront: to grow up *all the way*—mentally, physically, academically, socially, emotionally, and spiritually. The key not only involves knowing how to work through the process, but how to recognize what may be contributing to our perpetual adolescence.

978-1-57312-577-2 156 pages/pb **$17.00**

Psychic Pancakes & Communion Pizza
More Musings and Mutterings of a Church Misfit
Bert Montgomery

Psychic Pancakes & Communion Pizza is Bert Montgomery's highly anticipated follow-up to *Elvis, Willie, Jesus & Me* and contains further reflections on music, film, culture, life, and finding Jesus in the midst of it all. This collection of musings is firmly rooted in time and place— twenty-first-century Starkville, Mississippi—yet ventures into everything from Hurricane Katrina to the Super Bowl Saints, from Ellen DeGeneres to Charles Manson, and from suicide to salvation. And, there's a little Elvis and Willie thrown in for good measure!

978-1-57312-578-9 160 pages/pb **$16.00**

Reading Job (Reading the Old Testament series)
A Literary and Theological Commentary
James L. Crenshaw

At issue in the Book of Job is a question with which most all of us struggle at some point in life, "Why do bad things happen to good people?" James Crenshaw has devoted his life to studying the disturbing matter of theodicy—divine justice—that troubles many people of faith.

978-1-57312-574-1 192 pages/pb **$22.00**

The Role of the Minister in a Dying Congregation
Lynwood B. Jenkins

In our success-driven culture the topic of dying congregations is taboo, yet that is a reality many pastors and congregations struggle through with little guidance for discernment. In *The Role of the Minister in a Dying Congregation* Jenkins provides a courageous and responsible resource on one of the most critical issues in congregational life: how to help a congregation conclude its ministry life cycle with dignity and meaning.

978-1-57312-571-0 96 pages/pb **$14.00**

Sessions with John (Sessions Bible Studies series)
The Vocabulary of Grace
Robert B. Setzer, Jr.

Immersing us in the Gospel of John, this study explores themes that point to transformation, that is, to becoming a new person by trusting in and following Jesus. These studies offer Jesus' "words of life" to a new generation of believers. Those who prayerfully ponder and strive to live these words will discover that they still have the power to breathe God's peace and presence into every believing heart.

978-1-57312-5260-4 144 pages/pb **$14.00**

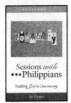

Sessions with Philippians (Session Bible Studies series)
Finding Joy in Community
Bo Prosser

In this brief letter to the Philippians, Paul makes clear the centrality of his faith in Jesus Christ, his love for the Philippian church, and his joy in serving both Christ and their church.

978-1-57312-579-6 112 pages/pb **$13.00**

Sessions with Samuel (Session Bible Studies series)
Stories from the Edge
Tony W. Cartledge

Tony Cartledge takes readers on a journey through these important segments of Israel's history. In these stories, Israel faces one crisis after another, a people constantly on the edge. Individuals like Saul and David find themselves on the edge as well, facing troubles of leadership and personal struggle. Yet, each crisis becomes a gateway for learning that God is always present, that hope remains.

978-1-57312-555-0 112 pages/pb **$13.00**

Silver Linings
My Life Before and After Challenger 7
June Scobee Rodgers

We know the public story of *Challenger 7*'s tragic destruction. That day, June's life took a new direction that ultimately led to the creation of the Challenger Center and to new life and new love. Her story of Christian faith and triumph over adversity will inspire readers of every age. 978-1-57312-570-3 352 pages/hc **$28.00**

Telling the Story
The Gospel in a Technological Age
J. Stanley Hargraves

The church has an ancient story to tell with one underlying theme: God has broken into human history to share with humanity an invitation to relationship. From the advent of the printing press to modern church buildings with LCD projectors and computers, the church has adapted the means of communicating the gospel. Adapting that message to the available technology helps the church reach out in meaningful ways to people around the world. 978-1-57312-550-5 112 pages/pb **$14.00**

This is What a Preacher Looks Like
Sermons by Baptist Women in Ministry
Pamela Durso, ed.

A collection of sermons by thirty-six Baptist women, their voices are soft and loud, prophetic and pastoral, humorous and sincere. They are African American, Asian, Latina, and Caucasian. They are sisters, wives, mothers, grandmothers, aunts, and friends.

978-1-57312-554-3 144 pages/pb **$18.00**

To Be a Good and Faithful Servant
The Life and Work of a Minister
Cecil Sherman

This book offers a window into how one pastor navigated the many daily challenges and opportunities of ministerial life and shares that wisdom with church leaders wherever they are in life—whether serving as lay leaders or as ministers just out of seminary, midway through a career, or seeking renewal after many years of service. 978-1-57312-559-8 208 pages/pb **$20.00**

Transformational Leadership
Leading with Integrity

Charles B. Bugg

"Transformational" leadership involves understanding and growing so that we can help create positive change in the world. This journey is not for the faint of heart or those who think leadership is achieved by learning a set of skills. On the contrary, effective leaders know that they have to be willing to change if *they* want to help transform the world. They are honest about their personal strengths and weaknesses, and aren't afraid of doing a fearless moral inventory of themselves.   *978-1-57312-558-1 112 pages/pb* **$14.00**

Written on My Heart
Daily Devotions for Your Journey through the Bible

Ann H. Smith

Smith takes readers on a fresh and exciting journey of daily readings of the Bible that will change, surprise, and renew you.

978-1-57312-549-9 288 pages/pb **$18.00**

When Crisis Comes Home
Revised and Expanded

John Lepper

The Bible is full of examples of how God's people, with homes grounded in the faith, faced crisis after crisis. These biblical personalities and families were not hopeless in the face of catastrophe—instead, their faith in God buoyed them, giving them hope for the future and strength to cope in the present. John Lepper will help you and your family prepare for, deal with, and learn from crises in your home. He will also help you help others in crisis.   *978-1-57312-539-0 152 pages/pb* **$17.00**

Cecil Sherman Formations Commentary

Add the wit and wisdom of Cecil Sherman to your library. After 15 years of writing the Smyth & Helwys Formations Commentary, you can now purchase the 5-volume compilation covering the best of Cecil Sherman from Genesis to Revelation.

  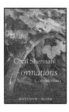  

Vol. 1: Genesis–Job   *1-57312-476-1 208 pages/pb* **$17.00**
Vol. 2: Psalms–Malachi   *1-57312-477-X 208 pages/pb* **$17.00**
Vol. 3: Matthew–Mark   *1-57312-478-8 208 pages/pb* **$17.00**
Vol. 4: Luke–Acts   *1-57312-479-6 208 pages/pb* **$17.00**
Vol. 5: Romans–Revelation   *1-57312-480-X 208 pages/pb* **$17.00**

Clarence Jordan's Cotton Patch Gospel

This four volume set recasts the stories of Jesus and the letters of Paul and Peter into the language and culture of the mid-20th century South. Born out of the civil rights struggle, these now classic translations of much of the New Testament bring the far-away places of Scripture closer to home: Gainesville, Selma, Birmingham, Atlanta, Washington, D.C.

Matthew and John   *1-57312-422-2 128 pages/pb* **$14.00**
Luke and Acts   *1-57312-423-0 176 pages/pb* **$16.00**
Paul's Epistles   *1-57312-424-9 192 pages/pb* **$16.00**
Hebrews and the General Epistles   *1-57312-425-7 96 pages/pb* **$14.00**